Brett Whiteley Art & Life
1939–1992

Brett Whiteley
Art & Life

New Edition

Barry Pearce

With contributions
by Bryan Robertson
and Wendy Whiteley

Exhibition research
Charlotte Hayman

in association with
The Art Gallery of New South Wales

LENDERS

Archer M. Huntington Art Gallery, The University of Texas at Austin, Texas, United States of America: plates 33, 41, 43, 53
Art Gallery of South Australia: plate 135
Art Gallery of Western Australia: plates 80a-f
Artbank: plate 82
Ballarat Fine Art Gallery: plate 106
Castlemaine Art Gallery and Historical Museum, Victoria: fig 10
Marlborough Fine Art London: plate 116
National Gallery of Australia: plates 22, 36, 37, 39, 94
National Gallery of Victoria: plates 50, 113
Newcastle Region Art Gallery: plate 155
New South Wales Government: plates 4, 78, 108, 114, 120, 125, 128, 154
Queensland Art Gallery: plates 17, 123
Tate Gallery, London: plates 10, 131
University Art Museum, University of Queensland Richard and Arija Austin: plate 91
Alan Boxer: plates 40, 56
Joseph Brown: plate 49
Martin Browne: plate 100
Philip Bacon: plates 72, 99
Gayle and Geoffrey Cousins: plate 156
Robin Gibson: figs 2, 4, 5, 6, 59
Ray Hughes: fig 25
Hogarth Galleries: plates 92
Holmes à Court Collection: plate 84
Lou and Brenda Klepac: fig 28

All the private collectors who wish to remain anonymous

PHOTOGRAPHIC CREDITS

All works of art reproduced in colour were photographed by Suzie Ireland from the Art Gallery of New South Wales with the exception of:
Art Gallery of Queensland: plate 123
Art Gallery of South Australia: plates 135
Artbank: plate 82
Mark Ashkanasy: plates 11, 14, 15, 24, 26, 28, 30, 47, 49, 51, 64, 69a-b, 70, 76, 97, 101, 118, 122, 126, 150, 151, 153
John Austin: plate 84
Australian Galleries: plates 62, 161
John Bolton (courtesy of Bridget McDonnell Gallery): plate 16
Christie's: plate 116
Bryan Hand: plates 72, 99
Lloyd Hessey: plate 155
George Holmes: plates 32, 33, 41, 43, 53
Heidrun Lohr (courtesy of Martin Browne Gallery): plates 89, 98, 100
National Gallery of Victoria: plates 50, 113
Marlborough-Gerson Gallery, New York: plate 81
Rex Moir: plate 91
Bruce Moore: plates 22, 36, 37, 39, 94
John Pilkington: plates 6, 35, 44, 157
Sotheby's: plates 75, 107
Chris Stacey: plate 17
Richard Stringer: plate 144
Tate Gallery, London: plates 10, 31
Greg Weight: plates 9, 48, 65, 87, 90, 117, 130, 139, 148, 149
Daryl Wiseley: plate 106
Greg Woodward: plates 46, 80a-f

While every effort has been made to trace the photographers, the authors are unable to credit those responsible for plates 152 and 156.

ACKNOWLEDGMENTS

Many people and institutions have contributed to the organization of this project, incorporating a major publication as well as a touring exhibition. We thank the following from The Art Gallery of New South Wales: Suzie Ireland, photography; Sherrie Joseph, copyright and reproduction department; Sarah Keogh, graphics department; Alan Lloyd, Stewart Laidler, Paula Dredge, Simon Ives, Rose Peel, Ranson Davey, Sun Yu, Yang Yan Don and Bill Lamont, conservation department; Susan Schmocker, Kay Truelove and Stevan Miller, library; Ljubo Marun, Emma Smith and Mathew Piscioneri, registration department; Simone Aquilina, Leanne Primmer, Debbie Spek and Helen Kidd, administrative services; Belinda Han-rahan, marketing; Jan Batten, publicity; Margot Capp, sponsorship; Anne Flanagan and Stefanie Tarvey, exhibitions management; workshop and installation staff; Bridget Pirrie and Peter Raissis, volunteer proofreaders. We also thank for their cooperation the following staff from institutional lenders: Betty Churcher, Mary Eagle, Tim Fisher, Warwick Reader and Jane Hyden, National Gallery of Australia; James Mollison, Timothy Potts and John McPhee, National Gallery of Victoria; Doug Hall and Timothy Morrell, Queensland Art Gallery; Ron Radford, Art Gallery of South Australia; Paula Latos-Valier, Art Gallery of Western Australia; David Bradshaw and Annette Larkin, Newcastle Region Art Gallery; Margaret Rich, Ballarat Fine Art Gallery; Anne Brodie, Holmes à Court Collection, Perth; Peter Perry, Castlemaine Art Gallery; Pat Sabine and Christa Johannes, Tasmanian Museum and Art Gallery; Nicholas Serota, Tate Gallery, London; Sue Ellen Jeffers and Mere-dith D. Sutton, Archer M. Huntington Art Gallery, University of Texas at Austin; Fran Considine Cummings, Gold Coast Art Gallery; Ross Searle, Perc Tucker Regional Gallery, Townsville; Dianne Heenan, Rockhampton City Art Gallery. We are grateful to the follow-ing for help towards the location of works in Australia: Anne and Stuart Purves of Australian Galleries, Robin Gibson, Philip Bacon, Martin Browne, Eva Breuer, Ray Hughes, Joseph Brown, Lauraine Diggins, Chris Deutscher, Bridget McDonnell, Kathie Robb of Christie's, Jane Clark and Justin Miller of Sotheby's and Clive Evatt and Ace Bourke of Hogarth Gal-leries, Sydney; and the following artists for their reminiscences: Tim Storrier, Michael Johnson, Lawrence and Edit Daws, David Christian, Peter Wright, George Gittoes and John Olsen. Special thanks to Beryl Whiteley, Arkie Whiteley and Fran Hopkirk; also Mal-colm Tweedie, Christian Quintas, Sara Ducker and Jennifer Clare, as well as the support of friends too numerous to mention. Lydia Burns has been curatorial assistant on a part-time basis and our thanks for her valuable contrib-ution. Finally, and most importantly, our deepest gratitude to Charlotte Hayman, Assis-tant Curator, who has been involved with the retrospective and publication from inception. Charlotte's work at all levels, including liaison with lenders, arrangement of photography, research and preparation of the catalogue, chronology and bibliography – not to mention countless other essential tasks she has carried out for the whole project – has been conducted with the utmost grace and reliability. Indeed she has been the backbone without which it would simply not have come to fruition.

PHOTOGRAPHIC CREDITS (pp i–xii)

i & ii. Ladbroke Grove, London, 1961:
© Kerry Dundas
iii. Pembridge Crescent, London, 1963: photographer unknown
iv. Lavender Bay, Sydney, c. 1980s: still from ABC documentary *Alchemy* © Peter Cose
v. With Wendy, Lavender Bay, Sydney, c. 1980s: still from ABC documentary *Alchemy* © Peter Cose
vi. Gasworks Studio, Waverton, Sydney, 1972: © Greg Weight
vii. With Arkie, Chelsea Hotel, New York, 1968: photographer unknown
viii. Gasworks Studio, Waverton, Sydney, 1972: © Greg Weight
ix. Gasworks Studio, Waverton, Sydney, 1972: © Greg Weight
x. With Joel Elenberg, Lavender Bay, 1980: © Graham McCarter
xi. With *Reason and Sense*, Lavender Bay, 1978: © Greg Weight
xii. Drawing Francis Bacon, London, 1981–82: © John Edwards, The Estate of Francis Bacon

FRONTISPIECE (p. 2): Reiby Place, Sydney, 1985, © Graham McCarter

This book was first published on the occasion of the Brett Whiteley Retrospective at The Art Gallery of New South Wales

Exhibition sponsored by Optus Communications

First published in Australia in 1995 by Thames & Hudson Australia, Wurundjeri Country, 132A Gwynne Street, Cremorne, Victoria 3121

First published in the United Kingdom in 1995 by Thames & Hudson Ltd, 181A High Holborn, London, WC1V 7QX

New paperback edition 2004
Reprinted 2024

Brett Whiteley © 1995 and 2004 The Art Gallery of New South Wales
Designed by Adam Hay, London

British Library Cataloguing-in-Publication Data
A catalogue record for this book is available from the British Library

ISBN 978-0-500-28548-0

Printed and bound in China by Toppan Leefung Printing Limited

Be the first to know about our new releases, exclusive content and author events by visiting
thamesandhudson.com
thamesandhudsonusa.com
thamesandhudson.com.au

FSC
www.fsc.org
MIX
Paper | Supporting responsible forestry
FSC® C104723

Contents

Sponsor's Preface

Optus Communications is proud to have the opportunity to present the Brett Whiteley Retrospective on national tour to all states and the Northern Territory from September 1995 until the end of 1996.

Brett Whiteley was one of the most exciting artistic talents to emerge in Australia in the last forty years. As a painter, sculptor and draughtsman, the images he has left with us are testament to the enormous talent and vision that pushed art to the very edge of possibilities. To an extent, there are similarities between the artist and Optus – an emerging force in Australia with a vision focused on pushing telecommunication service delivery to new heights.

This exhibition covers the period from the late 1950s to the last few years of Whiteley's life. Many of the works have never been shown in Australia and have been lent from a number of private and public collections in England and the United States.

Optus would like to thank The Art Gallery of New South Wales for staging the exhibition and to note the magnificent job that curators Wendy Whiteley and Barry Pearce have done in pulling together this spectacular and truly representative collection of one of Australia's greatest artists.

There is no doubt that the Brett Whiteley Retrospective will entrance and fascinate those who visit the exhibition as it travels throughout Australia over the next fifteen months.

Bob Mansfield
CEO Optus Communications

Foreword

Brett Whiteley had an extraordinary and intensely charismatic energy. It was an energy that endowed him with a consuming and quicksilver curiosity. Inevitably he attracted an image of a person of fleeting associations, with ideas, with issues, with art even and, most particularly, with people like him, who had that natural instinct for enquiry into the diverse attractions and often the deeper recesses of the human psyche. Thus it is that the seemingly cliché-ridden Whiteley public persona has tended to subvert the image of Whiteley the artist. This exhibition, a selective review of the achievements of a tumultuous and creative life, seeks no greater objective than to place him where he belongs: as a truly creative and individual spirit in the annals of twentieth-century Australian art.

Of course, like two of his heroes, Modigliani and Bacon, the person can never be separated from the art; the creator and the created are synonymous and, for Whiteley, art was as much an essential of life as life was an essential of art. It was a creed rich in opportunity for an artist devoted to the exploitation of the human figure, just as he was devoted to the exploration of the human opportunity in life. He was an indefatigable figurative artist who enriched his subjects – landscapes, Lavender Bay, birds, trees, animals, autobiographical orgies – with an indelible human sensuality. It was not the human condition that Whiteley explored but the human experience, and the expression of that experience naturally touched upon the delicacies of texture and sensuality that so engaged him and which he then so passionately passed on to his work.

Whiteley may always be linked with that somewhat quixotic image of a man travelling through life at a pace that permitted only a momentary touching, encounters of tantalizing brevity and an almost care-less disregard, but that was the inevitable nature of a man who so sought the mirage of freedom. There is a sense of liberation in his art which is captured in that unequivocal delight in the experience of the moment, the indulgent sensuality and the satisfaction and fulfilment of the moment. Whiteley's investigations have no profounder aspirations than to immortalize the experience, and this he achieved with unrelenting imagination, individuality and ultimately an immense and humane beauty. That beauty is enshrined in his drawing: the sweeping if at times laboured lines, the varied detail of imagery evoked in his views and landscapes, and above all in his delight in capturing the visual expression. Whether the enveloping line of a nude, the seemingly random lines of a Parisian balcony, the rich roundness of the Olgas, a bird, a tree or a flower, the texture of sensuality was for him an essential mark of human experience and involvement.

This exhibition has been in our minds for many years, and was discussed with Brett well before his death. Indeed it was something that he, naturally, was to be closely involved with and looked forward to with a mixture of eager anticipation and nervous uncertainty. In his absence the main mantle for conceiving and delivering the exhibition and the accompanying book has fallen to our Head Curator of Australian Art, Barry Pearce, working in conjunction with Wendy Whiteley. I acknowledge with gratitude the great commitment they have displayed in the thoroughness and the intelligent observation that they have brought to bear on the whole project, ably assisted by Charlotte Hayman. Our thanks also to the Whiteley family for their co-operation throughout.

Edmund Capon
Director

The London Years
Bryan Robertson

Brett Whiteley arrived in London in 1960 at the most auspicious moment in this century for the reception of Australian art by the English and the well-being of resident or temporarily expatriate Australian artists. Russell Drysdale, Sidney Nolan and Arthur Boyd had each in turn made a considerable and recent impact on collectors, critics and the general public.

As the Director of the Whitechapel Gallery since 1952, I had already presented the Nolan retrospective. By 1960, Nolan had lived in London for a decade, causing a minor sensation with his show of cinnabar-red paintings of eroded mountain ranges and deserts at the Redfern Gallery in 1952, and achieving what can only be termed star status with his 1957 retrospective exhibition at the Whitechapel Gallery. Boyd arrived in London rather later, in 1959, showing with acclaimed dramatic force an early group of *Bride* paintings at the Zwemmer Gallery in 1960 and with the promise of a retrospective exhibition at the Whitechapel Gallery in 1963 – that date, and the show, I offered immediately after seeing Boyd's very moving paintings at Zwemmer's.

In London I also became friendly during the fifties and sixties with Roy de Maistre, who had been living and working in England since the 1920s and was one of the earliest friends of Patrick White during his youthful stay in London in the thirties, and of the nineteen-year-old Francis Bacon. All three men were close friends. Sitting in de Maistre's studio on an Art-Déco couch designed thirty years earlier by Bacon, I became increasingly interested in Australia, Australian art and in the creativity of an exceptional number of Australian writers, designers, dancers and singers who appeared to be reaching a peak of recognized activity.

There were numerous other excellent painters from Australia also living and working in London in the fifties and sixties, apart from Nolan, Boyd and de Maistre. These artists included Francis Lymburner, Louis James and Tony Underhill, with longish visits from Frank Hodgkinson, John Olsen, Leonard Hessing, Albert Tucker, Leonard French and John Passmore. Lawrence Daws arrived in England around 1960.

The favourable climate for Australian art in England was helped by the existence in London since the 1920s of the Redfern Gallery in Cork Street, founded by a New Zealander, Rex Nan Kivell, and directed through the fifties and sixties by his partner, Harry Tatlock Miller, an Australian and life partner of Loudon Sainthill who, with a few other Australians, exhibited occasionally at the Redfern. The great artist Ian Fairweather had exhibited at the Redfern before the war, reputedly sending his paintings rolled in newspaper with hardly any other packing from Bribie Island, just off the coast of Australia.

My growing concern for Australian art developed quite independently, largely through friendships with Nolan, de Maistre and Boyd. I commissioned a text from Colin MacInnes for the catalogue for the 1957 Nolan retrospective and this formed the basis for a slightly longer text in the first comprehensive monograph published on Nolan (Thames and Hudson, 1961) which I edited and to which Kenneth Clark and myself also contributed separate texts. Clark was a very good friend to Australian art for a long while. He acted as the official buyer in London just after the Second World War for the National Gallery of Victoria through the Felton Bequest, and in the late forties visited Australia, came across Sidney Nolan's paintings and became Nolan's first and most famous patron outside Australia. In the fifties Clark presented the first Nolan painting to the Tate, one of the red paintings of eroded mountains. Clark bought other works by Nolan over the years, including one of the largest and most beautiful of the 1957 *Bracefell and Mrs Fraser* series from the retrospective at Whitechapel, to which he had contributed a catalogue preface.

This will, I hope, give some indication of the propitious scene in London for an Australian artist when Brett Whiteley, just arrived from Italy, walked into the Whitechapel Gallery in the summer of 1960 and asked to see me. He seemed almost absurdly young and boyish and was in fact only about twenty-one, slight in build, restless, wiry, at once cheeky and delicate in his approach – I was thirty-five, and he didn't at first quite know how to take me, or deal with me – and pink-faced from the Italian sun, wearing T-shirt and cotton pants, with an almost round crop of tight, red-gold curls, subtle and jokey in talk, darting about all over the gallery, filled with wit and bravado and enthusiasm for Europe, for Italian painting – for life. He was naturally intrigued to know that I was planning a big show of Australian painting for Whitechapel for the following year. Plans were in the penultimate stage. Brett danced and feinted round me like a friendly boxer, full of questions and challenges: a born goader to anyone even remotely in authority.

I had visited Australia for the first time in February and March of 1960, ostensibly on a lecture tour for the British Council covering Perth, Adelaide, Melbourne, Tasmania, Sydney and Brisbane, but really working night and day to visit studios and galleries and meet as many artists and collectors as possible with the idea of presenting a broad-based show of Australian painting at Whitechapel. In talk with Nolan and the just-arrived Arthur Boyd in 1959, I had learned of an impending 'official' show of Australian painting planned and selected by what was then a very conservative Art Advisory Board and scheduled for the Tate Gallery some time in 1961. There was the probability that a lot of good things, including the work of many painters, would be excluded from this show at a time when abstract painting or even a degree of fantasy were equated at Australian official level with degeneracy, or at least with valueless bohemian self-indulgence. Officials wished to present a rosy vision of Australia to the outside world, not carcasses in deserts, or surrealism or abstraction. It seemed the most useful thing to do, to present in London not a rival show to the official Tate exhibition but a complementary survey that might redress any imbalances and feature work by younger artists as well as the seasoned veterans – who were still, themselves, an unknown quantity in London.

Almost immediately after Brett and I met for the first time at Whitechapel, he introduced me to his elegant, blonde and surprisingly youthful mother, Beryl Whiteley, who had separated from his father and settled in London. Brett arrived in London with Wendy: an exceptionally pretty and swiftly intelligent girl, with a great sense of clothes and style, in looks and spirit made for the sixties, full of wit and humour to match Brett's. They had been involved with each other since childhood, and were married almost at once, with a big party at Knightsbridge – the first of a good many parties given by Brett's mother.

I became a friend of the family, with gaps when Brett moved on to the US towards the end of the sixties with a Harkness Commonwealth Fellowship, settling in New York in a penthouse studio at the Chelsea Hotel with his wife and daughter, Arkie. We kept in touch later through his mother back in London. But in those earlier years, Brett quickly became part of the London art world, a familiar figure at private views. He formed a group of friends, often drinking in the Elgin pub in Ladbroke Grove opposite his first small apartment, not far from the crowded Portobello Road street market. It was at the Elgin that Brett met people who had known Christie, the infamous serial killer, who was to be an early source of inspiration. Close to Brett at this time was Mick Johnson, another talented young painter from Australia who lived in the same building and was funny, hard up and enjoying the sixties. The English painters David Hockney and Roger Hilton, whose work Brett admired, and a number of other young Australian painters also lived in the same area.

Shortly after Brett and I met in the gallery, he was able to show me a group of recent paintings and some drawings, made in Italy (where he'd enjoyed a travelling scholarship, his first time out of Australia) and in some cases completed in London. Seeing Brett's work for the first time absolutely bowled me over. There had been nothing visible in Australia. This was one of the great moments of my life in any studio. The paintings were of startling maturity, richness and spiritual and imaginative poise, perfectly at ease in their medium and wholly original. It was hard to believe that they were by such a young artist. The images weren't merely sophisticated or knowing but totally realized in depth, filled with youthful panache and energy and above all a personal vision.

Three large paintings in particular stood out. As they were untitled, we called them after their principal colour: *Red Painting, White Painting* and *Black Painting*. I chose them for the show at once, knowing that they would provide the perfect youthful climax for the Australian exhibition, serving as its focal point

Figure 1
WENDY AND ARKIE AS A BABY 1964
Charcoal on paper, 56 x 76.2 cm

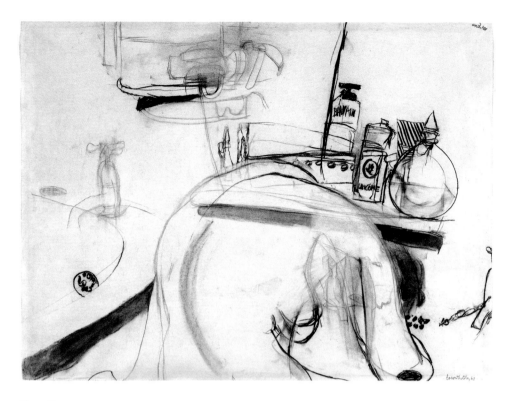

Figure 2
BATHROOM DRAWING 1963
Charcoal on paper, 54 x 76 cm

and star attraction. And this they did in spades, hanging together with considerable presence on the far-end wall of the gallery in 1961 and dominating a strong and lively exhibition. *Red Painting* was bought by the Tate Gallery; *White Painting* was sold to the Contemporary Art Society, at that time based in the Tate Gallery but existing quite independently, through members' subscriptions, to purchase contemporary art and distribute works among public galleries in England with insufficient funds for contemporary art. *Black Painting* was marked 'not for sale' by Brett.

There was a big press for the Australian show, in which Brett often figured with considerable praise. Although many other works were sold from the show – including a cool, semi-abstract, nocturnal *Nude with Moon* painting by Godfrey Miller, also to the Tate Gallery – Brett had plainly arrived on the scene. The show was a perfect vehicle for his youthful début in London.

His paintings touched me particularly because of the way in which they pushed landscape painting into a new area, in which the land itself seemed to be filled, packed, *instinct* with human association, remnants, occupancy. The paintings were very sexual: I don't mean that penises and vaginas, breasts and buttocks were swirling around in the paint; sexuality was somehow below the surface, like a semi-buried civilization in a Middle Eastern *thel*, or ancient burial mound. Flowing contours merged one into another; shapes were rounded and obliquely human; colour in most of these paintings in the late fifties and

Figure 3
STUDY FOR SUMMER AT SIGEAN 1962
Charcoal and mixed media on paper, 73.5 x 115 cm

early sixties was restricted to Indian reds, ochres, cinnamon, black and white, browns and dull yellows.

Brett pushed abstract concepts to the very edge, retaining always a sense of place, of habitation and events in the calm of aftermath. You could see the stylistic references, the points of contact with other art, with the way, for instance, in Australian art, that Drysdale handled rocks and desert. There were slighter Australian links with other mentors, and with de Kooning of the *Excavation* period. Brett's great loves in European art were Duccio, Cimabue and Piero della Francesca, seen at length in Italy – and he loved Piero's *The Baptism of Christ* and *The Nativity* in London's National Gallery. He also had twentieth-century heroes, such as William Scott, Arshile Gorky and Francis Bacon.

I gave a dinner party at the Café Royal after the private view of the Australian show and, at Brett's request, invited Bacon so that Brett could meet him. I knew that Francis would be more sympathetic to the figurative aspects of Australian painting than he was to most contemporary art – he ridiculed all abstract art but made frequent use of its props and devices in his own painting. I don't know whether he saw the show, but he was waiting at the Café Royal, amiable and sober. He and Brett took to each other, talked and argued all evening and kept up a lively friendship over the years. Later, Brett developed a respect and liking for Bridget Riley, paradoxically enough. He asked after these two artists when he was away from London, although he was always far closer to Bacon.

Robert Hughes came over for the show. I had invited him in Sydney to contribute a long preface to the Australian catalogue, and Hughes wrote an excellent essay, his first commission outside Australia – he was about twenty-three at the time and still working as a painter, although writing was soon to capture all of his time. Not long after his arrival in London, Hughes secured a job as regular art critic for *The Observer*, working for John Douglas Pringle – who had worked

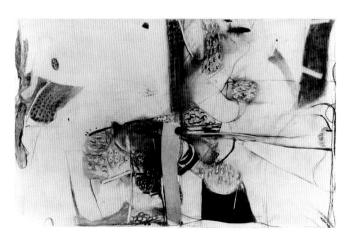

in Australia – and living a vividly picaresque life in Maida Vale. Pringle was behind a lot of the generous press coverage given to Australian art at this time.

Also around this time, in 1961, Barry Humphries appeared in late-night sessions at Arthur Boyd's home in Highgate or at Charles Blackman's rented house nearby. Brett came to these very funny gatherings sometimes: he and Sidney Nolan became particularly friendly – Sidney was always alert to the new element in town – but the Whiteleys really had their own friends. Gradually, Al Alvarez the poet and critic joined the gatherings, and as a Boyd admirer, the young Tom Rosenthal, then working for Thames and Hudson, which in the sixties published the first monograph on Boyd, as for Nolan.

There were a lot of crowded and informal parties at my flat in Chelsea, to which Brett and Wendy came often, as well as to parties at the Whitechapel Gallery after the opening of each show. Brett certainly met Rauschenberg in London at my flat, and Robert Motherwell and Helen Frankenthaler when they were over from New York, as well as Clement Greenberg, Rothko and Newman. For this was still the time when American art was having its maximum impact in Europe and most centrally in London. At Whitechapel the series of exhibitions started by the epoch-making Pollock show of 1958 was strongly under way with retrospectives for Kline, Guston, Tobey, Rothko, Motherwell, Frankenthaler, Louis, Krasner, Johns and Rauschenberg. For Brett, there were developments in figurative painting to consider, from Larry Rivers, Jim Dine, Warhol, Rosenquist, Lichtenstein and the great wave of Pop Art.

Interwoven with these arrivals in London were Whitechapel's *New Generation* shows, of painting in 1964, and of sculpture in 1965, which formalized the arrival on the scene of Bridget Riley, David Hockney, John Hoyland and Allen Jones, with Brett included among them. In the sculpture exhibition, there were fantastic works in new, synthetic, brilliantly coloured materials by Phillip King, William Tucker, Roland Piché and David Annesley among others, mainly working in assemblage directions encouraged by Anthony Caro.

Like the rest of his generation, Brett had to come to terms with the advent of American art. Although for young artists in the sixties, New York seemed increasingly the place to be, I don't believe that the example of American painting was much use to him, except in terms of increased scale common to all painters at the time and, marginally, the influence of Rauschenberg's 'combine' paintings, in separated canvases deployed like diptychs or triptychs on to which photos or texts or objects were occasionally collaged. And London was not wholly given over to American art. As well as important shows of Calder, David Smith and de Kooning at the Tate, Brett would also have seen superb official shows of Rouault, Chagall, Magritte and Giacometti, among many others.

Although Brett made trips away from London, to Paris, back to Italy, to Sigean and to Majorca where, at Deya, he and Wendy became friendly with Robert Graves, it should be remembered that Brett worked centrally in London, and worked very hard. London was still the swinging playground of Europe and the US. Girls shopped at Biba's, Mary Quant's miniskirts gave place to ethnically inspired creations by Zandra Rhodes, Ossie Clark designed simpler clothes using lovely fabrics by his wife, Celia Birtwell, and both designers were immortalized by David Hockney in a double portrait. This was the time of Ravi Shankar and the rediscovery of Indian music, flower power and love-ins, the Beatles and the Rolling Stones, Peter Cook and Dudley Moore performing at *The Establishment*, poor Barry Humphries prancing around night after night as Fagin in the long-running, unsinkable musical *Oliver!* We read *Domus, Metro, Art International, Studio International* and *ArtForum*. The art dealer Robert Fraser and Mick Jagger were driven off in handcuffs by the police on dope charges, and Richard Hamilton made an artwork of the press photo of the event.

Figure 4
STUDY FOR CHRISTIE *c.* 1964–65
Charcoal and brown conté on paper, 16.7 x 24.5 cm

Figure 5
FRANCIS BACON *c.* 1964–65
Charcoal on paper, 16.6 x 24.5 cm

Figure 6
RITA NELSON *c.* 1964–65
Charcoal and mixed media on paper, 16.7 x 24.5 cm

Brett was in the middle of this with Wendy and his cronies and kept his head, enjoying a lot of the action but always working hard. Apart from de Kooning, who was loved in Australia, his new connections were somewhat anachronistic: Bacon and Matisse. He spent a lot of time studying the big *L'Escargot* collage at the Tate. He walked a lot, exploring London, districts like Paddington near Notting Hill Gate, and he enjoyed the parks. He was popular everywhere because of his absolute directness of approach, his buzz of enthusiasm and his wry humour.

He had to deal with success, which can be as tricky to handle as failure for a young artist – Brett was still in his twenties – and a lot of attention. He was an amazing achiever at this stage, always seeming to win prizes or gain scholarships. He was generous to his friends: he gave me, for instance, a small perfectly beautiful, richly glowing landscape-based semi-abstract painting, and later some drawings over the years, which I treasure. As a painter, he showed great strength and confidence, sticking to his figurative principles unfazed by a lot of very fashionable abstraction, from abstract expressionism to Op Art. He made many friends and sold a lot of work.

Hans and Elsbeth Juda became fond of the Whiteleys as well as buying Brett's work for their collection. Hans Juda had founded and then edited a beautifully produced fabrics magazine *Ambassador*.

Their spacious and elegantly modern apartment was the scene of many crowded gatherings. One such party – in which Brett and Wendy are visible, with a lot of other members of the art world – was photographed by Lord Snowdon and reproduced in the book *Private View*, an account of the London art world written by myself and John Russell, published in 1965. For the book's launch, the Snowdons gave a dinner party at Kensington Palace for most of the artists, officials, critics and collectors who appeared in the book, and Brett and Wendy were present there and for the party later that night at the Royal College of Art.

In 1961, not long after the successful Australian show at Whitechapel, the Australian Government asked me if I would serve as a commissioner for the Australian participation in the newly created *Biennale de la Jeunesse*, an international showcase for young artists to be launched in Paris with great fanfares. Malraux was Minister of Culture and France was more lavish than usual over cultural affairs. Canberra left the choice of artists to me and my fellow commissioner, the elderly painter Moya Dyring, who had lived for decades in Paris. Out of touch with recent Australian painting, she handed the choice of artists for the Biennale to me. Each country was allowed three artists. With Moya's agreement, I chose Lawrence Daws, Charles Blackman and Brett Whiteley to ring the maximum changes. We put up a powerful group of works and Brett won on a unanimous vote the first prize for Australia. Nobody in Paris seemed to have heard of Australian painting before, and the show caused a good deal of excitement. This was the first Australian participation in an international art exhibition of this kind, and we were all jubilant. Brett and Wendy were in Paris with the other painters and Moya Dyring threw a fine party in her studio. It was a very good moment: to see the success of Australian art extending beyond London.

From his first arrival in London Brett was casting around for a commercial gallery, and was included in a group show at McRoberts and Tunnard. His first one-man exhibition was held in March 1962 at Matthiesen's, an old established firm with fine, spacious premises in Bond Street which had always specialized, with considerable distinction, in old master paintings and drawings. It was warmly received. Soon after, Brett moved onto a new series of paintings of a female nude bathing. They were sensuous images, often quite erotic in their plunging, swooning arabesques – like Matisse on speed. Each nude, stooping or reaching, had great presence, thinly but lusciously painted in a slightly lighter palette than before, with flashes of pale blue and yellow to offset the familiar Whiteley near-monochrome.

Somewhat earlier, Brett had become obsessed for a mercifully short period with the story of Christie, a pathological murderer of young women who used a chair, gas and tubing for his crimes in Rillington Place, Paddington, not far away from Brett's studio. For a long while, I could only look suspiciously at Brett's convoluted and passionate nudes in tubs, semi-abstracted as they were, but the Christie preoccupation soon passed, culminating in the Christie–London Zoo exhibition at the Marlborough New London Gallery in 1965. The bathroom nudes really had been a celebration of women bathing, free of sinister undertones. In some ways they were not dissimilar in essence to what Degas said visually with such radical lack of sentimentality about the beauty and vulnerability of women washing themselves seventy years earlier, but in a different language: Brett's images were post-Matisse and perhaps even post-Bacon.

Brett's brilliance as a draughtsman grew all the time he was in London, and so did his painting. But the fascination that the Christie story had for him rang a warning bell. He was tough-minded, sceptical, irreverent and very much his own man with a highly origi-

Figure 8
CRAB *c.* 1964
Charcoal and wash on paper,
62.6 x 48 cm

nal talent, prodigiously gifted at both drawing and painting. But he was also compulsively impressionable, and some of the things that Brett got excited over seemed sometimes to be questionable, too near to visual journalism, or if from more exalted sources, not quite fully digested. He had a deep love for Rembrandt, Masaccio, Piero, the Impressionists, van Gogh, Picasso, Matisse, de Kooning and Bacon. His discovery of Rimbaud later in the decade excited him greatly and yet it produced what I felt was weaker, or confused work. His sensitivity and intelligent insights were never in question, but he talked sometimes of Rimbaud or van Gogh almost like a record sleeve – too excitable, too exclamatory, oversimplified. Occasionally, I saw signs of this in his work. He sometimes confused sensation with feeling. But eventually he usually disproved my misgivings in a marvellous drawing or painting.

I think that Brett's dichotomy, if he had one, was summed up in the choice of music that was nearly always playing on the hi-fi if you visited his spacious studio in London in an elegant and quiet part of Kensington. As you walked in, you'd hear either Vivaldi's *The Four Seasons,* or one of the concertos for various instruments and strings – or Bob Dylan, who became a lifelong passion for Brett. In these two musical extremes lay Brett's dilemma: the struggle to remain a serious artist when artists were increasingly

Figure 9
SWINGING MONKEY *c.* 1964–65
Charcoal, ink and collage on
paper, 76.2 x 54.4 cm

Figure 10
BATHROOM DRAWING 1962–63
Conté on paper, 54 x 70.5 cm

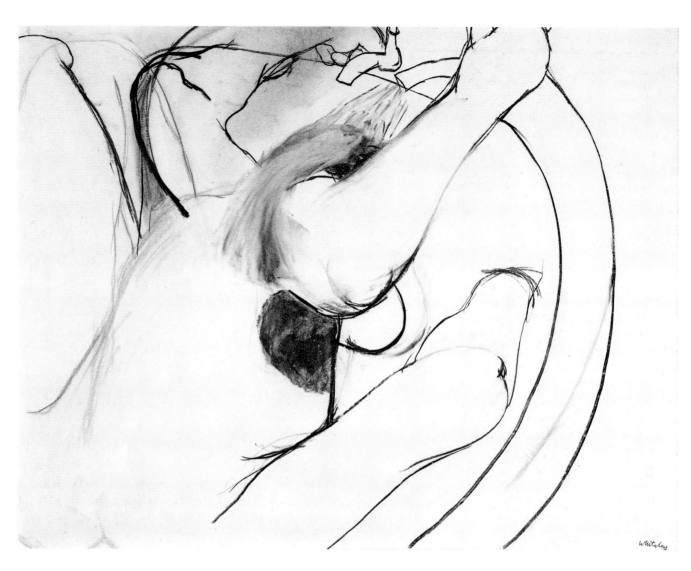

accorded the status of pop stars, and sometimes trivialized their work in the necessary balancing act. The transcendence and formality of Vivaldi at one extreme, the singer immersed in life and the world at the other.

Brett's time in London was a good period in his life. He worked hard, as he always did of course, but perhaps with less strain than in later years. The decade moved on and the swinging scene ran out of energy and focus. In art, minimalism, politico-social art, conceptual themes and art-and-language arrived and painting itself, including Australian painting, was pushed to one side. In Biafra, in Vietnam and Cambodia, in the poor black districts of American cities, and in the prison riots at Attica, violence increasingly dominated the world. The 1968 students protest in Paris, in sympathy with the strike of the Renault workers, had its grim echoes and repercussions among poor and disaffected art students in London turning also against some of the art world excesses of the sixties. As opposed to the world of

poetry, say, or music, too much money had passed hands: art was in a state of surfeit. The days of the cheerful sexual revolution, a lot of humour, innocent pot-smoking, incessant parties, happenings, buoyant travel, much gaiety and open dialogue, seemed to recede into the past.

I acted as a referee when Brett applied for a Harkness Fellowship, which granted an artist two years in the US. New York still seemed the place to be: Brett got his fellowship; it was time to move. I greatly valued our later meetings over the decades in New York, Paris and London. In the mid-seventies, he and Wendy stayed in my house in London while I was in Australia and he had a show at the Marlborough Gallery. Brett's life had changed irreversibly by then, with serious drug addiction. But in the sixties, his youth was wonderfully well spent in London. It was a time of heightened perception and swift reaction, when the art world was extraordinarily open, internationally, and in the first flush of success, Brett made the most of it.

Persona and the Painter
Barry Pearce

The greatest obstacle to appreciating the art of Brett Whiteley may be his life and his death. He is the antithesis of a painter about whom we know nothing and whose works make entirely their own argument. During more than two decades following Whiteley's return to Australia in 1969, after he had created a presence in the art worlds of London and New York, as well as harvesting cultural landscapes far beyond Europe, art critics were both beguiled and constrained by the way he looked, what he had to say, and the stylish manner with which he presented his exhibitions. Everyone was compelled to come to terms with his persona if they wanted to consider his work. Many found themselves between Scylla and Charybdis. Damned if they liked him, damned if they did not, their critical dilemma was intimated by Donald Brook in 1970 when he wrote: 'Brett Whiteley seems to have moved toward a new attitude, in which the status of the art object and the role of criticism are altered out of recognition.'[1]

Few artists can be judged through their work with utter purity. The sculptures of ancient Greece may

have been stripped of their biographical sources by interminable wars and medieval neglect, but by the time they were discovered by the Renaissance, there was a Vasari to sow the history of art with the personality cult. This cult reached its peak in France during the late nineteenth and early twentieth centuries. Indeed when Whiteley, then twenty-one years old, visited Paris in 1960, he made a special visit to Montparnasse to pay homage to one of his heroes whose personal legend once threatened to overshadow his art. Amedeo Modigliani had come to Paris from Italy in 1906 at about the same age that Whiteley did, his existence dramatized with affairs, brawls and drunkenness whilst he struggled to maintain the idealism of his youth. Whiteley recorded a telling comment in his notebook: 'I am now in Modigliani's country. This has been my secret, strange and abnormally mystical ambition to sit alone…to retire entirely from everything and everyone that is important – and allow my understanding (or maybe it's my misunderstanding) of how environment can mould, shape or even stain the personality of a genius.'[2]

Modigliani epitomized those artists who, during the years leading up to the First World War, drifted into Paris to create careers in painting inseparable from the way they lived. Theirs was a kind of idiosyncratic independence which appealed strongly to Whiteley. That visit in 1960 might have been seminal for him, except that he had already established strong tendencies for a self-determined life in art at a remarkably young age, long before he left Australia. As he said to Phillip Adams, 'about eleven I decided, and I quite deliberately decided, that I would go into an art which I didn't have to answer to anyone; that apart from a framer, and plausibly a dealer, it would be a one-man band.'[3]

In 1955 Whiteley wrote to his mother Beryl from Scots boarding school in Bathurst, a town in western New South Wales, asking her to find him a book on the works of Augustus John and Jacob Epstein, as well as a second-hand easel. He was then sixteen years old, and pondering seriously the constellation that would guide him. It has now entered folklore how he discov-

Figure 11
SELF PORTRAIT AT 16 1955
Oil on board, 26.5 x 26 cm

Figure 12
THE ARTIST PAINTING IN
THE BUSH, ULLADULLA, 1958
Photograph by David Christian

Figure 13
**THE ARTIST AT LINTAS ADVER-
TISING AGENCY, SYDNEY,**
c. 1956

ered a small book on the work of van Gogh in a church in Bathurst. By his own account this was in 1952, when he was thirteen: 'That morning, returning to school by bus, I remember the poplar trees were bare for winter; they now seethed with new lines, they were thickets of energy.'[4] It is interesting that in Whiteley's notebook, started during his first year in Europe in 1960, and which contains many lists of great artists who were shaping his ideas, there is hardly a mention of van Gogh. Nor does a reference to van Gogh appear in any letters to his mother, in which he communicated his enthusiasms in quite extensive detail. Yet he had been to Paris on several occasions and seen numerous van Gogh paintings in museums and exhibitions both there and in other European cities, and certainly looked at his works in the National Gallery in London.

This matter is worth considering from the outset only because as Whiteley grew older, the trace ele-

ments of his artist's journey which began in childhood became ever more important to the romantic image that he had of himself, and he may have been inclined to exaggerate them. Given his later anxiety to deal with van Gogh there may be no reason to doubt this germinal legend, but the impression could prevail that the work of the Dutch master was more formative than it actually was. An association may perhaps be drawn between Whiteley's painting *The Soup Kitchen* of 1958 and van Gogh's *The Potato Eaters* – similar subject, similarly clumsy – although Whiteley's work, which he laboured at for three months, is really related to the Australian figurative painter William Dobell, with a side reference to Modigliani. In fact there were far more persuasive and immediate influences coming into play; not to mention Whiteley's internal combustion, which would have driven him to draw and paint even if he had not looked at an art book or stepped foot inside an art museum.

Early in 1956 Whiteley's art teacher expressed surprise that his intention after leaving school was to spend only a year or two at East Sydney Technical College, then the premier art school in Australia, without finishing the course. Meanwhile, in his last months he sat at the back of classrooms sketching whatever took his fancy, be it 'a wren that landed on the tree' or 'the hills, the sort of caressed breasts of Bathurst'.[5] He was focused on his vocation, to which the prospect of art courses was becoming rather incidental. By June he was in Sydney, working at the advertising agency Lintas, and there was no further thought of studying full-time. Rather, he and his friend from Lintas, Michael Johnson, became wanderers and raiders of evening courses in and around the city, in particular John Santry's sketch club in Northwood, and Julian Ashton's life-drawing classes. Before he left school, however, one experience was of special importance.

In 1954 he visited a one-man exhibition of the paintings of the Australian master Lloyd Rees at Macquarie Galleries. Rees was then fifty-nine and moving towards the prime of his incredibly long career. Decades later, as Rees was close to dying, Whiteley wrote to him a moving tribute, recalling the boyhood impression of that exhibition comprising works painted in Italy and Paris: 'The thrill of discovery walking into that little gallery and seeing for the first time – landscapes, big and tiny, that looked to me as if they had every influence in the world in them... these little pictures signed in the corner L. Rees, seemed to have filtered and sometimes dredged the whole of Europe through them.'[6] He described how through the older artist's work he discovered that painting could be an adventure, something to be risked, ragged back, restarted, extended, changed, violated. One did not have to sit in front of a landscape and simply cover the canvas until it was completed.

At The Art Gallery of New South Wales Whiteley was able to see two wonderful masterpieces by Rees, *The Road to Berry* (1947) and *The Harbour from McMahon's Point* (1950). The first was a tiny landscape with the understated sensuousness of line that Whiteley was to expand in spectacular fashion in later years, and which he would come to regard as one of the three greatest landscapes ever painted in Australia; the second was a celebration of the harbour that would become one of his own most inspiring subjects. With Michael Johnson, Whiteley scanned the harbour shores and cliffs for the vantage points where Rees had found his motifs, tracking through the process of how he might have seen it, and exploring the interval between what was perceived and what could be

invented. Unfortunately very few works of this period have survived, but Whiteley's interest in different approaches to painting was already developing in a broad way. Johnson recalled: 'I would go to Brett's house at Longueville and he had a little glass-house at the side of the house. The plants had been thrown out and it became a studio. I was amazed when I went over to see his work – I was into Degas and Botticelli and people like that – the very second day after Brett got the job at Lintas, and there it was, the blue period of Picasso, working-class people in singlets, bony looking characters and so forth. I was quite staggered that Brett was painting out of history books.'[7]

Whiteley was of the modern era, highly receptive to whatever currencies of the moment he could tap, and it must be said that although Rees impressed him it was more the works of Russell Drysdale and William Dobell that led him towards the first important phase of his painting during the late 1950s. Something in the warm pigments of the drought and Hill End pictures of Drysdale, and the compact figure compositions of Dobell, in contrast to the soft atmosphere and idyllic spaces preferred by Rees, seemed to accord with the mood of contemporary painting. Even Sali Herman's Sydney street scenes with their scraped, peeling-wall impastos, made Whiteley think further about the painterly values that existed independently of the subject.

Then, when he began to look at reproductions of international contemporary art at Carl Plate's Notanda Gallery, and in various books available in Sydney, the windows of possibility opened even faster, as he combined with white-heat enthusiasm the sources of art with the sources of life. There was Michael Seuphor's illustrated dictionary encapsulating just about every approach to abstract painting until 1958, Herbert Read's *Contemporary British Art*, and Marcel Brion's *Art since 1945*, which contained an essay by Herbert Read on British painting. As Johnson recalled, 'He had this determination to be an artist that made him more adventurous than the stodgy students at Ashton's. We read these little Penguin and Pelican books obsessively and used to go down in the evening on Thursdays to the soup kitchen and we would draw these derelict characters there...Modigliani played a big role at that stage – in drawing people, characters.'[8]

One who stood out in these publications was the British artist William Scott. Read's essay carried a colour plate of one of Scott's most beautiful paintings of 1957; a squarish still-life abstraction with ochre, white and Prussian blue shapes nuzzling the left and upper sides of a picture plane suffused with glowing orange. Whiteley was especially responsive to this image, and it is possible to see that if he was reluctant to plunge into full abstraction, he could at least flatten his compositions based upon landscapes around the old gold-mining towns of Sofala and Hill End by pushing his horizon line to the very top edge, the way Scott was doing with his table tops. Until Whiteley met Roger Hilton and Francis Bacon a few years later, Scott was to hold the strongest spell on him of any British artist.

Inevitably, Whiteley thought about going to Europe. However, there were events connected with his personal life beforehand which would profoundly affect his psychological make-up, and had more than a little impact on the development of his art. Although he was perceived from childhood to have a rocket-propelled personality, some of his close friends from Lintas observed that he appeared to be going full speed at the world with a sense of seeking compensation. There was a solitary and shrewd streak in him that avoided intimacy, a disquiet it seemed, which he protected by moving fast.

In about May 1956 his mother left for England on an extended holiday, but it was not simply a holiday as far as the family was concerned. Brett felt abandoned, and had threatened to leave school if she went through with it. In Perth en route she received a telegram saying that he had made good his threat, and she was urged to return. He had walked out, burned his books – 'wandered down and stayed under a bridge with some metho drinkers for four days, wandered back into the city, and began existing, painting'.[9] Beryl continued her journey, and after returning to Sydney in October to devote her energy to the wedding of Fran, Brett's older sister by two years, she returned to England the following June for good. The marriage with Clem was over. Within three years the Whiteley household had fallen apart.

The period until Whiteley himself left Australia at the end of 1959 was important for his relationship with his father. Clem was happy for his son to be an artist. He had a creative flair himself, a facility in layout for advertising work, and had produced colour gravure reproductions of the paintings of Dobell, although with greater enthusiasm perhaps than business instinct. He was, however, pragmatic enough to insist that Brett get a job with Lintas so that he could have something to fall back on. A young painter could do far worse than be employed by a company that was exceptionally supportive of artists improving their practice. Whiteley was allowed some Fridays off so that he could have three-day weekends in the country, visiting towns such as Ulladulla, Bathurst, Orange, Sofala and Hill End with his Lintas friends, camping in deserted barns and houses, making

pictures, getting drunk. David Christian, the photographer of the group, remembers packing a two-seater car with a box: 'Brett was like a child. He jumped in the back and off we'd go.'[10] The main part of their cargo apart from booze, bread and cheese would be high-quality art materials procured illicitly from Lintas. On Monday mornings at tea-breaks the senior staff of Lintas, under art director Brian Weekes, would give constructive criticisms of the work that the young artists had brought in from their weekend activities.

Sometimes the friends would just stay around Sydney with an occasional lazy Sunday at The Art Gallery of New South Wales. Apart from the classic Australian paintings there, one favourite work of Whiteley's was a Graham Sutherland painting which he discovered through Drysdale, a semi-abstract called *Welsh Mountains* (1937), with the light of a setting sun in the cleft between two hills. Other times they would sketch together. Michael Johnson recalls one day the group of them sitting in The Rocks doing pen drawings: 'I spent three hours and had three lines down. Max Cullen was there and he had five lines down. Brett had produced enough drawings in this time for an exhibition. They were a package, a quick package. Moreover the contrast between us was that he could get two people into his composition and I could only get one. He was interested in the conflict within the picture space. That was his way, a natural thrust and parry.'[11] Whiteley's life was jammed with thrust and parry as he worked hard at his art. While at home in Longueville he did his part to help Clem keep the semblance of a family together.

Full speed at the world. That was the way he discovered alcohol at the age of seventeen, the first stimulant of many on a long and dangerous road: 'I found alcohol took the edge off things. That gave me an enormous leap…I remember the first glass of beer I had, the euphoric asparagus squeal off the top of my subconscious was just amazing. I was up on a chair doing a very bad rendering of Fred Astaire.'[12] This could have been a description of the way in which he fell in love with Wendy Julius.

His intoxication for Wendy, who became his lover, marriage partner, friend, critic and combatant for the next thirty-two years, was immediate. He saw her in 1956 at a coffee shop in Rowe Street, a favourite haunt of art students. Her beauty was a miracle of nature, with pale skin, black hair, and electrifying blue eyes. A mutual friend took her to Clem's house, and there she met Brett for the first time. He invited her to accompany him to John Santry's sketch club, and soon discovered that her drawing was much better than his: 'He was quite worried by that in a way. It also started to engender that competitive thing, to push it further, winning, winning, winning all the time. Very driven to be on top, very fascinated with power, always.'[13] This aspect recalled by Wendy of their early relationship is an instructive one as far as Whiteley's work is concerned, because in spite of general admiration in later years for his natural gifts as a draughtsman, he never considered his early drawing to be very good. Indeed he felt that he only really broke through with this side of his talent in the bathroom series of 1963, celebrating the sensuous beauty of Wendy's body, and the intensity of his feelings towards her. In a way she was the making of him as a figure draughtsman, not only as an inspiring subject, but also because if there was something in another he admired, he was impelled to gather speed and overtake.

It was time to get out of Australia. Some of Whiteley's Lintas friends had already left for London, and Wendy had her own fantasies about following in the footsteps of her great aunt, the painter Kathleen O'Connor, who had recently returned after living for many years in Paris. Wendy encouraged Whiteley to apply for the Italian Travelling Scholarship at The Art Gallery of New South Wales, to be judged by Russell Drysdale in October 1959. He was not all that hopeful of winning, for there were established artists putting in for it, fourteen entrants in all, and each required to submit four works. However, Drysdale responded very strongly to Whiteley's paintings, recognizing in the young man a willingness to adapt a traditional ethos of Australian landscape painting, echoing perhaps the mood of his own palette, to a contemporary idiom of abstraction. Three months earlier Whiteley had given up his job at Lintas to devote himself entirely to painting. Now, with the award of the scholarship, he was able to live in Italy for ten months to study the great works of art there. With tremendous excitement he departed by ship in the new year, and stopped in Naples on his way to Rome.

Beryl gave him a lot of support in Europe. She leased an apartment for him in Rome near the top of the Spanish Steps where he stayed for three months. He visited London, then Paris at Easter, moving on to Florence, where Australian sculptor Stephen Walker was living and working on a similar scholarship. Here Whiteley continued the kind of painting he had been doing in Sydney, but devoted much time looking at works of art, fathoming what could be useful for his own repertoire of style and procedure. Whiteley described himself at this period as an art-historical virgin, unprepared for, and ignorant of, the great Italian artists of the past, as he wandered like a dazed tourist through churches and galleries. He continued to produce a mixture of landscapes and abstractions, including a painting of the Spanish

Figure 14
WENDY SLEEPING 1973
Pen, brush and brown ink on paper, 29.9 x 33.4 cm

Steps. Meanwhile, there were traumas at home.

Wendy had been living at Clem's house, and was employed at his decorator's shop, but now quit to get jobs elsewhere, trying to earn enough to join Brett in Europe. One night when he was drunk Clem confessed to her that he feared they would never come back. Beryl was gone, Fran had moved to New Zealand; the family had completely fragmented. In this context, when Clem died just three years later, Brett could hardly deal with it. It haunted him for the rest of his life, partly out of guilt, partly out of a fatalistic pattern to which he felt bound. He imagined that he might not live beyond his early fifties, and he turned out to be right. Unity and division, life and death: these were dichotomies that would inform so much of his work for the next three decades.

Wendy joined Brett in Paris and they moved to Florence, where they stayed for the remainder of his scholarship until November. A notebook of this year and the next in London is an astonishing compression of data reflecting an attempt by Whiteley to reconcile his very real passion for the artists of the past with the need to be a painter of the moment. He discovered the early Italian painters Cimabue, Duccio, Giotto, Masaccio and Piero della Francesca, linking their styles to the flat, abstract qualities of the Byzantine tradition rather than to what he considered to be vulgarities of perspective in the later Renaissance. For example, in the Piero paintings he saw in London, Whiteley looked not so much at the spatial qualities as the spare, dotted landscapes in his backgrounds. He continued some of the Bathurst-style abstractions for a while, for he remained something of a wild colonial boy who never lost his interest in the Australian outback, but he made an imaginative connection between the warm palette of Drysdale, the honey-coloured panels of Duccio, and the ochres and creams of the old Italian walls and buildings that he saw every day. Meanwhile, in his notebook he jotted down aphoristic comparisons between the old and the new, abstraction and recognizable content, and compiled endless lists of artists in and out of favour as he continued to assess them almost daily. These spiralled through his writing like interminable riddles: 'So and so up so and so down Cézanne's blue vase up van Gogh down Utrillo down…Giotto up Corot up eventually stay up except bad painting. Titian, Tintoretto, Bacon and of course W.S.'[14]

He wrote down comments on artists from Uccello to Rothko, the latter of whom he said, 'His paintings issue a strange personal struggle with serenity and agitation', reflecting already Whiteley's fascination with oppositional forces. He made thumbnail sketches of works that he saw in his travels between Italy, Paris and London, by such artists as Zoran Antonio Music, whose work he saw at the Venice Biennale, Bonnard, Modigliani and Marquet, to name a few. But especially prevalent are several based on the contemporary French painter Alfred Manessier. Whiteley most likely found in Manessier a brief alternative to William Scott. With their abstract shapes softened at the edges like tiles and templates tumbled on a river bed, his paintings were seen to mitigate the hard geometric style that Whiteley so despised.

He certainly got something from the American painter Philip Guston, with numerous sketches of wobbly boulder forms similar to Guston's drawings of the 1950s. David Christian remembers that in Whiteley's London studio in late 1960 or early 1961 'he had some Guston pictures torn out of catalogues and magazines and he had them up on the wall'.[15] The association is appropriate, considering Dore Ashton's description of Guston in 1960, which could have been written for Whiteley: 'There are always two voices arguing in him, and he is given to extravagant pursuit of paradox, even in conversation.'[16] Nevertheless, this was just one part of a massive cornucopia of artists' names and verbal images that Whiteley scattered on paper and in conversations which is impossible to simplify. His was a kind of computer greed for all the things that tantalized his curiosity, and in fact his own words would often threaten to obscure rather than clarify. One particular statement indicates that he knew, in a bewilderingly rich artistic labyrinth, he had to hold some sort of instinctive thread that would prevent him losing his way: 'Go to the unfamiliar, go to the end, the whole way the unexplored but even in this passage a piece of cotton in the cave…not so much to find your way back to artistic

safety but just as an assurance of ground covered.'[17]

Michael Johnson turned up in Florence, and he and Whiteley made a journey in August to the Venice Biennale. Here Whiteley was inspired especially by Music as well as by Alberto Burri and Afro. He liked Victor Pasmore, Eduardo Paolozzi and Hans Hartung (who won the prize), but was disappointed in the Americans, except Guston, 'a poet, he refreshed my eye'.[18] On the way back to Florence they stopped at Bologna, travelling on a Vesta motorbike to Grizzana to visit Giorgio Morandi, the venerated master of Italian painting who was nearing the end of his life. Whiteley's interest in this artist was not as obtuse as it may seem. Morandi mainly painted still lifes in quiet celebration of the dignity of common objects on a table with plain, almost colourless backgrounds. Given that still lifes were also the essential source of William Scott's abstractions, these two painters belonged to the same spiritual stable. Years later Whiteley was to pay direct homage to Morandi in a number of restrained, but sonorous still-life paintings.

Johnson has said that there were two Americans who influenced Whiteley then above all others in those early days: Richard Diebenkorn and Arshile Gorky, each in their different ways straddling the arenas of figuration and abstraction, with Gorky more rich with surreal, erotic possibilities. Lawrence Daws, the Australian painter who arrived in London from Italy at the end of 1959 and met Whiteley a year later, confirmed Johnson's observations, although he also mentioned that Whiteley liked the work of the Japanese-American artist Kenzo Okada.[19] Okada's work had an important reference for Whiteley's early abstractions, as well as his later preoccupation with Japan.

Ultimately, this complex libretto of experiences and influences must be set aside to consider the purely visual evidence of what Whiteley was doing. Some of the most interesting drawings he made in his 1960–61 notebook were based upon a trip to the Cotswolds with Beryl and her friend John McCarthy soon after Whiteley arrived in England. Whiteley made several such excursions on weekends. Fragments of landscape – hills, bushes, telegraph posts, roads with traffic markings – are drawn as seen from inside the car. In some, the windscreen forms an inner frame, its contours running close to the sides of the picture plane, creating a tension between the curve and the rectangle. Small shapes, such as the rear-view mirror, or the knees of a passenger, come in from the edges, activating the perimeter of the composition. It may be stretching things to say that a hybrid shape between rectangle and oval can be traced back to Whiteley's drawing of a cricket match when he was seven years old, but certainly it was an archetype that may be found in a number of his abstractions during the early 1960s. The frame-within-a-frame, inside-outside device for landscape became a recurring one, reaching a climax with his views of Sydney Harbour ten years later. Whiteley developed an acute ability for activating large empty spaces by sensitive disposition of forms or lines huddled around the edges.

The Cotswolds sketches have a link to three superb abstractions that Bryan Robertson included in his Whitechapel exhibition of recent Australian painting in 1961. Their deep throb of colour, textures which ranged from radiant, fresco-like glazes to creamy impastos interrupted here and there by slabs of collage, and jostling, overlapping forms which occupied an ambiguous pictorial territory between landscape and erotic figuration, created a sensation. He had now distanced himself a little from the coolness of William Scott and moved closer perhaps to the sensuousness of Roger Hilton, whom he was to befriend later in London. Gorky's influence too was much in evidence.

One of the Whitechapel paintings was purchased by the Tate Gallery. It had the stunning red colour derived from an old barrel of tomato powder that Whiteley had procured from an art shop in the back streets of Florence.[20] The Tate acquisition made Whiteley the youngest artist ever represented in its collections. Quite suddenly his status was in orbit. He began to win international prizes, exhibit in London, and corporate and private collectors began to purchase his work. Bryan Robertson has written evocatively of Whiteley's arrival and phenomenal success on the London art scene during the 1960s, but there are aspects of the relationship between Brett and Wendy at the time which are especially worth noting in so far as they influenced their movements and impacted on the development of his work.

When they arrived in London at the end of 1960 the Whiteleys went straight to Ladbroke Grove, where Michael Johnson was living. They found a place in the same apartment building, in an area where there were many Australian and English artists living and working. But here Whiteley's early success and the rich feast of exhibitions, art museums and interaction with the art scene were counterbalanced by more basic realities of survival. They had just two rooms and it was winter. Restriction of space exacerbated the arguments which had always been part of the passion between them. Wendy got a job in a boutique in Knightsbridge, and her existence became divided between working and playing the role of housekeeper at home. 'Ladbroke Grove was a nightmare,' she said, 'very rough, right next to the station opposite the Elgin pub, where every Friday night someone would be murdered, or there'd be a fight. The Jamaicans who lived in the area too were all smoking pot, which I read as being madly exotic, but it was all so filthy, absolutely filthy.'[21] Often when she came home from work Brett and Michael had been to the pub and the place would be a shambles. After helping Beryl move to a new flat in Knightsbridge, Wendy was invited to stay with her in New York for two months during the summer of 1961. In accepting the invitation Wendy virtually walked out.

This chain of events is inextricably linked to three groups of works that followed over the next three years: the Sigean landscapes; the bathroom paintings; and the Christie series. They formed the structure against which much of Whiteley's reputation would be measured thereafter. After Wendy returned from New York Whiteley began to talk of marriage, partly because of the anxieties he had developed over her absence. She wanted to get out of Ladbroke Grove, away from the pub life and the constant stress of living quarters overlapping with studio space. Whiteley could be messy in his work habits, with little regard for separation between his area for working and that for day-to-day living. Consequently, their marriage, which took place soon after his successful first solo exhibition in London at the Matthiesen Galleries in March 1962, was a conscious attempt to improve things between them. It also turned out to be a significant event for Whiteley's work, for their honeymoon in Sigean, in the south of France, led him to produce the most elegant abstract paintings of his career, paintings that signified a mood of harmony between nature and humanity that is special to the Mediterranean landscape. More pertinently, they reflected an equilibrium that he felt between himself and Wendy. The reason was quite simple: for the first time they now had no conflict of space, and were free from the emotional demands of other people.

The Matthiesen exhibition had sold reasonably well. The interpenetration between figurative and landscape forms in his work was duly noted in the reviews. He had moved away from the free-floating shapes of William Scott and now made them interlock and overlap, but no English writer was quite in a position to adopt Bryan Robertson's perception and enthusiasm for the precocious resonance between Whiteley's Australianness, his response to early Italian Renaissance painting, and his ability to absorb the current ideas of European and American painting: 'His arrival on the European scene in 1961 was dazzling; never had youthful precocity seemed so disconcertingly substantial, deep and alert in its light, its texture, its fabric…its spirituality.'[22] The recognition that Whiteley received at this time happened so fast that there was a real danger of overheating. The period in Sigean was therefore a salvation. For during six months there, surviving on an income from the Prix International at the Paris Biennale, and secure with a contract from the Marlborough Gallery in London, he did not have to deal with criticism, galleries and the selling of pictures. He could just lose himself in painting and drawing.

They heard about the small town of Sigean near the Spanish border through the Australian artist Wendy Paramor. Clem had arrived in London for the wedding, accompanied Brett and Wendy to Paris, where he bought a car and drove them through France to the Pyrenees. Here Brett and Wendy stayed at the house of George Sheridan, an American painter they had met in London, whilst Clem went on to further tour Europe. This was the last time Whiteley saw his father. Paramor then arrived and told them about two large empty double-storey buildings in the middle of a vineyard at Sigean. They packed their things into her truck and left straight away. When they got there, there was no electricity and no water apart from a well-pump. But it was paradise. There were fruit trees, fish from the lake, and as Whiteley later told Sandra McGrath, 'we just watched the sun ripen the grapes, and painted'.[23] The creamy colours of dry hills dotted with olive trees were straight out of Piero. Art became life. He wrote to Lawrence Daws, 'I have discovered the dot.'[24]

Figure 15
SIGEAN 1963
Charcoal on paper on card,
65 x 50.5 cm

The Sigean paintings and drawings also represented a crossroads between abstraction and figuration. His magnum opus of the period, the triptych *Summer at Sigean*, executed during 1962 and 1963, summarizes the position which he had reached. McGrath has written at some length about the work, and how although its resolution after considerable struggle resulted in one of the greatest paintings he would ever make, it was almost too conclusive. In this regard Whiteley was concerned about the potential dead end of abstraction. Referring to artists like Kline and Rothko who had arrived at an ultimate essence, he asked Michael Johnson, 'Where do you go from here?'[25] Formalism had come hard at them, and would continue to do so even though Pop Art soon arrived on the scene. He decided that he must go against the grain. At the same time, he felt compelled to make the sensuous forms of Wendy, which pulsed through the hot colours and mysterious transitions of edges in *Summer at Sigean*, far more explicit.

The Whiteleys travelled by car to Spain, stopping at Barcelona, and then to Majorca, where they stayed at George Sheridan's house and met the English poet Robert Graves, not to mention several Australian artists who were living there. They went to New York next, staying for a fortnight before returning in November 1962 to London, where they settled into a new flat in Pembridge Crescent, near Notting Hill Gate. With more room than they had had in Ladbroke Grove, Whiteley was ready to embark upon a major new series once they had gotten through a bitterly cold winter.

In early May 1963 Whiteley received news of his father's death. He did not cope with this well. He did not want to go back to Australia for the funeral and visit the house at Longueville, where in his boyhood bedroom, he made his first serious drawings of whatever he saw across the bay. As far as he was concerned, someone else could tidy up his father's affairs. Anger, it seems, was his best way of grieving, but he felt too guilty about Clem to be angry. Fran said that both she and Brett had great admiration for their father: 'He was a fantastically nice man – with a real sense of decency. Brett used to say he was a poet, but Brett was closer to his mother because she challenged his mind. His mother was Brett's love of difficulty, whereas daddy would be making people laugh.'[26] Whiteley may have felt that he had contributed to Clem's sense of loss by following his mother to the other side of the world. In some ways he only came to deal with his grief through the Christie series the following year, when he introduced questions of death and evil into his subject matter. Meanwhile, he threw himself with passion into his bathroom series.

Although the Sigean abstractions had comprised various close-up sections of the naked figure, in the bathroom pictures Whiteley brought a single nude right up to the picture plane, closing in on it as if he might reach out and tenderly caress the forms of his beloved while drawing and painting her. There was still a good deal of abstraction in this series, but the erotic ambience was more intimate, as if the eye got so close it could only see the figure as a sequence of shapes, looking up, down, inside and around it in a way which Tom Rosenthal described as 'a kind of Proustian tour'.[27] The slabs of pinks, ochres and creams from Piero's frescoes were still evident, but now joined by the acid blues and greens of the tiled walls and accoutrements of the bathroom. When the series was shown at the Marlborough New London Gallery in 1964, English critics pointed out the references to Bonnard and Bacon but were perhaps more descriptive than effusive.

Norbert Lynton wrote in the *New Statesman*: 'Whiteley is on the side of Degas. It is the girl's distorting, necessary gestures that hold his attention, and the conflict between the hard fact of taps and geyser and her slippery, slumping back. He draws her moving body as though the static so-called life-model had never existed, almost as though he had never before seen a naked body, and at times the repeated and smudged marks of his charcoal jell to deliver an aesthetic kick of unexpected sexuality.'[28] Another writer referred to the spatial detachment that Whiteley may have gleaned from Piero, and Kenneth Coutts-Smith wrote that 'Whiteley sees the figure completely integrated with its environment, the curve of the bath, a wash-basin, taps, are seen almost as if they were sensory extensions of the figure itself. Time also is concretised, the movement of an arm is fixed into sequential positions in space, and as such give an existential flavour to his work.'[29] The reviews were a mixture of coolness and condescension maybe, but amongst them were the most serious comments Whiteley had received to date in London.

His next series caused consternation, even with some of his most ardent admirers. The connection with Bacon in the bathroom series had already been underlined, and now Whiteley decided to follow Bacon's lead more directly with a series of paintings on the theme of the necrophile murderer John Christie. Bacon, it seemed, had challenged the dominance of American abstraction with images of civilization's dark side that could not be denied as powerful and valid expressions of the current state of humanity. Rejecting abstraction almost completely, Whiteley saw Bacon's path as a suitable one to follow, and even a means to come abreast with him in reputation. He

Figure 16
BATHROOM DRAWING 1963
Charcoal on paper, 76.5 x 55.8 cm

also felt compelled to flip over the celebration of idyllic beauty and show that sex could manifest itself in ways that were evil and destructive.

The original idea for the Christie series had occurred to Whiteley when he was living at Ladbroke Grove, not far from Rillington Place, where the murders took place during the 1940s and early 1950s. He walked the streets and frequented the pub where Christie had been. 'It was a general contemplation of that aspect of London – the mixup of races, the asphalt pimping sort of Ladbroke Grove beer-bottle stuff, the violence in London. I feel very sad for a man like Christie. He crystallises the life around him…he could no more control his madness than the world can control its energies. I feel afraid on all levels, from Christie to the White House.'[30] Posing as a doctor, Christie had lured women, mainly prostitutes, to his house, persuading them that he could cure their ailments with a special balsamic inhalant. Whilst they were inclined in a canvas chair he would release gas into the mask, and after they had ebbed slowly into unconsciousness he raped their bodies and hid them in the walls. Of all the research that Whiteley did from newspapers, police files, visits to Madame Tussaud's, and especially through texts which had examined the case extensively, one confounding factor emerged above all others: the image of Christie himself.[31] With his high intelligence, prim appearance, balding head and glasses, and restrained but impeccable manners, he presented himself as the least likely perpetrator of such horrible crimes. Whiteley asked how it was possible to recognize evil, and from a photograph of Christie painted one of the most haunting and disturbing portraits in the history of Australian art, symbolizing the dysfunctional aspect of human existence, just as Arthur Boyd had done in his studies of heads in Melbourne twenty-six years earlier, and Albert Tucker in the mid-1940s with his depictions of criminals painted from newspaper photographs.

The paintings in the Christie series explored the forms of female bodies in various stages of their fate; including Hectorina McLennon holding the mask before her face whilst the figure of Christie released the gas; and the dead body of Kathleen Maloney being ravished by her killer with a macabre, pathological pleasure. Each of these works featured the death chair cradling the victims against dense, impenetrable backgrounds of purplish-brown or ultramarine, strangely compelling in their impact of flesh still radiant with the ghost of the departing life-force. But for all their drama and brutality, none encapsulated the paradox of Whiteley's theme as succinctly as his small Christie portrait. It was here that the artist was least sensational, and yet most insidiously effective in his projection of the image of evil as a sad and frightening aspect of the human condition.

Again English criticism was subdued, if not shocked. During the exhibition of the Christie series at the Marlborough New London Gallery in October 1965, John Russell wrote: 'The paintings themselves are carried out in an eclectic idiom which skates at high speed across the top of the matter in hand. Whiteley the persevering student of a detestable subject is continually over-ruled by Whiteley the Australian wonder whose charm, bluff, cheek and astute raiding of idioms from all over (Bonnard to

Bacon) empower him (literally, in this case) to get away with murder.'[32] Australian writers were hardly less sympathetic. Robert Hughes, a friend and admirer, later questioned the veracity of the artist's experience of real horror and human suffering. Even Whiteley himself, in his letter to Lawrence Daws in September 1964, questioned whether he should go on with the series just after he had started it: 'I think now that it's better to think about: and it means more that way than actually seeing it, or making something that looks like it…the subject is too turgid.'[33] He may have been aware here of the risk of pursuing a kind of miscreant journalism.

Undoubtedly there was much more to it than mere journalism. To begin with, there was Whiteley's internalized preoccupation with his father's death. Beyond that his interest in the question of evil was obsessive, and he genuinely felt that he could be a fellow traveller with Bacon on a quest to uncover its meaning. Whiteley and Bacon in fact developed a friendship, and the latter's ironic pessimism cannot be disassociated from what Whiteley was trying to do. A curious letter was drafted by Whiteley to Bacon in his notebook of 1970–72. It seems that when he last saw the British painter, the younger artist was puzzled and irritated by Bacon's comments on the question that burned in Whiteley for an answer. Whiteley had written, 'By attempting to define and comprehend that nature of evil, does one in anyway alleviate it, or does one merely become the vehicle and perpetration of the very harm one wishes to understand?'[34] He then wrote: 'Dear Francis…The last time I saw you, in New York, you could only recommend that I just go *and do it*. Good advice. Even if you'd considered that there's little else to say to someone who inquires at execution level…making it easier to lie, or to kid, you only answered that there isn't any answer to evil. How come you've been answering for years Francis? So much for Germany and the northern spirit! How easily the Asians recognise it.'[35] What he did not quite realize was that Bacon's aesthetic solutions were his own kind of catharsis. Whiteley wanted to imagine what it was like to feel the flames of hell sear his conscience, and he was not far away from exploring that theme on a gigantic scale.

Painted and exhibited in London at the same time as the Christie series were the London Zoo pictures, which served as an essential companion, especially in the context of Bacon's caged figures. But Whiteley's spirited paintings and drawings of giraffes, monkeys and lions may also be appreciated in terms of his ongoing feeling of connection with the animal and bird kingdoms. He had always loved visiting Taronga Park Zoo in Sydney, and as a child his sister Fran

Figure 17
AFTER CHRISTIE HAD FLED *c.* 1964
Charcoal on paper, 35.7 x 76.7 cm

recalled, 'He was mad about eggs, loved their shape and symbolism…I was almost crucified for stealing eggs from a bird's nest for Brett. His huge appreciation of nature was evident from childhood – he rejoiced in the optical look of the world, and delighted in making art out of it.'[36] One powerful piece of sculpture from the London Zoo works, *White Sacred Baboon* (1965), was carved from a gnarled olive tree root which Whiteley had found on a road near Deya, Majorca, and carted back to the village in a wheelbarrow. Much later in his career, Whiteley made a series of zoo drawings in Sydney, but birds and animals in their natural habitat were also to become important for him after his return to Australia.

Brett and Wendy's daughter Arkie was born in November 1964. She was almost one year old when the Christie–London Zoo exhibition was finished, after which the Whiteleys decided to visit Australia. Exhibitions had been arranged for early 1966 at Kym Bonython's galleries in Adelaide and Sydney, including the Christie–London Zoo pictures, and then later in the year a show at the Australian Galleries in Melbourne, to which several Australian works were

added. His return home was eagerly awaited. The news of his success preceded him, and at the end of 1965 Robert Hughes wrote an article for *The Bulletin* which projected a tantalizing image of the larrikin genius, while summarizing in inimitable style the essence of Whiteley's achievement up to that moment.

Hughes met Whiteley in London in August 1964. The artist was then living at Melbury Road, in a studio once owned by the Pre-Raphaelite painter Holman Hunt. It comprised a large white room with a Gothic roof and a small extra room for a bed, and was his most capacious working space since Sigean. Hughes wrote of him: 'There is something about this nuggety, bristling 26-year-old, with his tangled conversation, eclectic mind and terrier-like curiosity, which is unlike most young English painters.' He continued, 'Every painting of Whiteley's is a roll in the hay with the muse of art history: as soon as an issue about the nature of art or perception was raised by another painter – Gorky, de Kooning, Bacon, Giacometti, Rauschenberg, Johns, Warhol, Piero della Francesca, Uccello, Masaccio – Whiteley was into it, either painting his way through it or arguing it out. His intellectual appetite is matched by no other Australian painter I've met. Like Arshile Gorky, with whose early years Whiteley's have much in common, his outstanding act as a painter is the decision not to be original – not to narrow his style into the crippling uniqueness of a trademark, but to keep it open, and to preserve the flow of ideas between his art environment and his own experience.'[37]

It seems that Jackson Pollock's widow Lee Krasner had considerable admiration for Whiteley, for Hughes reported her as saying, 'I don't know whether Brett's going to be as good as Arshile Gorky was, but he's got the same sort of tenacity. When he sees a painter he admires, he meets his work head-on, and paints straight through the middle of it. He doesn't try to find a way to avoid the influence and look original.'[38] Finally, Hughes was rather more generous about the Christie series in this article than he was in his book *The Art of Australia*: 'The aesthetics of murder: five whores die that Whiteley might work his way through Jasper Johns and Francis Bacon…The fact that Whiteley could take a subject so loaded with journal-

istic associations, and turn it into art, is the measure of his power for transformation. His show was patchy, a bit capricious sometimes, but alive with promise and achievement.'[39]

The Whiteleys arrived in Australia at the end of 1965 after five years' absence, and were struck by its difference, as if they had stepped into an Eden way behind the pace of the rest of the world. It was the beginning of summer, and they were able to stay at a house in Whale Beach, north of Sydney. The dazzling sands and waters, combined with intensely blue skies and the smells and sounds of the bush, charged Whiteley with new possibilities for his work. More than that, the six months' stay in Australia had an impact on his whole idea about what it meant to be an Anglo-Celtic European in that part of the world. From being an artist soaked in the cultural milieu of Europe, he began to think that through his paintings he might activate a change in the way Australians perceived their identity as neighbours of Asia. His figure draughtsmanship blossomed as his eye explored the lissom, sun-tanned torsos on beaches, but he also

Figure 18
WENDY ON CUSHIONS 1976
Charcoal on paper, 56 x 76 cm

26

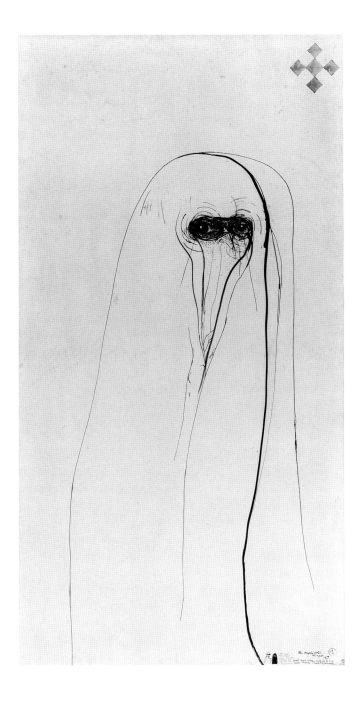

Figure 19
**THE MAJESTIC HOTEL,
TANGIER** 1967
Pen and ink and gouache,
brush and ink, pencil on card,
160 × 85.5 cm

Figure 20
**ALI AKBA KHAN PLAYING THE
SAROD** *c.* 1978
Charcoal and ink on paper,
55.8 x 73 cm

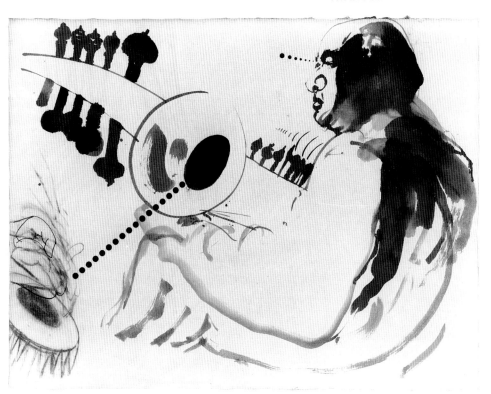

moved more emphatically into three dimensions: not only through sculpture, but also the devices he had begun to use in the Christie series of constructing windows and boxes within his pictures. He attached to the surfaces of his paintings plaster build-ups and found objects such as fur, shells and cardboard boxes with product names, together with written statements and word symbols.

The Pop language and collagist vernacular of contemporary American art became useful for this development, but it was almost as if Whiteley decided to relinquish the subtleties of metaphorical language in totally flat painting because its audience base was, and always would be, restricted. By creating something people could touch or catch their clothes on, they might take greater notice of the fact that a painting was an object which had something to say, and could touch political and social nerves reaching beyond the normal domain of art. At about this time, Whiteley was also stepping up his courtship with the notion of charisma. Sandra McGrath, Whiteley's biographer and one of his most enthusiastic apologists, wrote in 1967: 'Bob Dylan…folk-singer, a mouthpiece for the young, a sort of old-young, in fact articulates in song and verse what Whiteley to some extent seeks to convey in paint – a sort of convulsion of the soul… where opposites meet and merge into one. They are both concerned with the violence and potential destruction of the world.'[40] Dylan was one of many musicians Whiteley would pack into his baggage of cult heroes. However, unlike Dylan, who transformed ideology into music and poetry, Whiteley ran the risk of making the poetry of painting into prose.

On their way back to England from Australia the Whiteleys stayed in Calcutta for ten days. The shock of what they saw there echoed the sense of contradiction that Whiteley had explored in his Christie images, except now he created works which conveyed duality as a rhetorical declaration rather than allowing it to emerge mysteriously from the *frisson* of a singular image. In London he worked during the last half of 1966 on two major paintings referring to his recent experience: *Calcutta*, which contrasted the floating form of a sitar player with photographs of street beggars, and *Fidgeting with Infinity*, a predella based on Piero's *The Baptism* traversed by a brutal, hard-edged highway flanked by a pink fibreglass figure referring back to the female victims of the Christie series, and a horrendous image of emaciated famine victims presided over by vultures.

When these works were displayed at the Marlborough New London Gallery in October their impact on the general visitor was startling. Also included in the exhibition were studies resulting from a two-month holiday in Morocco, a stay in Majorca, and paintings and drawings from Australia. But especially in the Calcutta works, there were critical questions about the issues of duality. A serious disjunction was discerned in that either the gravity of a subject, such as the poverty of India, was being trivialized by gimmickry, or the paintings simply failed as formal propositions. Whatever it was, reviewers remained unmoved. Keith Roberts wrote in *Burlington Magazine*: 'And yet there is something decidedly superficial about his style, which is confident rather than powerful, and not without vulgarity…at almost every point one cares to look in the present exhibition, one senses an artist for whom what is up to date, both in terms of style and public mood, is emotionally important. It is hardly surprising that Mr Whiteley should have chosen an Indian theme at a time when mysticism is a current fad.'[41] This reviewer obviously missed the point of Whiteley's concern with conflicting realities and could not possibly have foreseen that Whiteley's interest in Eastern cultures would eventually bring about a reductivism in his art that was a salvation, but he was correct in identifying at that moment a tendency which was to become calamitous during the two years following Whiteley's imminent arrival in New York.

He was awarded a Harkness Fellowship to study in the United States for two years. Ever since their brief stay there in 1962 New York had fascinated him for its energy, and no doubt for its reputation as the centre of the world art scene. And of course it was home to two icons of modern French painting that Whiteley revered above all others, after he had seen reproductions of them during his formative years in Sydney in the late 1950s: Matisse's *The Red Studio* (1911) in the Museum of Modern Art, and Gauguin's *The Yellow Christ* (1889) in the Albright-Knox Art Gallery, Buffalo. The former in particular was to inspire Whiteley's magnificent group of Lavender Bay interiors in Sydney during the early 1970s, and the latter to make an important connection to Whiteley's later landscapes and his interest in Japanese art. Michael Johnson confirmed that of all the paintings they analysed and ingested during their early years, these were the two works Whiteley talked about most, and constantly. But there were other things to get out of his system in New York before these influences became manifest in a major way.

The Whiteleys cruised across the Atlantic on the last voyage of the *Queen Mary*, arrived in New York at the beginning of November 1967, and headed straight for the Chelsea Hotel. Other Australian artists had stayed for periods at this downtown Manhattan home to

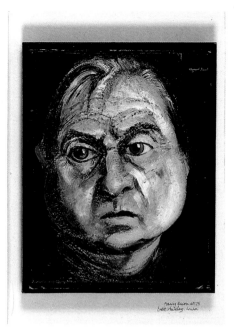

Figure 21
FRANCIS BACON AT 75 1984
(Triptych) Mixed media on paper
and board, 36 x 75.7 cm

writers, poets, artists and musicians, as well as push-
ers and prostitutes, who were living at the edge of
American society and yet feeding its creative essence.
America was then an agonized cauldron of change, as
old values were challenged by new, edifices of political
power and ideology undermined by protests and
assassinations, and alternative lifestyles extolled by
writers and poets of the beat generation. The Vietnam
war was at its worst, and lines of battle between
Americans themselves were drawn across the whole
spectrum of society. At first Whiteley loved it, saying
that the city was like 'a living sculpture', with everywhere the prevalent New York yellow 'in the taxis, in
the mustard, in the Kodak boxes and Con Edison con-
struction tents, in the sanitation trucks'.[42] It was at
once the colour of optimism and madness. At the
Chelsea they were able to procure the penthouse
given up by a professor from Yale University who had
been there for fourteen years, a largish room with a
small staircase leading up to the kitchen. Its best
attraction was access to a roof-garden, where
Marlborough-Gerson was to stage the opening of
Whiteley's first exhibition with them in May. He started work on that show in November, renting an empty
office for a studio across the road from the hotel.

But he soon began to fear America too: its inter-
necine violence, its potential to destroy, but most of
all its indifference to cultures outside its own border-
lines. His work showed signs of an attempt to
fit into a cultural pattern with which he was uncom-
fortable. Reviewers of his exhibition were good-
natured about the apparent moral consistency of
his political messages, and admired especially the
drawings of lovers copulating, but unfortunately

the tenuous combinations of fibreglass, oil paint,
photography, electricity, steel, barbed wire, and in one
instance rice and a hand-grenade, consigned a good
number of the works to oblivion. They were not made
to last. What was notable in the exhibition, however,
was the expanded ambition of the hero paintings.
There were two works dedicated to Bob Dylan, two to
Gauguin, one to Brendan Behan, and his first of many
to van Gogh. The composition of *Vincent* (1968) was
constructed around a floating head – copied from a
self-portrait by the Dutch painter – connected to an
open razor by a serpentine blood track. Zoom-lines
also linked the head to an Arles landscape drawing,
and a collaged, double-headed arrow pointed to the
words 'life' and 'art' in symmetric opposition.

Vincent had an immediate context for its conception. A fine self-portrait by van Gogh could be seen in
the Metropolitan Museum of Art, but there was at any
rate a lot of interest in the artist in New York when
Whiteley arrived. A huge exhibition of ninety watercolours and drawings was opened in mid-November
at nearby Philadelphia Museum of Fine Art, and *Time*
ran an article about a fanatical Los Angeles sculptor
who had cast a large head of van Gogh, intending to
offer it to the town of Arles.[43] In December the following year Whiteley attended Francis Bacon's exhibition
opening at Marlborough-Gerson. The two artists
spent much of the evening drinking whisky and talking art in a back-room. One wonders if they touched
on Bacon's own passionate tribute to van Gogh ten
years earlier, paintings which Bacon later considered
to be 'follies'. Whiteley may have missed Bacon's big
retrospective at the Tate Gallery in 1962 because he
was living in Sigean, but one of the British artist's

most impressive paintings of the time, *Study for Portrait of van Gogh IV*, was presented to the Tate by the Contemporary Art Society in 1958 and to be seen hanging there throughout the early 1960s. During this time Whiteley tried to purchase one of Bacon's paintings, *Landscape near Malabata, Tangier*, and later painted a tribute to it in one of his van Gogh works.[44] All these were far more potent connections with Whiteley's obsession than a church in Bathurst.

In the meantime, observers in Australia were giving Whiteley's work their unequivocal approval. He held an exhibition at the beginning of 1968 at Bonython's gallery in Sydney which included mainly Australian works, and the so-called *Tangier postcards*. James Gleeson wrote: 'One of the characteristics of his art is a tendency to crowd the most telling details into the periphery of the painting and leave the central area devoid of incident. He delights in throwing the composition into an unbalanced state and then by feats of brilliant dexterity, holding it in improbable and breathtaking equilibrium.'[45] Surprisingly, support came from Donald Brook, the most acerbic of Australian art critics: 'The proximity of the sordid, the beautiful and the banal is managed with a sense of dramatic contrast as strong as Yeats' in that peculiarly indigestible line...but love has pitched his mansion in the place of excrement.'[46] For Brook this was strong praise.

In New York the atmosphere of the Chelsea Hotel was extraordinarily stimulating, but also damaging. The relationship there between Brett and Wendy became complicated. In an era of newly perceived social and sexual freedoms the dividing line between what was permissible and impermissible became blurred. At the Chelsea, where parties lurched from one room to another, the Whiteleys each had affairs with other people – perhaps with a sense of compensation or revenge, or for other reasons it is beyond the scope of this essay to explore – but it is certain that jealousy and mistrust contributed to the stress of Whiteley's feelings about America and subsequently to the mood of his work. Conflict of values had already pushed Wendy towards suicide in London, and he in turn became threatened whenever she showed any sign of independence. 'He was so angry and jealous,' she said. 'He didn't trust women in general, nor did he trust relationships, but at the same time he needed it badly. We did a lot of experimenting, but it didn't provide any answers.'[47]

Hovering ominously above all this was the spectre of drugs. Whiteley was a hard drinker, but apart from the odd experience with LSD, a lot of smoking of marijuana, and dabbling in various other drugs, they did not become too involved with hard substances at that

stage. The connotation of drugs was rather less sinister during the 1960s, their enhancement value argued eloquently by the current generation of artists. However, the Whiteleys certainly witnessed first-hand the destructiveness of heroin abuse, and were more cautious about it then than they have been given credit for. Whiteley told Janet Hawley many years later, 'I know heroin is lethal. I saw evidence of that when I lived in the Chelsea Hotel...with Jimi Hendrix and Janis Joplin and others into extremes. I'd use booze and grass to expand my consciousness, but never touch heroin...I never embraced it and said, let's get the bags in and go to the horizon...There has always been this urge in me to be supernaturally sober.'[48] It was not until several years later, after he had left New York and returned to Australia, that he would go down that darker road, and justify his use of chemical stimulants, fixating on the heroes of art and literature whom he could describe as 'addictive personalities'.

One more aspect may be explored further as part

of the climate in New York that was building towards Whiteley's most ambitious work of art, and which had not a little to do with the ambiguities that threatened to tear him apart: his use of written language. Intelligent rather than intellectual, Whiteley was not a good reader of literature. He was not easily able to plough through books, but rather skimmed them to pluck whatever took his interest, whether from the critical writings of Baudelaire, the poetry of Rimbaud, or a biography on the life of Einstein. This was reflected in the way he used words in his paintings and drawings. Riddles, descriptive passages, anecdotes were often placed on pictures for their visual impact rather than an essential meaning. His style was one of free association that had much in common with beat poetry, although the Australian critic Elwyn Lynn wrote that at their best, Whiteley's inscriptions could have a William Blake-like quality, exhorting the reader towards a moral rage, or a more exalted plane of thinking.[49] Occasionally Whiteley might hit the mark with profundities, but he did not have the intellectual structure or discipline to do it consistently enough to really earn him credit as a literate artist.

One contemporary writer Whiteley read carefully was R. D. Laing, the British psychiatrist who was esteemed for his study of schizophrenia and madness, conditions that Laing deliberately induced in himself in order to understand them. It is tempting to think that Whiteley may have been thinking about his own splintered approach to art when he looked at Laing's book *The Divided Self*, which was published in 1960. Laing proposed that insecurity about self-existence elicited a defensive reaction in which the ego might split into separate parts, generating classic psychotic symptoms. The self-portraits Whiteley began just before New York included heads fractured or distorted towards the creation of another self, or double identity, and even his paintings of such heroes as van Gogh, Gauguin, Dylan, Rimbaud and Baudelaire were a means of assuming the essence of someone else.

The crisis of his life at this time, the fragility of his marriage, his disillusionment with the society around him, the questions about where he had come from, who he was, where he was going, all found voice in Whiteley's painting *The American Dream*, which he started at the beginning of 1968. This massive, eighteen-panelled work had trauma and failure all over it, simply because Whiteley's intentions were absurd. He aimed for nothing less than to challenge America and change it. Anger and frustration exploded throughout the central section with streams of blood and pus mixed with the detritus of a decadent society; a black-and-white image of an electrical storm crackled across a dead, flat ocean juxtaposed against a lurid

mushroom cloud; and at each end glimpses of earthly paradise held tenuously at the fringes of disaster. It was not so much a painting about America as a portrait of Whiteley himself, whipping up hell and heaven to extend the possibilities of art far beyond what it could achieve.

'I was determined myself to produce a monumental work of art that would summarise the sensation of the impending necessity for America to own up, analyse and straighten out the immense and immediately seeable MADNESS that seemed to run through most facets of American life…As the work began I still considered myself an outsider, a foreigner, a white Asian staying in America for a short time, unable to objectify the separation I felt from needing to behave as most Americans did. But as the work progressed…it developed into a struggle within myself to own up, analyse and straighten out.'[50] His drinking increased to the point of serious danger to his health. At one point he did not know what to do next with the painting. His father's brother had just died at about the same age as Clem had, and Whiteley, with a sense of foreboding, locked himself in his studio, drinking himself into a coma. Wendy had to have the door broken down, and on two occasions she took him to hospital with alcohol poisoning.

The American Dream was never exhibited in America. Marlborough-Gerson refused to take an interest in it. In July 1969 Whiteley abandoned it and flew to Fiji, the paradise he had projected in the far right-hand section of the work, a place of Baudelairean tranquillity and happiness. Wendy stayed behind to finalize the successful boutique business that she had established with her friend Liz Sheridan, and went to London to tidy up the Melbury Road studio and sublet it.

He stayed in Navutulevu Village, about a hundred kilometres from Suva. Just before Wendy and Arkie arrived to join him, Whiteley wrote to his mother, expressing his immense relief at leaving America, 'We were born into hell and have pressed 10 conscious years…all of us, into getting around it, getting into it, trying to salvage trying to salvate! And all we have apart from wrinkles and yellow tongues is a kind of speedy humour about survival. I am glad to leave there.'[51] At first Fiji was everything it promised to be. The rustic simplicity of the lifestyle was for the Whiteleys a universe away from New York. It was Gauguin's Tahiti, Donald Friend's Bali. But as with those artists, Whiteley found the idyll not entirely consistent. He continued in his letter, 'Everything is such a sort of stoned state…I walk around with a bunch of violets in my hand and a sledgehammer and a grain of sand in my head. I am happy.' Then a glimmer of apprehension: 'The Lost and Last paradise, but I am still waiting: the place seems to be overrun with Eves but don't know what to make of the Polynesian mind. Maybe it's so simply contented my complexity is sort of envious and refuses to comprehend without some poisons. They are determined not to dislike anything. I can't stand that sort of purity having soaked myself in scepticism and by nature am magnetised to bitterness.'[52]

Nevertheless, Whiteley was more than satisfied with the work he was doing. He celebrated nature at its most luxuriant and made evocative drawings of the local people. Themes such as birds, palms and water were a prelude to his later landscapes in Australia: 'Rain the last few days. Started to work directly again in front of nature, way out on a hill. Worked all afternoon. Ecstasy! On the way home a torrent hit the top of the car ruining it.' And there were moments of sheer beauty which only words could capture: 'Just stare at the myriad of leaf changes for hours. Swallows flash. Sun comes on for you minutes like a search light then hides off behind a grey veil. Out on the reef half a mile out an inner roar like New York a bit, an inner thunder. Always.'[53] Then, after five months, paradise ended quite suddenly.

Hiring a barn in Suva, Whiteley presented an exhibition of his paintings which stirred a lot of positive local interest. The intention was to go back to Sydney, raise some money, and arrange permanent immigration to Fiji. However, as with many colonial outposts, officials harboured deeply reactionary attitudes, especially to such an off-beat family. Whiteley had talked to someone about drugs, and at 7 a.m. the morning after the opening the apartment was raided by police. They found some opium that Whiteley had purchased from a Chinese man two days before. He was arrested, and the Whiteleys were told to get out of Fiji as soon as possible. A week later in November they sailed into Sydney Harbour. The press rowed out to meet them. 'Word had gone ahead that the disgraceful Whiteleys were on their way and not to be missed.'[54] Apart from their brief visit in 1965, they had been away from Australia for exactly ten years.

Shortly after their arrival in Sydney the Whiteleys looked for a house in the country, somewhere near the sea with a disused barn that might be used for a studio. They stayed at a friend's vineyard, near the country town of Cessnock ,about which he wrote, 'the worst dump on earth. The only culture in the town is rust.'[55] Fiji, or Sigean, could not be re-created so easily. They came back to Sydney and found a flat at Lavender Bay, above that of the painter-architect Rollin Schlicht. It was a time for working out mixed feelings concerning Australia: 'Very affluent it is, the place looks rich, but the place's soul goes right back to the convict beginnings – bitter as lime juice…God America with all the shit and pain going on there really seems like a great nation because it fought and built and experimented and did it…and if it matures (which it might) those scars will be earnt [sic] and are real. Here they haven't struggled like that out in front…Imbeciles! Nowhere has speeded towards vulgarity of the human spirit at such a rate as Australia.'[56] He found an ally for his sentiments in the Australian writer Patrick White, who began to collect his work. A fondness developed between the two men, but unfortunately their relationship soured later when Whiteley painted White's portrait.[57]

He held a colossal exhibition in June 1970 at the Bonython Art Gallery in Sydney which included *The American Dream* and works he had made on the themes of Australia, and Fiji, a dazzling cacophony of landscapes, animal sculptures, parodies of Aboriginal burial poles, and a large homage to Baudelaire, whose writings edited by Enid Starkie he had read in New York. Laced throughout were statements warning Australians about the vulgarity of America, the vulnerability of the natural environment and the foolishness of ignoring Asia. From this and the subsequent show at Australian Galleries in Melbourne, art critics departed stunned, with a mixture of dismay at Whiteley's half-baked polemics and unrestrained admiration for his artistic vision. Donald Brook questioned the unrelentingly high pitch of his style, and the manifesto look of the assemblages, adding 'he is rapidly giving ground to the commonplace poet and the pretentious sage'.[58] The rest of the Sydney reviewers more or less allowed themselves to be swept up with the sheer energy of the event which, with its presentation of plastic, fur, feathers, leather and electronics, as well as the conventional materials of painting and drawing, almost defied conventional criticism.

In Melbourne, however, one critic summarized Whiteley's achievement more evocatively than anyone else. Unfortunately, his essay was not available to a wide Australian public, but Alan McCulloch's review in *Art International* is worth quoting extensively: 'However briefly the edges of his art have touched those of say Bacon, or the Pop-period Warhol, a sizzling dichotomy of highly individual, simplified forms has resulted. There have also been spells of eclipse and reappearance, and from it all we get a vision of a youthful, wraith-like luminary protected from a hostile world mainly by a finely attuned, acutely perceptive eye, extraordinary capacity for tuning in to the global atmosphere and rhythms of the time and a powerful talent for large-scale drawing. All this sensory, cerebral and technical equipment is kept lubricated, ready at all times for instant action…

'It was as if he had opened the windows of his Australian-conditioned soul to a series of lightning flashes that then crystallised as hallucinatory fixed images through a remarkable ability for total recall. In the language of mainly drawing, he was postulating a Joycean reassessment of the new nine muses: zoology, ecology, botany, sociology, sex, narcotics, pollution, travel and political science…and if in the general evocation of images ranging in complexity from the horrors of Vietnam and the consequent possible collapse of *felix Australis*, to the poisoning of land and sea masses by chemicals, we seemed to be witnessing a performance rather than attending an exhibition…the constant in Whiteley's work remained the tense, all-embracing rhythm. It leapt across oceans in a succession of writhing, twisting, alternately taut and relaxed delineations of organic forms that pulsated with individual life and character.'

McCulloch concluded: 'One is continually aware of the conflict between Whiteley the artist, Whiteley the participant in the social upheavals and excesses he portrays, and Whiteley the professional entrepreneur – a role that might well lead him eventually, like Warhol, into film-making,' but, 'As observer and delineator of the waning kingdoms of animal and bird life Whiteley is a remarkable artist, perhaps because in these relatively uncontaminated domains he is motivated more by love than despair.'[59] There would be little to match the concentrated exuberance of this assessment for the remainder of his career.

The climactic nature of Whiteley's exhibitions in 1970 was underlined by the artist's concern that he avoid predictability: 'At this moment,' he said, ' you reach for the furthest opposite: To be perpetually shifting and not holdable, to be mercurial and Zen!'[60] He now began work on a series of portraits, some self, some family and friends, but mostly of personalities of history and contemporary life who fascinated him for their energy and their power to effect social change. He prepared these works in a studio that he had found in an old abandoned gasworks building not far from the house at Lavender Bay. An exhibition of them, dedicated to the People's Republic of China, was held at Bonython's in Sydney in February 1972 and then moved to the Australian Galleries in Melbourne. After his exhibitions in 1970, the show caused disappointment and a lot of anger.

In spite of Whiteley's involvement with the Yellow House in Sydney in 1971, where appropriation was part of an intelligent pursuit of the creative life, Whiteley's experimentation with an oriental style was seen as unconvincing, and many of his exhibits regarded as

'stage props' and 'montage tricks' used merely for effect.[61] Bernard Boles in Melbourne was perhaps the most sympathetic, and pointed out an influence rarely mentioned, that of the London-based American artist Ron Kitaj: 'Kitaj constructs allusive riddles with fragments both from learned books and urban ephemera, to creat a visual poetry hinting at the complex layers of experience'; although he felt that Whiteley by comparison kept his antipodean audience in mind by using lines with fairground simplicity.[62] A few interesting and beautiful works came out of this phase, including the large *Portrait of Arthur Rimbaud*, inspired in part by Enid Starkie's 1962 book on the poet which Whiteley had asked his mother to send to him in Fiji. He wanted to know why Rimbaud, who envisaged that he might sail to happiness, or God, through art, had given up his cause so early. Both Rimbaud and Baudelaire were amongst the most important role models for Whiteley's self-

Figure 23
THE MOST BEAUTIFUL MOUNTAIN 1969
Pen and ink and wash, 56.5 x 51 cm

image as artist, as they were for many others of his generation.

Portrait and persona paintings continued to be produced throughout the 1970s and the 1980s, including the zealous van Gogh series. His self-portraits, apart from those of his adolescence, had been started just before New York, and Whiteley's return to Sydney prompted memories of his family and the way he had been shaped by it. He wondered how much he had really changed from that child at Longueville who did little poems and drawings, ears prickling at household dissent, hoping for pacification maybe, and to receive a piece of love in return: 'one gets into the habit of having an invented world as opposed to the external world – the external world is so repugnant. It's a natural schizing and I became addicted to the split.'[63] These remarks shed some light on the escapist nature of Whiteley's themes during his last two decades, but especially the portraits.

The one work of his first few years back in Australia which summarized Whiteley's state of mind in all its myriad accumulation of influences was *Alchemy* (1972–73). Like *The American Dream* this was another self-portrait on a gigantic scale, except that there was not the fierce political agenda in its conception. Spread over eighteen panels, it may be read right to left as a vision of earth, ocean and sky, through transmutations of flesh, genitalia, fornication and landscape, ending with a white sun and serpentine tentacles set against a gold background using panels with which Whiteley had portrayed Yukio Mishima in 1972. Mishima was a Japanese writer who committed *seppuku* in 1970, having decided that the gap between art and action could only be closed effectively through ritual death. Literary mythology has it that his final vision, as the knife cut into his flesh, was of an exploding sun which lightened the sky for an instant. This vision in fact became the technical beginning of *Alchemy*, as Whiteley developed his composition from left to right. But the work can be read either way, or even from the centre, where an image of the word 'IT' holds the fulcrum between opposing ideas.

Completed in the gasworks studio, *Alchemy* also reflects angst in Whiteley's personal life at that time, from early 1972 until January 1973. Cause and effect worked in reverse too, for the toll of drugs and alcohol on Whiteley's health while he was painting *Alchemy* was extreme. His intentions were now much more personal, but he had, once again, tried to extend the capacity for art to change society. He could not help feeling that he might entrance masses and move them with his statements like a thinking pop musician. When it was exhibited at the Bonython Gallery in Sydney in January, *Alchemy* was accompanied by

a catalogue comprising images and words from Whiteley's notebooks. Collectively it fails to make much sense – quotes from Huysmans, Bacon, Hughes, Laing, Dante, Dylan and so on, mingle with Whiteley's own anecdotes – however, there are occasional flashes which get to the nub of the artist's concept: 'Alchemy is the business of seeing what doesn't exist'; 'The quest is the transmutation of Self'; 'Most of this painting was first seen with the eyes closed in the pitch of night, awake'; or the often quoted, 'Art should astonish, transmute, transfix. Work at the tissue between truth and paranoia.'

It seems that Whiteley anticipated people pointing out the connections of his Surrealist imagery with the fifteenth-century Flemish painter Hieronymus Bosch, when he wrote a note for critics: 'I didn't look at Bosch once while painting any of this…If I wanted to make a picture about Bosch or make a picture using Bosch, uplifting Bosch, it would have an utterly different look. This painting is about my inner paddock, which maybe means that all inner paddocks have similarness.'[64] There is no doubt, however, that the Flemish master played an important part in both *Alchemy* and *The American Dream*. On the way back to London from Morocco in June 1967 Whiteley went to Madrid to see the Bosch paintings there, and was overwhelmed: 'Incredible!…What care and such menacing twitching really seen not invented images,' he wrote in a postcard.[65] But his description in the following year of America with 'ribbons of violence squealing from the T.V., the dying capitalism of Bull America debowelling itself' took the reference beyond Bosch when he began looking at the writings of Paracelsus.[66]

Paracelsus, or Theophrast Bombast von Hohenheim, was an early-sixteenth-century Swiss alchemist intrigued by the possibility of turning base metals into gold. He also wrote a book on surgery and a clinical description of syphilis. An idea associated with his theories was that beauty is something merely perceived on the surface of the skin, for what lies underneath and may effuse from the orifices is another quite opposite, repulsive reality. The dichotomy between the seen and unseen, relevant to the practice of Surrealism centuries later, was in perfect accord with Whiteley's thinking. Moreover, he drew from the old alchemical interest in changing base metals to gold, a metaphor for painting as a vehicle by which life could become transmuted into art. Through all the rich passages and details of this important work, that became its single, unifying idea.

The critical response to *Alchemy* was, possibly with a sense of relief after Whiteley's portraits exhibition, enthusiastic. Nancy Borlase saw it as a journey to the state of serenity and oneness with nature after passing through monstrous horrors of temptation in modern life.[67] Daniel Thomas noted its Asian quality, like a picture story on screens in a Chinese or Japanese tradition, beginning with earthly, erotic impregnation and ending with the source of all life.[68] Indeed, in the exhibition catalogue Whiteley proclaimed, 'a great transmutation is at hand in Australia. The shifting from white techno consciousness to a higher more naturally based Asian view of reality.' Remarkable though its impact was, *Alchemy* was to endure a rocky path of ownership before its eventual purchase by the New South Wales state government in 1994.

All but drained physically and emotionally by *Alchemy*, Whiteley recovered his strength and began a low-key series of paintings and drawings on the theme of waves, which he exhibited in the middle of 1973. Following this he left with Wendy and Arkie for England and Europe via North Africa and the Middle East. They visited Harar in Ethiopia where Rimbaud had stayed for most of his life. It was a recuperative journey, for the sake of both Whiteley and his relationship with his family. After a few months in England they returned at the end of the year to Sydney, where, on the proceeds of a large retrospective exhibition of drawings at Bonython Gallery, they purchased the house at Lavender Bay in June 1974. This signified the beginning of what may be regarded as one of Whiteley's greatest periods of painting, and also his real rebonding with Australia; a centring, as it were, of his universe. For until then most of his work in the first four years back may be seen as a kind of crossing-over process from London and New York.

The house had comprised two flats, which they soon joined with a tower extension, enabling a bedroom to be built under the roof. Meanwhile, the second floor was opened up with archways and windows overlooking Lavender Bay. This part of the house, elegantly decorated by Wendy with Brett's works, rugs and objects collected on their travels, and combined with stunning harbour views in all their variation of mood and tone through the windows, became the leitmotif for a series of paintings quite spellbinding in its sense of equilibrium. It seemed that Whiteley had let go, at least for the time being, the angst of the last six years and the overpowering need to be a popular prophet and shaman. During his exhibition of the series at the Australian Galleries in Melbourne in November he told a critic that words were difficult to grasp and that he wanted to forget what he had written.[69]

Robert Hughes's account of Lee Krasner's enthusiasm for Whiteley, that he confronted his influences head on, painting his way through them without pretension, was no more appropriate than now. His Lavender Bay paintings from 1974 were a clear

homage to Matisse, and in particular to his *The Red Studio*, which Whiteley had always loved. The title of one work, *Henri's Armchair* (1974–75), declares the debt plainly. Whiteley's interiors make rather more concession to deep pictorial space than Matisse's, and there is nearly always a little disturbance in them, like a pebble striking a still pond, be it the vibrating contours of a chair, or ghost lines indicating that someone was in the space just a few seconds ago; or maybe the presence of the artist himself, drawing at the edge of the composition, peering into his cage. Unlike Matisse, Whiteley never emptied his ego completely from such subjects. In fact one, *Self-Portrait in the Studio* (1976), which shows the artist's face in a hand mirror at the bottom of the picture, was awarded the prestigious annual Archibald prize for portraiture at The Art Gallery of New South Wales for 1976.

Other Lavender Bay paintings, such as the large scale *Big Orange* (1974), *The Balcony 2* (1975) and *The Jacaranda Tree* (1977) incorporate the broad panorama of Sydney Harbour; totally flat picture planes without horizons, dominated by orange or ultramarine blue with boats, bridge, buildings and little pockets of nature distributed masterfully. These were the paintings he described later as 'soaking in perfume', especially the colour ultramarine, which he said 'hits my nervous system in such an exciting way',[70] feeling that

Figure 25
SUNDAY 1973
Pencil and charcoal on paper,
49.5 x 45.3 cm

intensely private of all his paintings, with the momentary perfection of flowers and fruit counterpoised by beads, vases and platters from the day-to-day surroundings of the family. Table tops lifted to the upper edge of compositions recall William Scott, whose abstractions gave Whiteley his first real understanding of the picture plane and showed him how to command its most elemental potential for dispersing shapes in a painting. However, one area of his work which he pursued with equal enthusiasm at this stage, and has tended to be underrated, was his sculpture.

His first sculpture was made in the 1950s and again in the early 1960s as part of the Christie series, such as *Christie's Chair* (*c.* 1965). During his New York period and first couple of years in Sydney Whiteley put a lot of energy into assemblages, not to be confused with the stand-alone sculptures in which Whiteley met nature half-way, adapting his ideas to the ready-made forms of tree branches and trunks he found in the landscape. These had their beginnings in *White Sacred Baboon* carved from an olive tree root in Majorca in 1964 and continued in various works executed at the Melbury Road studio in London for the Christie–London Zoo exhibition, then in the nude studies of *Her* (*c.* 1975), for which he made countless drawings at Lavender Bay. The latter were carved from mangrove wood, and mounted on stands of sandstone and metal reminiscent of the forms of Brancusi, thereby creating a collision between the organic and the geometric.

Another side to his sculpture included wistful adaptations of old shoes into birds; combinations of stuffed animals and plumbing pipes; birds and animals fashioned from wire and palm fronds, sometimes cast into bronze; shark teeth set in plaster; egg totems; and the persistence of an idea which began in miniature in 1983 and developed through versions of various scale towards a huge installation outside The Art Gallery of New South Wales in 1991. This was entitled *Almost Once*. Two matchsticks, one live, the other burnt, are the emblem of 'Endlessnessism', and Whiteley's life-long preoccupation with opposites, yin and yang, life and death.[71] All of these works, together with the ceramics which he began to decorate during the 1970s, comprise a three-dimensional oeuvre which bears examination in its own right.

The spirit of Lavender Bay was carried into themes of birds and landscapes which Whiteley painted during the next fifteen years, works that were joyous responses to an optical world without pain. He had made paintings of central Australia as early as 1970, but these contained something of a polemical rather than poetic purpose. As he moved around the countryside of New South Wales – Oberon, Marulan,

it also contained a sense of rightness which amounted to a moral imperative. The only hint of the house in *The Balcony 2* is a pattern painted in delicate calligraphy near the base of the composition, and white lines placed casually next to three sides of the picture, representing a vast window opened up for the grand escape. Whiteley's ability to project curvilinear movement and electrify empty spaces in these very large paintings was extraordinary. He could also evoke the poetry of the bay on a small scale in different schemes of grey, cream and plum brown depending on the time of day and weather, or the decorative mood that took him. But for its big-scale orchestration, *The Balcony 2* is one of the greatest creations of sustained ecstasy in the history of Australian painting.

Completing the trilogy of Lavender Bay themes is a series of still lifes painted during the late 1970s in which Whiteley paid tribute to a medley of artists, including Bonnard and Morandi. These are the most

Carcoar, Bathurst – and to the Glasshouse Mountains in Queensland, where he often stayed with his friends Lawrence and Edit Daws, he painted and drew the landscape in all its seasons with a tendency he called 'Chinese'. It was not so much the style of the works which gave him this idea as the repetition of certain motifs in nature that might symbolize states of mind. For example, the arabesques of rivers meandering into the distance from the bottom to the top in some pictures echo the flight paths of birds which are soul-lines of the artist's relaxed journey through his private domain. Here it is not fanciful to think of Whiteley's bird paintings as self-portraits. He had always loved them since childhood and in his last phase of work birds became symbols of both domesticity and free-dom. It is not surprising that he held special exhibi-tions dedicated to the theme, the last in his Surry Hills studio in 1988, four years before his death.

Birds, rivers, trees, rocks, ponds, skidding insects, shy mammals, spaces alternately cluttered or uncluttered; such elements and passages were dis-pensed throughout Whiteley's landscapes in various combinations, and he brought them together with elegiac majesty in a large painting exhibited at Surry Hills entitled *Autumn (near Bathurst) – Japanese Autumn* (1987–88). This major work, for which he did several smaller studies, is restrained to the point where its stillness hums quietly with Whiteley's gene-sis, returning to the landscape where as a boy it first occurred to him that he could be a painter. Compris-ing two main sections with small, spare, floating shapes nudging the edges like the abstractions of William Scott, but now in an idiom that belonged entirely to Whiteley, a central panel is given to the calligraphic drawing on paper of a willow tree. This, combined with a rich brown lacquer colour dominat-ing the rest of the painting, also recalls the Japanese screen tradition which informed the work of Kenzo Okada admired by Whiteley in the early 1960s, and anticipates Whiteley's visit to Japan during in the autumn of 1988. It was his first trip to the country whose artists and ancient philosophies he had admired for so long.[72]

For all this focus on landscape Whiteley did not neglect the other subject equal for him in inspiration, and whose history began with those hybrid forms of his abstractions in the early 1960s: the female nude. He had articulated it with power and sensitivity in the bathroom and Christie series, and then during the summer of 1965 and 1966 found its perfect setting in the beaches of Australia. His notebooks and studio contents suggest that the drawing of the female nude was a constant activity for Whiteley throughout his life, be it classic studies of Wendy, torso drawings for

sculpture, erotic sketches of lovers, or photomontages cut up and rearranged in a Cubist manner from illus-trations in magazines.

In 1981 he mounted an exhibition of recent nudes at his studio in Circular Quay, Sydney, with paintings, drawings and sculpture made since 1975. The cata-logue contained a credo by the artist which today's politically correct society may find objectionable, but it is fascinating to see how the images in that exhibi-tion balanced on the boundary between overt male desire and misogyny. One of the finest paintings, *The Letter (to Anna)*, 1980–81, reads at distance like a deco-rative cut-out, then from a closer view the figure has shallow modelling which invests it with a tender erotic ambience. A portrait of Anna Elenberg, wife of sculp-tor Joel Elenberg, who died of cancer in 1980, it floats, swooning in grief, against a background resounding with cello-like resonance to the night sky above. Many of the other works, however, challenged the notion of

Figure 26
STUDY EXTENSION TO THE DIVIDED UNITY *c.* 1972–73
Pen and ink, pencil and wash on card, 73.6 x 44 cm

Figure 27
PROVENCE LANDSCAPE 1982
Pen and ink and mixed media on
paper, 182 x 120.5 cm

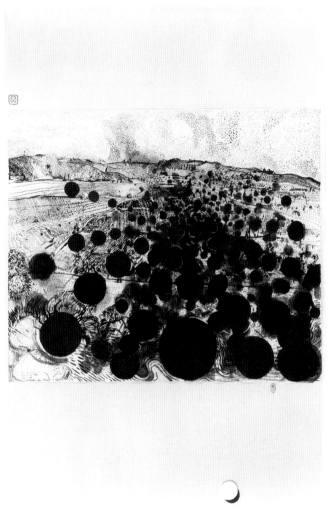

sensuality with extreme distortion which hovered just
this side of the grotesque, even of mutilation, recalling
an enigmatic comment that he wrote in a notebook:
'The me in her is the thing that disgusts me. Ego trying
to die by blaming the fact onto sexual prowess.'[73]

The dark side: it was an inescapable part of the
equation of Whiteley's life to the end. In 1978 he painted a portrait of himself which he called *Art, Life and
the Other Thing* and entered it for the Archibald prize
for portraiture. The immediate attention that this
work received in Australia on winning amounted to a
public announcement of Whiteley's struggle with the
thing that was killing him. It was a triptych with a tall
central panel containing an exceptionally elongated
image of himself, with head vibrating into the splitting
persona evident in earlier drawings, and holding a
sketch of William Dobell's Archibald-winning portrait
of Joshua Smith; a parody no doubt on the debate
about distortion and modern art that Dobell's work
had engendered back in 1944. Flanking this panel on
the upper right was an angelic photograph of
Whiteley, and on the lower left the painted image of
an entrapped simian beast howling for a syringe being

offered, slightly out of reach, by a pale hand. Whiteley
was then thirty-nine years old and he was not expected by many of his friends to live beyond forty.

It was a credit to his physical resilience that he did.
Alcohol had been part of his life since leaving school,
experimentation with stimulants and hallucinogenic
substances *de rigueur* in London and New York during
the 1960s, and then in about 1974 the circumscribed
lease of his addictive life was established when he and
Wendy became serious users of heroin. It was such a
casual development, as it so often is: a friend is asked
to 'score' and comes back with heroin from the street;
a collective act doomed to end in loneliness. As
Whiteley's life became more illuminated by public
attention over the next two decades he was forthright
about his problem in the many articles and interviews
which appeared, and openly admitted his fear of losing his ability to continue his work without drugs.
There were many desperate attempts to shake off the
beast that would eventually destroy his marriage and
him. In 1984 he said to Jane Singleton, 'I remember in
the 60s if you smoked a bit of grass that you could see
down the canyon of a picture much quicker because
of the race or something inside the marijuana. It
could help sharpen a bit some pictures. I think a
whisky and orange can uplift a drawing enormously.'[74]

Unfortunately, such comments gave rise to an exag-
geration of how much Whiteley's art was a product of
drugs, and a simplistic myth became exploited
through the mass media, explaining the existence of
his gift on one hand, and his squandering of it on the
other. Certainly Whiteley admitted using stimulants to
hype himself to resolve the difficult resolution of
major works such as *The American Dream* and
Alchemy. What may not be commonly understood,
though, is that by and large addicts come to need
drugs for their sense of well-being and normality,
rather than the continuing fabrication of some fantastic mental experience. Indeed, on those rare occasions

Figure 28
**BULBUL'S NEST IN
AVOCADO TREE** 1976
Brush, pen and ink and wash on
paper, 68 x 101 cm

Figure 29
EXPANDINGNESS 1983
Ink and charcoal on paper,
74.5 x 104 cm

when Whiteley consciously depicted drug visions – for example, his so-called 'smack' pictures – he produced the most self-conscious and least interesting works of his oeuvre. To a degree this may be said of his exhibition on the theme of van Gogh at The Art Gallery of New South Wales in July 1983.[75] He proposed a theory about Vincent's dot-dash method, which went against his own way of working, and which he linked to an Einsteinian 'atomic' vision. But in the end, the main thrust of the exhibition was really Whiteley's confrontation with addiction, and a need to deal with the violence that he felt was within. As art, the efficacy of many of these works was on dubious ground.

There is no doubt that Whiteley's impulse to take drugs and his drive to make art were interwoven. During the late 1970s he began to visit clinics with Wendy. This was about the time when the book on his work by Sandra McGrath was being published, an event that was not enough to blanket the difficulties of withdrawal. He wrote to his mother at the beginning of 1979: 'I can tell you it's been the most miserable difficult confusing deeply distressing gaoled 12 days my mind has ever had to spend. Not so much

craving the drug, but feeling the desolate panic that there doesn't exist any sort of future, so intertwined had I become with this false lover, so powerful had its control over our lives become…I have had to virtually become reborn to the world. Our friends looked on, then looked away as Wendy and I headed slowly, setting sun like towards inevitable destruction and death.'[76] In 1985 Whiteley bought an old T-shirt factory in Surry Hills which he converted to a studio. Shortly after, Wendy went to England to receive further treatment. She had already been counselled that to be free from addiction they would both have to stop using. Not for him: a second separation in 1987 preceded their divorce. Whiteley formed other relationships, and for a period found the female companionship he needed with Janice Spencer, whom he had met at a Narcotics Anonymous meeting. Spencer tried to help him overcome his addiction, became a model for his late figurative work, and travelled with him abroad. Christian Quintas continued to help him with the affairs of the studio as he had done for several years.[77] For much of the time during his last year or so at Surry Hills, however, Whiteley was living alone.

The letter to Whiteley's mother quoted above was the most poignant he ever wrote: 'Firstly let me congratulate you on your wisdom. I think it's the finest letter I've ever received from you...in that the scorpion intolerance, hurt, fear for my drug problem has been replaced by the facility of love, a love you have always found difficult to spawn, understandable by one peek at nanny and pa, a difficulty I, indeed, have inherited from you to a degree...still it accounts for our vigorous independence.'[78] The ambiguities that Whiteley exploited for so long, now came home to roost. Donald Friend touched upon this state when he wrote, 'I have never come to terms with the shadow that periodically falls over my mind and turns everything to bitterness and frustration: to dispel it I turn...to the illusory warmth to be found in the act of love. But that is not love itself, which I need in my despair.'[79] In Whiteley's hunger for physical intimacy, reflected through the sexual themes of his art, emotional intimacy was not part of the game. In his last days he finished up with neither.

Nothing could contrast more starkly with Whiteley's death than that of his friend Joel Elenberg. Elenberg was a talented young sculptor whom Whiteley met in Melbourne in 1970. They became magnetized to each other as physical opposites: the sculptor tall, dark and Jewish; the painter short with Anglo-Celtic skin and red hair. When Elenberg became ill with cancer, Whiteley made him the subject of anguished drawings and paintings which he exhibited in 1980, the year the Whiteleys took him to Bali to die. As Joel slipped towards the penumbra of death, he could feel the presence of those who loved him. When Whiteley's body gave up the fight in June 1992 in a motel at Thirroul, a coastal town south of Sydney, he was utterly alone. Only a month earlier he had been discussing his retrospective with The Art Gallery of New South

Wales, following his exhibition there of his recent drawings of Paris.[80]

Friends were shaken but not surprised. They had seen too many miraculous recoveries. In the months that followed, the women who had been closest to Whiteley were left to sort out what they had created in him, and what he had created in them. Critical assessment of his art became drowned in the media blitz, inextricably entangled with personal controversy. Three years before he died, he said with Huysmans-like intensity, 'I am determined to crush a coloured picture from that area within me that is game and wild and intoxicated...Can I do it?', describing in his mind's eye a fabulous garden that he would like to paint, saturating his palette with a dazzling array of colours.[81] This is a vision which lingers. For that which will be appreciated in his work by future generations may not be quite the same as what is admired today. When the more erratic quests of his personality have been peeled away, like excess clothing from a public prince, Brett Whiteley's achievement will stand on the quality he in his deepest conscience most cared about: being a painter.

Notes

1. Donald Brook, 'Painters, poets, sages', *Sydney Morning Herald*, 18 June 1970.
2. Artist's notebook 1960-61, private collection.
3. Artist interviewed by Phillip Adams, radio 2UE, Sydney, September 1986.
4. Brett Whiteley, *Another way of looking at Vincent van Gogh*, Melbourne, Richard Griffin, 1983, unpaginated. Book launched in conjunction with an exhibition at The Art Gallery of New South Wales, Sydney, July 1983.
5. Phillip Adams interview, op. cit.
6. Letter to Lloyd Rees, 21 September 1988, possession of Jan and Alan Rees, Sydney. Rees wrote a reply to Whiteley 23 September, and died in Hobart in December. Both letters were published in full in Good Weekend, *Sydney Morning Herald* magazine, 3 July 1993.
7. Michael Johnson interviewed by author, Sydney, 25 May 1994.
8. Ibid.
9. Phillip Adams interview, op. cit.
10. David Christian interviewed by author, Sydney, December 1994.
11. Michael Johnson interview, op. cit.
12. Phillip Adams interview, op. cit.
13. Wendy Whiteley interviewed by author, Sydney, 5–6 January 1995.
14. Artist's notebook 1960–61, op. cit.
15. David Christian interview, op. cit.
16. Dore Ashton, *Philip Guston*, New York, Grove Press, 1960, p. 5.
17. Artist's notebook 1960–61, op. cit.
18. Ibid.
19. Lawrence Daws interviewed by author, Beerwah, Queensland, 17–18 August 1994.
20. Sandra McGrath, *Brett Whiteley*, Sydney: Bay Books, 1979, p. 34.
21. Wendy Whiteley interview, op. cit.
22. Bryan Robertson, 'Innocence and experience', *Spectator*, London, 5 November 1965.
23. McGrath, op. cit., p. 35.
24. Letter to Lawrence Daws, 9 September 1964, possession of Lawrence Daws, Queensland.
25. Michael Johnson interview, op. cit.
26. Fran Hopkirk interviewed by author, Milthorpe, New South Wales, 6 December 1994.
27. T.G. Rosenthal, 'Ancient and modern', *The Listener*, London, 5 November 1965.
28. Norbert Lynton, 'Voyeurs', *New Statesman*, London, 8 May 1964.
29. Kenneth Coutts-Smith, 'Brett Whiteley', *Art Review*, vol. XVI, no. 8, London, 2–16 May 1964.
30. Robert Hughes, 'The Shirley Temple of English art? Brett Whiteley's splash in the mainstream', *The Bulletin*, Sydney, 18 December 1965.
31. The two principal texts were Colin Wilson's *Encyclopedia of Murder*, London: Barker, 1961; and Ludovic Kennedy's *10 Rillington Place*, London: Victor Gollancz 1961.
32. John Russell, 'Brain, brawn and blood', *Sunday Times*, London, 17 October 1965.
33. Letter to Lawrence Daws, op. cit.
34. Artist's notebook 22, *c. 1970–72*, artist's estate, Sydney.
35. Ibid.
36. Janet Hawley, *Encounters with Australian artists*, St Lucia, Queensland: University of Queensland Press, 1993, p. 40.
37. Hughes, op. cit.
38. Ibid.
39. Ibid. Hughes wrote in his *The art of Australia*, London: Pelican 1970, p. 298, 'The Christie paintings were a highly polished exercise in this kind of figure-field relationship. But their weakness was in the experience that began them. Whiteley has no vision of evil. His comments on the monster of Rillington Place were, therefore, tinged with artificiality: the act of painting was a way of gathering vicarious experience. One did not feel that Whiteley knew anything about the agonies and horrors he was painting… By this I do not mean to imply that Whiteley's paintings were trivial or vulgarly kinky – only that he was not equipped to deal with the experience with which they were ostensibly concerned… So his innate bounce and sensuality filled the gap, quite incongruously.'
40. Sandra McGrath, 'Profile: Brett Whiteley', *Art and Australia*, Sydney, June 1967.
41. Keith Roberts, 'Current and forthcoming exhibitions', *Burlington Magazine*, London, November 1967.
42. Quoted in the 'Art' section, 'Painting: Plaster apocalypse', *Time*, 10 November 1967.
43. 'Electricity in water', *Time*, 10 November 1967.
44. See John Rothenstein and Ronald Alley, *Francis Bacon*, London: Thames and Hudson, 1964, p.152, cat. 215, illus. The painting in question was dated 1963. According to Wendy Whiteley, Bacon took Whiteley's portrait of Rembrandt as a possible exchange, but returned it shortly to Marlborough. See note 4. Whiteley's tribute painting was *Walking down a street at Palm Beach thinking about Vincent*, 1972.
45. James Gleeson, 'A landmark in painting', *The Sun*, Sydney, 7 February 1968.
46. Donald Brook, 'A huge talent', *Sydney Morning Herald*, 8 February 1968.
47. Wendy Whiteley interview, op. cit.
48. Hawley, op. cit.
49. Elwyn Lynn, 'Erotic obsessions', *The Bulletin*, Sydney, February 1968.
50. McGrath, op. cit., pp. 87–88.
51. Letter written July or August, shortly after his arrival in Fiji, possession of Beryl Whiteley, Sydney.
52. Ibid.
53. Ibid.
54. Bruce James, 'Wendy's world', *Mode*, Sydney, August-September 1994.
55. Letter to Beryl Whiteley begun on voyage from Fiji to Sydney, and completed after some period in Sydney, possession of Beryl Whiteley, Sydney.
56. Ibid.
57. After initial resistance Patrick White bought several of Whiteley's works from about the beginning of 1972. He later presented these to The Art Gallery of New South Wales. When Whiteley received unkind press this year White sent him a supportive letter. In reply Whiteley proposed that the author might try to influence his publisher to use one of the artist's paintings for the cover of his next book, *The eye of the storm*, saying, 'Your work has such a powerful effect upon my spirit it literally takes me hours to come out of the delicacy of one of your silences'. Whilst White was writing his autobiography *Flaws in the glass* during 1980 Whiteley painted his portrait. However the author became upset when the artist pasted on to the painting a list of loves and hates that White had written on a piece of paper. See David Marr, *Patrick White: A life*, Sydney: Random House, 1991, pp. 519, 600.
58. Brook, op. cit.
59. Alan McCulloch, 'Letter from Australia', *Art International*, October 1970.
60. McGrath, op. cit., p. 113.
61. Rodney Milgate, 'Dangerous rib tickling', *The Australian*, 15 April 1972. The Yellow House was an artists' collective based at 59 Macleay Street, Potts Point in Sydney between 1970 and 1972. The aim of the collective was to establish an artists' colony based on the unfulfilled dream of Vincent van Gogh. Each artist involved was given a room to create a thematic environment. In 1971 Whiteley spent a considerable time at the Yellow House, presenting with Wendy the so-called Bonsai Room. He also worked on the Hokusai wave in the stone room and painted his Rembrandt head which became an ongoing self-portrait. See exhibition catalogue *The Yellow House 1970–72*, The Art Gallery of New South Wales, Sydney, 1990.
62. Bernard Boles, 'Paintings by Brett Whiteley', *The Review*, 15 April 1972.
63. Adrian Reed, 'He climbed into his own picture', *The Australian*, 8 November 1969.
64. Statement amongst various papers, artist's estate, Sydney.
65. Postcard to Beryl Whiteley from Madrid, 20 June 1967, possession of Beryl Whiteley, Sydney.
66. Letter to Beryl Whiteley from New York, 1968, possession of Beryl Whiteley, Sydney.
67. Nancy Borlase, 'Whiteley's promised land', *The Bulletin*, Sydney, 13 January 1973.
68. Daniel Thomas, 'A literal autobiography in 18 Whiteley panels', *Sydney Morning Herald*, 11 January 1973.
69. Nancy Borlase, 'An unexpected Whiteley', *The Bulletin*, Sydney, 23 November 1974.
70. Phillip Adams interview, op. cit.
71. Donated by Whiteley in 1991, this work was installed in the grounds outside the Gallery building. According to the artist, it was conceived at the Chelsea Hotel, New York in 1968 when he was influenced by F. Scott Fitzgerald's view that 'there is no second act in one's life'. The earliest maquette however, is dated 1983, exhibited in *Another way of looking at Vincent van Gogh*. See note 4. The final version was executed with the assistance of sculptor Matthew Dillon. Endlessnessism is the name of a company formed by Brett and Wendy Whiteley: the term was used by both Brett Whiteley and Lloyd Rees as a description of eternity, although Whiteley also used it to refer to the process of abstraction. See letter to Bernard Smith, 1971; Bernard Smith Papers, State Library of New South Wales, Sydney.
72. According to Alison Brionowski, perhaps one of the last to conduct an official interview with him, Whiteley may have delayed his trip for the same reason as did certain other writers and artists, fearing that the reality of Japan would not measure up to their romantic idea of it. However, in his account to her of his five weeks there, spending most of the time in Tokyo and Kyoto, he said that he was not surprised at what he had discovered. Alison Broinowski interviewed by author, Sydney, February 1995. See also Alison Broinowski, *The yellow lady: Australian impressions of Asia*, Melbourne: Oxford University Press, 1992, pp. 149–51.
73. Artist's notebook 19, *c.* 1966–67, artist's estate, Sydney.
74. Artist interviewed by Jane Singleton, ABC radio, Sydney, *c.* 1984.
75. See note 4.
76. Letter to Beryl Whiteley, 29 January 1979, possession of Beryl Whiteley, Sydney.
77. Linda Van Nunen, 'The other side of Whiteley', *The Australian Magazine*, 31 October 1992. In 1994 the state government of New South Wales announced the purchase of Whiteley's studio as a public museum. It opened to the public on 18 February 1995.
78. Letter to Beryl Whiteley, op. cit.
79. Donald Friend's diary, May 1957, National Library of Australia, Canberra.
80. Whiteley had been visiting Thirroul – made famous by D. H. Lawrence in his novel *Kangaroo* – regularly for several years to cure himself in private, and to do some painting and drawing. His exhibition *Paris, 'Regard de Côté'* was held at The Art Gallery of New South Wales, April 1990. This comprised a series of gouaches, drawings and photographs made in Paris between June and July 1989.
81. Artist's notebook 25, 1989. This statement, dated 3 March 1989, was one of several written by the artist in preparation for Don Featherstone's film on him entitled *Difficult pleasure*. It reads in full: 'After seeing Bonnard's "Violet Countryside 1946 (c)" in the Readers Digest Collection at the NSW Art Gallery I am determined to crush a coloured picture from that area within me that is game and wild and intoxicated – I want a garden that is a smear of Cambodian lipstick, green and mauves and lettuce green and magenta purple and ultramarine and arctic pale blue with lemon yellow and orange and cadmium yellow against apple green and baby pink apricots. North Queensland. Can I do it?'

Recollections
Wendy Whiteley Interviewed by Barry Pearce

What sort of painting was Whiteley doing when you first met him?
It wasn't so much what he was painting, it was the way he went about it, the energy and the driven quality. When we met, Brett was seventeen and I was fifteen. He had a passion for the idea of being an artist which I shared. He went away for weekends to paint landscapes and began some nudes in his glasshouse studio that I posed for. It was highly sexual.

He has told a number of interviewers that in the very early period he found painting a way of escaping, to create his own world, a kind of sanctuary for himself.
He wanted to create his own world and move away from childhood. In order to do this we needed each other. We were curious and obsessive, and wanted to take things apart. Brett viewed contentment as a dangerous state – it was bovine. He needed to put his hand in the fire. That's what struck me when I first met him: I thought he had courage.

How much was art the cement of the relationship?
It was very much a shared love. Arriving in the Louvre in 1960 and seeing Giotto's *St Francis with the Birds* was one of the most powerful experiences we shared. We were holding hands and a charge zapped through us. There was the shared sense of wonder that whether looking at great art or being part of the attempt to make it, it was powerful cement. Each time it was like falling in love.

Leaving Australia was important for Brett's exploration of abstraction.
Abstraction for Brett was more about learning how to deal with aesthetics and emotion together to come up with something that was a unique vision. He learnt a lot from abstraction about how to bang one form up against another. He loved William Scott and Arshile Gorky. It didn't really matter what it was, whether it was figurative or abstract; the important thing was not to leave the canvas empty.

He had a secret admiration for Barnett Newman and Mark Rothko because they solved the problem of how you put two forms – or one form – on a canvas and think about the actual empty spaces more than about the two forms. Ultimately, though, he found pure abstraction a dead end. He felt you look at someone like Rothko and you can't repeat it. Brett

Figure 32
STANDING NUDE *c.* 1959
Charcoal on paper, 53.4 x 31 cm

returned to figuration because he needed to relate his work to what was around him: his environment. There was a constant amalgamation of influences throughout his life with both figuration and abstraction.

In the bathroom series, which came straight after the Sigean abstractions, there seems to be a rare sense of the artist approaching emotional intimacy. They are the most poignant dialogue between you and him in all his work.

It was an immensely pleasurable time. I had baths and he would just sit and draw while I was in there, then we'd make love or go and eat. It was very much an immediate response to our life. With both the Sigean abstractions and the bathroom series, the colour and the flattening of the form was an acknowledgment of his love of Piero della Francesca. The actual landscape and our lifestyle was closer to Piero's time than our own century seemed. We lived in these old abandoned farm buildings, which had been no electricity, no running water, and the most wonderful natural light. The surrounding countryside was very much like the background to *The Baptism of Christ* – the creams and the dry greens with the dots. And there was a large lake with a beautiful river and lots of trout. We were so happy there, and Brett was so excited about his work and where he wanted to go. I looked out the window one day when he was painting in the courtyard and there he was, scratching his head, building up this amazing electricity in this hair. He was so excited with his work.

Do you find it hard to modulate your enthusiasm from one phase of his life and art to another?

It is all connected, whether light or dark. And this is why I hate heroin addiction now – or can see it for what it is – because it makes you live life in a cocoon or vacuum, whereas the pleasure-pain principle has to exist. Brett's father died in 1963, and that raised a lot of questions about evil and death which Brett incorporated into his work. His fascination with Christie was just as much a part of our lives as the bathroom series or the Sigean abstractions were, and I wouldn't have enjoyed his company if it hadn't been so. Robert Hughes questioned whether Brett had the experience to deal with the complex issues of the Christie paintings – of course you've had the experience, unless you have grown up where nothing ever happens. Brett had pain in his life, and so did I and most of the people I knew. It was to do with the recognition that evil and ugliness, good and beauty, all coexist.

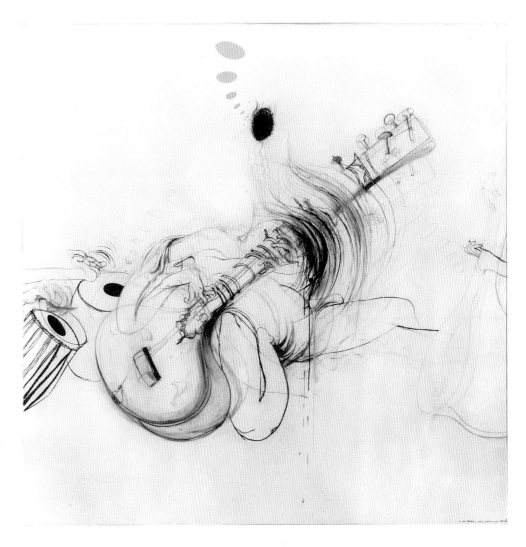

Did you have any apprehensions about Brett wanting to move from this blossoming period of your marriage – Sigean and the bathroom series – into the troubling area of the Christie murders?

I thought the change was totally natural, although I didn't particularly enjoy living in the middle of it. The fascination with Christie began when we were living in Ladbroke Grove. It was the first time either of us realized the sad and dismal loneliness of the lives that many people in the huge cities of Europe had to live and die in – and in the case of Christie's victims, almost unnoticed. At the same time, Brett was building a profound admiration for Francis Bacon and the way he seemed to deal with alienation while making beautiful paintings. It was only after our marriage, his increasing confidence with his work, the success of the Sigean and bathroom pictures, and the sanctuary and stability of the studio in Pembridge Crescent that he could really attempt the Christie pictures. Of course, even then he felt he needed to balance them with the zoo.

Figure 33
SHANKAR 1966
Charcoal and ink on paper,
213 x 203.2 cm

Did you share what was going on?
Mostly, yes. Apart from the time I left Ladbroke Grove because I couldn't marry my life with Brett and my working life in Knightsbridge. Our life together had a sense of inevitability about it, but both of us also clung to the notion that we could change it whenever we wanted. Later, in New York, it became difficult to share everything. There was a lot to do. It was exciting and glamorous on one side, and dark and dangerous on the other. The Chelsea Hotel was an island unto itself, a colony of its own. You could be extraordinary out on the streets or extraordinary in there. But once again I also had a business and Arkie to look after, and Brett had a separate studio.

Based in London you were able to travel extensively throughout Europe, but you also made trips to Africa and India. Brett wrote eloquently about the women of Tangier in his notebooks, what was his response to your first journey to North Africa?
When we first went to Tangier we found a whole floor of an old hotel on the beach called The Majestic, which was run by an ex-station master who didn't have a clue about how to run a hotel. We went to the markets, made friends with Achmid the alcoholic, travelled around on the buses, and Brett made drawings and portraits. He was very interested in photography and took wonderful photographs. One

day he went off with Achmid – who is in one of the *Tangier Postcards* – to the hashish dealer in the kasbah. About an hour later Arkie and I, very relaxed, were sitting on the beach when we saw this little ginger person charging by with his hair fizzing, hit the edge of the water and head out for the horizon until the water lapped his chin. He was completely off his face with hashish paranoia and stayed in the water until it wore off and he felt safe to come out.

It was a culture he didn't understand, and he could never have lived in it for long – he would have been in trouble very quickly. He felt very controlled by the Muslim morality but yet was fascinated by it. The veiled women both attracted and repulsed him – the power of the women's eyes communicated so much. Brett found it quite beautiful but quite frightening because as Westerners you could so easily break the rules. The kasbah was the perfect expression of it: a walled, inward-turning, secret place, with impenetrable mystery.

What about India?
Calcutta was incredible. With people sleeping in the streets, unbelievable heat, flies, dust and terrible poverty, it was a shock after Australia. We went to the meat market one day, which was both fascinating and horrific, and saw a huge banner advertising a Ravi Shankar concert. On the way to the concert we passed a ragged three-mile queue for a James Bond film, yet the Shankar concert was half empty. We sat there with the determined, rapt attention of Westerners,

while Shankar's family sat in front of us talking constantly through the entire show, commenting on every note. Brett was intrigued by Shankar's metronome foot hanging off the stage, beating time for the music. Even though we were there for a short time, India made an impact. *Fidgeting with Infinity* and *Calcutta* came from that trip.

Is it too harsh to say that New York was a shipwreck in terms of Brett's art, even if only in the sense of Baudelaire, that there had to be destruction in order to reconstruct?
New York in the late sixties was floundering. America was politically polarized, and there was a lot of intolerance and anger. But in the arts there was a great deal of experimentation. Both Baudelaire and Rimbaud were the poetic heroes, in the feeling that the old order had to be destroyed to make way for the new. Calamity had to happen. Brett pushed himself as they had done, to the absolute extreme, and that took its toll. *The American Dream* was Brett's response to New York and what was going on there. The centre panel looked like he vomited all over the canvas, which was painted in a kind of drunken state of rage and fear. In that sense he was fearful of analyzing too much, of going into therapy or counselling, unless there was someone to trust who would ride with him. So we counselled each other.

What about the actual practice of his art? I guess when I once said he was able to draw like a bird sings, it was misleading, many people don't realize how hard Brett actually worked to attain that quality of naturalness.
He did work very hard, and he loved working hard – and he set himself very high goals. The early work of the bathroom drawings, the Christie studies and the boxing match show the search and the struggle; the spontaneous marks and the nerve endings are there on the page. This is what he loved about Giacometti's drawings. Later, when he acquired a calligraphy brush and attempted to deal with his love of the Asian calligraphers and Matisse, it became even more important to judge the tension between discipline and freedom. Unless there is the tension at the same time as the flow, the work is facile. When there was that struggle and balance, his drawings were magnificent. Some believed it was all too easy. Students came around and said, 'give us some magic' – it drove him crazy.

Michael Johnson said that he admired Brett's greed, his 'want' to find out and to work at fabricating his own magic.

Figure 36
INTERIOR, LAVENDER BAY 1976
Pen and ink on paper,
76.2 x 57.2 cm

He wanted to know what alchemy was about, that sense of transformation which was both a joy and a curse – a desire to know everything, fascinated with a mystery but not being prepared to accept that there are a lot of things you may never know. The process of transformation was certainly involved in Brett's case, but he was looking for it in too many directions at once. He couldn't concentrate on one thing at a time and became really overloaded in New York. Marlborough's refusal to exhibit *The American Dream* certainly didn't help, it just catapulted him into absolute and fearful paranoia. He pushed himself to a physical and emotional limit with *The American Dream* and when his uncle died – Clem's brother – it was both an enormous shock and a catalyst. His decision to go to Fiji saved him.

What did the Fiji experience mean in the end?
Fiji was important for his sanity and our relationship. He was there alone for a couple of months before Arkie and I arrived, which was an essential break to learn that we could do things independently and that we missed each other.

What made Brett want to stay there?
We really did live in paradise there. Brett was painting

Figure 37
STUDY FOR GAUGUIN 1968
Pencil, ink, collage and adhesive
tape on paper, 35.3 x 55.7 cm

birds, landscapes, frangipanis, some of the Fijians.
It was Gauguin and Tahiti: you could sink into it.
We'd swim, and then there were the simple things
you had to do during the day. He enjoyed getting
wood for the fire, because it was tactile. There was
no machinery, except the batteries for playing
music and the car. It cost little. So the wrench from
this was hard, and we came back to Australia to a
great deal of publicity that was unpleasant. Brett was
angry because they had thrown him out of paradise.
There was a huge amount of chaos. We'd had this
wonderful show, and we were leaving it all behind. We
eventually drifted into staying in Australia, mostly
because we found this place in Lavender Bay.

*The first years back in Australia were successful in
terms of Brett exhibiting and selling work.*
His work certainly got a great deal of attention and
was reasonably successful financially, and it enabled
us to stay. We got a couple of dogs, started to accumu-
late, bought a bit of furniture. And we started to feel
okay about being back because a lot of people we had
known came back into our lives, and we made
some new friends. The Yellow House happened, and
people we had known in London started to drift back.
Of course, there was also Joel Elenberg, and so a real
life started to happen with some very close friend-

ships. It was also important that we established a
home for Arkie. There was the gasworks studio nearby
in Waverton. Brett always came home at night and
would go off in the mornings, so I didn't feel isolated
from him. I spent a lot of time around there anyway,
and he had space here as well. The downstairs in
Lavender Bay became the studio, and for quite a long
period of time he had two studios. He couldn't work
on the really big things in the downstairs studio.
Alchemy happened at the gasworks, partly due its
enormous space, so the picture just grew and grew
until it hit the other end of the wall. But he preferred
to live and paint in the same space, where there was
the freedom to get up in the middle of the night. That
raised the issue of having a daughter and a wife who
didn't necessarily want to stay up all night and have
the music pumping out. So it was a relief when he
would go to another space. What we both missed then
was the interrelation, the intermeshing all the time.

*There was consolidation and anguish in your first
four years back in Australia, and it certainly shows in
his work.*
There was the paradox of the success, because along
with fame there was the pressure to live up to and live
out the myth that the drug bust and Fiji had created. It
was the first time we had achieved front-page infamy,

and that had a big impact on our lives, as well as settling back into Australia.

In 1974 you bought the Lavender Bay house, and that was the year you both started using drugs on a serious level.

It was a very simple process. In 1974 a friend was around here one night, and during a conversation it came up that heroin was on the streets in Sydney, and that quite a number of people had begun using. It had come into Australia with the Vietnam war. American soldiers started to bring it in on R&R, then Australian soldiers. It had come out of the Chinese world, which we would never have had any access to. If there was any opium or heroin around, there were probably only a few tired old jazz musicians hooked into it, and we didn't meet them until much later on. But they were there and in the early 1970s had actually been using heroin for a number of years, very quietly through secret connections. It suddenly became a part of the culture in Australian society, and it was heroin not opium – very, very strong heroin, pure and lots of it. So Brett said, 'Let's get some'. He sent our friend off with a fist full of money, and about an hour later he came back with a little packet of rocks, and we all smoked it, laid back on the sofa and basically couldn't have cared less what each other did at all. We were completely, euphorically stoned.

What were the consequences?

It progressed into the whole tragic thing about the horrors of addiction and just not being able to put it down. Then you become caught up in a whole other world of dealers and other users. You spent a lot of time with some pretty crummy people, which made you mad at yourself, at them, at the addiction. In the early years it appeared to take away all the stress and felt free, then years later you wake up and realize it is a world that is very difficult to get out of. In my view complete abstinence from mood-altering chemicals is the only way out.

Of course this period of heavy drug use took place just after the completion of Alchemy, *but ongoing issues of Brett's state of mind can be located back to the conception of that work.*

I suppose we would have to begin with Brett's interest in people like Mishima, Hitler, Mussolini, and even pop stars, whose power to beguile large groups of people intrigued him. He had been struggling with various portraits of heroes to understand the principle of transformation and power. He was fascinated by pop stars and how they used their music, their

medium, and the way it brought them fame, money, power and attention. He also started reading a bit of Paracelsus, a bit of Bosch and so on. A book of Ronnie Laing's poetry got dragged out again, too, which was very existential and schizophrenic. Some great stuff came out of it, like Laing's theory about schizophrenia. Brett was not schizophrenic, but he was fascinated with the schizophrenic state of mind, in the sense of being split between good and evil – what did power mean, what was the price to pay, did it always lead to a dramatic event like Mishima's suicide? He destroyed his portrait of Mishima, joined the remaining panels, and *Alchemy* just grew from there. There is paradise in hell in it, and all those little details are both humorous and quite frightening. Beautifully drawn, it is like a recipe. All the alchemists had various recipes for going about the transformation. The thing of base metal to gold is the most meaningless bit. More important is the search for the Holy Grail, the connection between heaven and hell, animal and spiritual. This was Brett's recipe. I've seen people laugh when they look at it and I've seen people confused. Quite a difficult picture to take in, in one hit. You do have to travel the journey with it.

How about the Lavender Bay pictures?

Optical ecstasy. That's the strong Matisse connection. The inner journey into the dark side had been so tiring, that's why what Matisse said about art being an armchair for people to relax in appealed to Brett. He loved Matisse but knew little about his life.

Figure 38
PORTRAIT OF JOEL ELENBERG 1980
Charcoal on paper, 39.5 x 37.9 cm

Obviously they were very different people in their behaviour, but that's not to say that Matisse didn't have a dark side. He just managed it differently and didn't put it on the canvas. In a sense Lavender Bay was Brett's return to paradise, having come from a very anxious situation – and it is paradise. He said some quite tender things about it at the time, like 'I'm home again at last'. And yet that was a really dark period because we started destroying it by being locked into a chemical paradise which had its moments in hell.

The Lavender Bay period was also about the whole concept of beauty, with sumptuous, glorious pictures celebrating the harbour and the birds, and the table tops too. Sometimes the table tops were coded, in the sense that there were other things going on. The beads were mine, a special present he had given me, a symbol of my presence in Lavender Bay. There are certain things that were codes between us that people wouldn't necessarily see, except that it was repeated in different circumstances. Almost every drawing he made of me for a long time had bracelets.

The big self-portrait looking at himself in the mirror is extraordinarily honest in some ways. He makes no attempt to hide the fact that he is really somewhere else, and that it is not a particularly happy place. He looks very stoned and haunted, though of course the painting itself is very beautiful and is generally read as a sumptuous interior.

Figure 39
SENSORENO 1977
Ink and collage on paper,
20.3 x 25.4 cm

Senso reno. ziteen-opps

With Self-Portrait in the Studio, *what do you think the message is for us as spectators?*
He was trying silently to say, Stay away, this is not what it might seem. Look at this beautiful house and wonderful pictures and things. But there was another side – that's the duality of life – and that's where Brett's pictures moved away from Matisse's. It was an acknowledgment of Rimbaud: 'One evening I sat Beauty on my knees. And I found her bitter.' It is a wonderful painting, but he was warning himself and other people watching. It was the cage of his interior, his addiction, the window or a glimpse of possible escape into paradise: the escape from one's own psyche. The second Archibald portrait, *Art, Life and the Other Thing,* deals much more directly with the terror of addiction.

Every artist is alone in the end. It is ultimately a solitary act.
It is a solitary act in many instances to be a human being. I think most of us desperately struggle to be understood. Brett wanted to be understood even within our relationship. Yet we had an enormous amount of compassion for each other. It is not just a matter of being judgmental. His greatest fear wasn't death, it was abandonment. I think mine was too.

The sculptor Joel Elenberg was Brett's closest male friend. How important was his life and death to both of you?
Joel was not an addictive person, perhaps, or romantic in that sense, but Brett had a long period of mourning for him. As soon as we knew Joel had cancer there was a period of immense hope, then nothing more we could do. We went through the whole process with Joel, which was an amazing thing to do. It wasn't as if somebody just died suddenly. Joel felt it terribly unfair because he didn't think he deserved it, and he didn't. He was so young, and occasionally he blew his temper with us and would say, 'The two of you are ridiculous. Here I am dying and look at you.' He was trying to think of a way out of his disease and there we were abusing our power of choice. Joel handled his dying with great dignity. We'd gone to Bali because Joel didn't want to die in hospital. He was very thin and he had no hair. There was no more chemotherapy that he could have. So he said, 'I'd like to go somewhere warm and maybe exotic. I'd like to have a bit of paradise here on this earth.'

What about the actual death?
While Joel was in hospital we and his closest friends

would go backwards and forwards. Then we were all together in Bali in about mid-1980. When he went into a coma for about ten days, he needed full-time nursing. Anna, his wife, and I were actually bathing him when he died, and I said, 'Oh my God, he's stopped breathing.' I felt a rush of heat. Then Brett came into the room. Someone had just told him. He didn't say anything, just held him in his arms and sang. I felt grateful because there was so much Joel had dealt with about his own life, yet in the end he had actually helped Brett go through the process of grieving for his dad.

Were you disappointed about the potential in Brett that was lost because of addiction?
It was really the potential for him to rediscover the joyful side, the funny side and the beauty that was inherent in our lives and in Brett. During the years of addiction there were periods of time that produced wondrous paintings – the landscapes and rivers, the glorious bird show with Robin Gibson in 1979, the drawing shows – an extraordinary body of work. He was just defeated in the end. I know that people from the outside thought I was trying to destroy him or he was trying to destroy me, but it wasn't like that. It's not about vengeance. It's about what you're doing to yourself. But don't you really want to ask me if I think the heroin had a detrimental effect on his work?

Okay, make your statement.
Yes, I think it did. But I didn't see it until I returned from England in 1986, after a year off drugs myself. I felt really uneasy about the bird show in the studio, which he and Christian Quintas had set up in 1988. Was it because I was jealous or wasn't there for some of those pictures? I couldn't see a breakthrough in the work, but I didn't confront him with any of these things. At this stage I thought maybe he had been clean for a year, and this was just the beginning of something else. The fact that he actually got the show together I suppose was an achievement. But I felt that some of the paintings were dead, sitting solidly on the canvas, heavy, overworked.

Perhaps it had something more to do with the current distraction of his life, the trauma of the split with you and so on. Can you really make an exclusive link with the drugs?
When we were in London getting counselled, it was put to Brett the same way it was put to me: that he should close down all activities and just concentrate on getting off drugs. And he decided against it. That was probably the only way he would ever get

Figure 40
THE WILLOW TREE 1978
Charcoal on paper, 222 x 125 cm

into recovery, to stop worrying about painting for a year. But of course that frightened him. He thought he would never be able to survive. He always said, 'I wonder if they ever gaoled me, if they would let me paint. It would be okay if they let me paint and they can put me in gaol. But they probably wouldn't.' And treatment centres didn't let him paint either. So he couldn't see the centres as a way out of addiction.

When he started communicating with me again, it really did overwhelm me. But instead of trying to simplify his life and focus on getting off heroin, he just made it worse. At the end of his life, there he was, everybody vying for his attention, everybody trying to control him, and none of us could really help. I guess that in a way I feel I am helping through this retrospective.

Early Work

After leaving school in 1956 at the age of seventeen, Whiteley worked in Sydney for the advertising agency Lintas. Apart from evening drawing classes and sketch clubs he was largely self-taught. During the next three and a half years he produced several paintings containing qualities which he carried into his later work. His early inspiration came from a mixture of art and life experiences. On the one hand there were the books and reproductions of international painters such as William Scott, Arshile Gorky, Amedeo Modigliani and Pablo Picasso. Whiteley also looked at original Australian paintings by Lloyd Rees, William Dobell, Sali Herman and Russell Drysdale, whose palette and landscape forms influenced him profoundly.

On the other hand there were the landscapes around the country towns of Hill End, Sofala and Bathurst, not to mention the streets and buildings of Sydney, where he lived and worked. Their shapes, textures and colours became an indelible part of his repertoire as a painter. In fact, the ethos of the Australian landscape remained prevalent in his work, even after he left the country at the end of 1959 for Europe. He had been awarded an Italian Travelling Scholarship by Drysdale, who recognized in Whiteley a sense for abstraction then dominating the concerns of most young artists in Australia. Drysdale saw in Whiteley someone who was aware of, and prepared to accommodate, the traditions of recent painting.

Plate 1
CHARLOTTE LANE 1957
Oil on cardboard, 20.3 x 26.5 cm

Plate 2
THE SOUP KITCHEN 1958
Oil on canvas, 76.2 x 63.7 cm

Plate 3
MAN CONTEMPLATING *c.* 1959
Oil on board, 90 x 59.5 cm

Plate 4
SOFALA 1958
Oil on canvas mounted on board, 65.8 x 85.4 cm

Plate 5
DIXON STREET 1959
Oil on board, 81.5 x 119.8 cm

Abstractions

Whiteley arrived in Italy at the beginning of 1960 and stayed for about ten months. Basing himself first in Rome, then Florence, he spent most of his time looking at paintings in churches and museums, developing a particular interest in late Byzantine and early Renaissance artists, for example Duccio, Uccello and Piero della Francesca. During this period Whiteley made a few paintings that were derived from the goldfields landscapes he had painted in Australia but informed by the still lifes of British artist William Scott and the semi-erotic abstractions of the American Arshile Gorky.

After moving to London, where he remained for the next seven years, Whiteley continued to combine these elements – the earthy colours of Australia, as reflected in the paintings of Russell Drysdale, and the ambience of Italian painting and architecture – with powerful hybrid forms of landscape and the female torso. Such paintings glowed with a confident command of their visual sources while conveying an acute awareness of the current modes of abstraction. The three works shown in Bryan Robertson's exhibition of recent Australian painting at the Whitechapel Gallery in 1961 created a sensation, and the purchase of *Untitled Red Painting* (1960) by the Tate Gallery established Whiteley's international reputation.

After Whiteley married Wendy Julius in March 1962, they spent six months in Sigean, a town in the south of France near the Spanish border. Whiteley's most elegant and relaxed abstract work emerged from his idyllic life there. He saw for the first time the creamy slopes dotted with olive trees that had attracted him to the backgrounds of paintings by Piero, and he dispersed his shapes according to the general feeling of the Mediterranean environment. This phase climaxed with the triptych *Summer at Sigean* (1962–63), in which voluptuous erotic forms drawn from his studies of Wendy asserted a move away from both landscape and abstraction.

Plate 6
SOMEWHERE IN SUMMER 1961
Oil, tempera, collage, string and canvas on board, 183 x 213.5 cm

Plate 7
THE KITCHEN 1960
Pencil and gouache on board, 35.8 x 51.2 cm

Plate 8
GOLD MINING 1960
Oil, pencil and PVA on paper on board, 35 x 53 cm

Plate 9
PRELIMINARY STUDY FOR UNTITLED RED PAINTING 1960
Oil, charcoal and collage on canvas, 69.5 x 62.5 cm

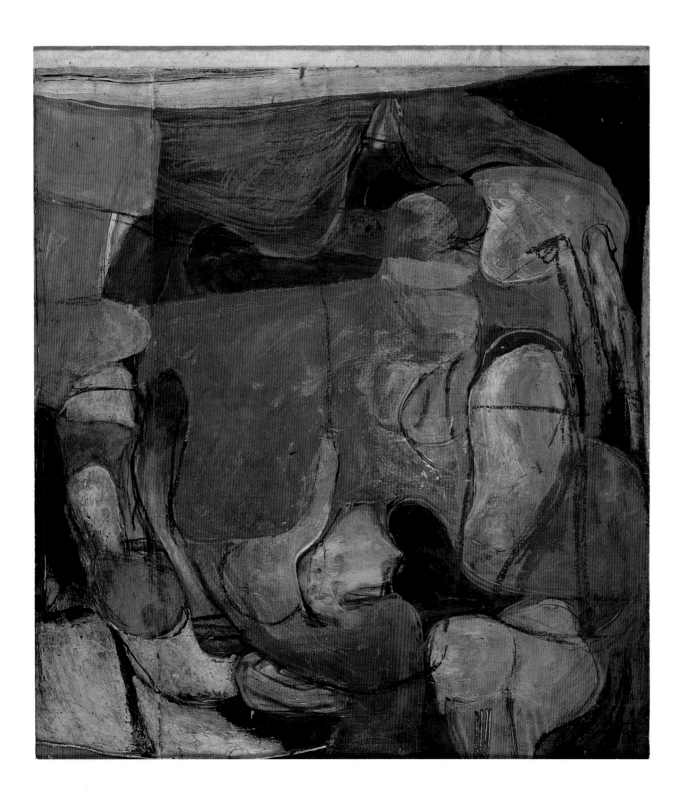

Plate 10
UNTITLED RED PAINTING 1960
Oil and collage on canvas,
132.7 x 186.1 cm

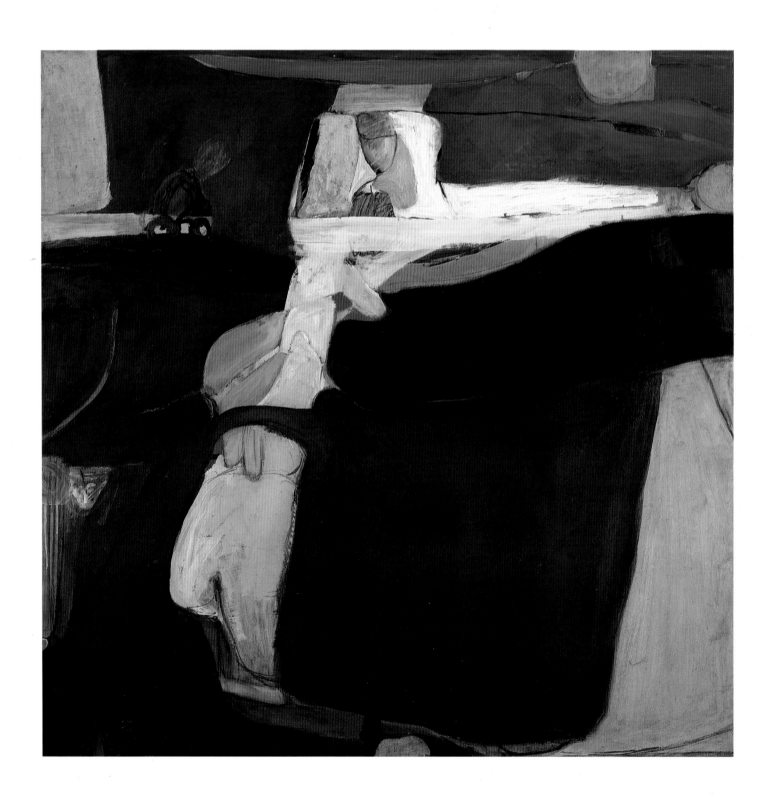

Plate 12
UNTITLED ABSTRACT *c.* 1960
Oil and charcoal on canvas, 86.5 x 115 cm

Plate 14
UNTITLED PAINTING 1962
Oil and mixed media on board, 122 x 127.7 cm

Plate 15
UNTITLED RED PAINTING 1961
Oil, newspaper, charcoal and resin on board, 152.4 x 152.4 cm

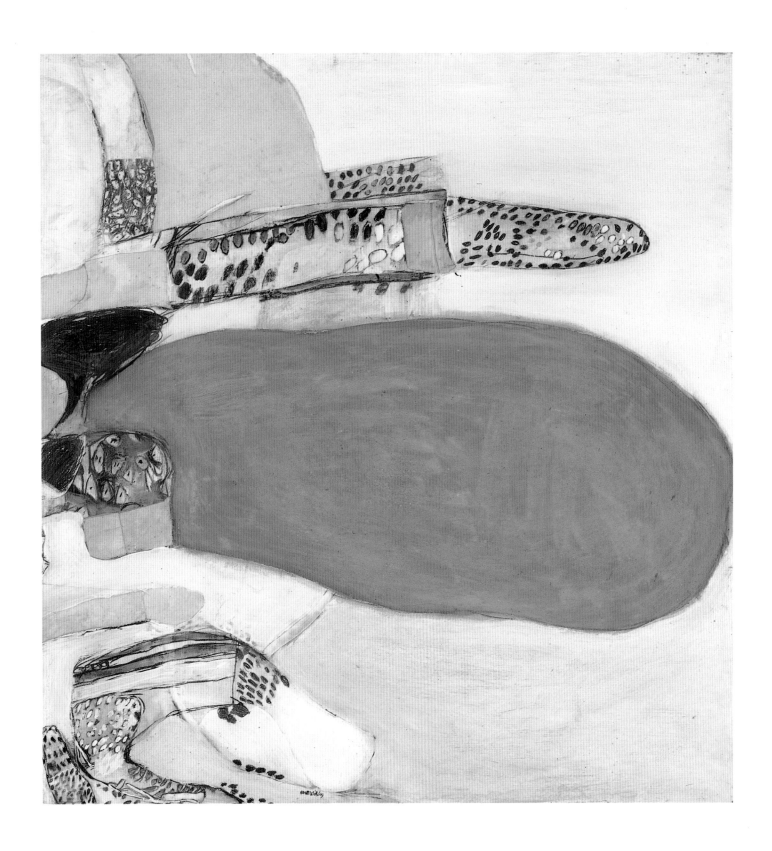

Plate 16
SUMMER FIELD PAINTING III 1962
Oil, tempera and collage on board, 122 x 127.5 cm

Plate 17
UNTITLED WHITE PAINTING II 1962
Tempera, ink, gouache, charcoal and collage on paper, 74.6 x 67 cm

Plate 18
UNTITLED DARK PAINTING 1962
Oil, charcoal, material, string and wax on canvas, 133 x 186.2 cm

Plate 19
WHITE PAINTING WITH COLLAGE 1961
Oil, collage, pencil, canvas, charcoal, newspaper and wax on board, 123.5 x 123.5 cm

Plate 20
TO ARRIVE AT A POINT OF 'CUBELESSISM' 1961
Charcoal, pencil, pen and ink, collage, material, oil and gouache on paper on card, 70.7 x 71 cm

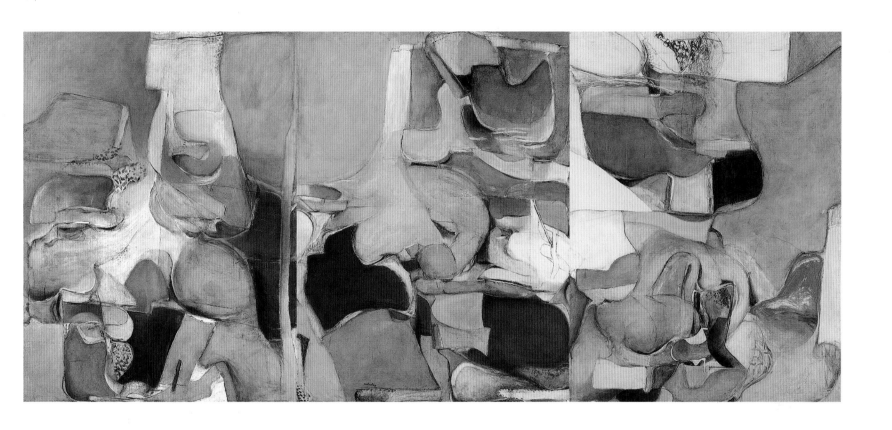

Plate 22
SUMMER AT SIGEAN 1962–63
(Triptych) Synthetic polymer medium, oil, charcoal, pencil, tempera on hessian and cotton gauze on composition board, 198 x 456 cm

Bathroom Series

Following their stay in Sigean, the Whiteleys travelled to Spain and New York before returning to London and settling in a new studio. The last Sigean abstractions that Whiteley worked on showed an increasing preoccupation with the female torso, though seen from a distance and in multiple forms dispersed across a shallow pictorial field. He then began his bathroom series, preserving the warm reds and honey colours of his abstractions while combining them with the bathroom's acid blues and greens.

Whiteley started to focus on the single figure, the naked form of Wendy in the bath, capturing the tactility and tones of her flesh with an intimacy rarely equalled in his later paintings of the same subject. Something of the colours and broad shapes of Piero della Francesca's works admired by Whiteley was retained, but there was a closer tradition of figurative painting making an impact on him, particularly through the work Pierre Bonnard and Francis Bacon. Indeed, one of Bonnard's most striking bath paintings was at the Tate Gallery, and Whiteley was impressed by a reproduction he saw in the studio of William Scott.

Whiteley exhibited his bathroom pictures at the Marlborough New London Gallery in 1964, and one painting was purchased by the Tate Gallery, the second in just a few years. Most importantly, the bathroom series signalled Whiteley's breakthrough as a figure draughtsman and his desire to make eroticism more explicit. In the catalogue to the exhibition *New Generation: 1964* at the Whitechapel Gallery he wrote: 'All the paintings I have made in the last four years have been concerned one way or another with sex and the desire to record sensual behaviour.'

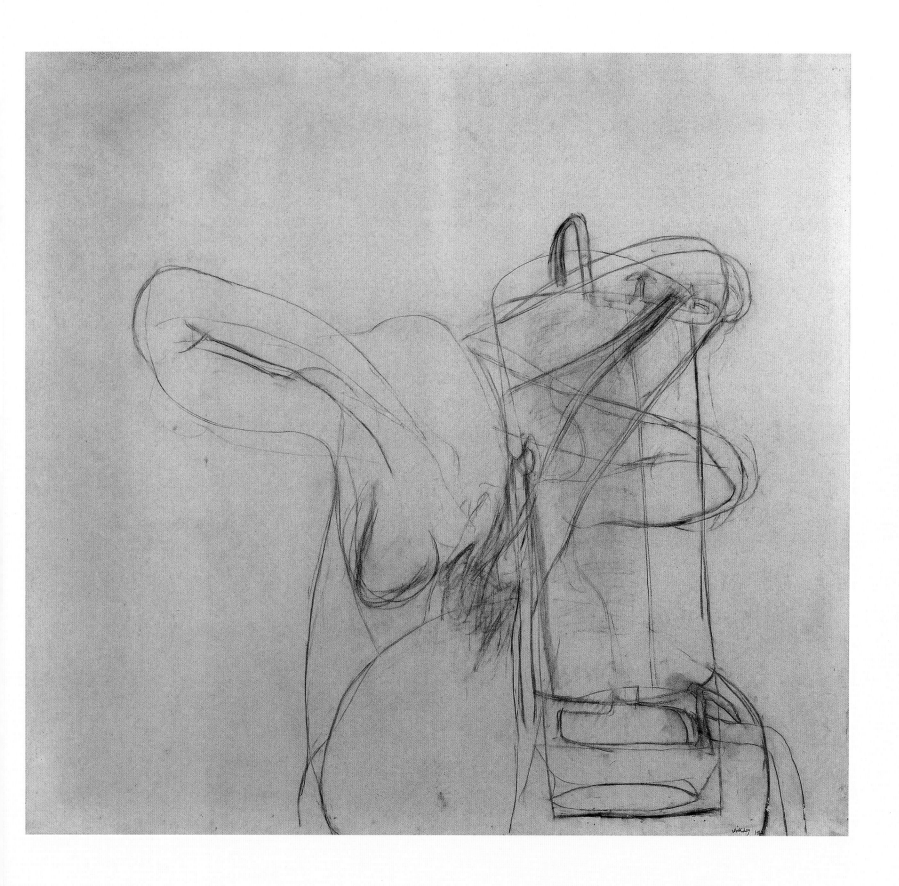

Plate 23
LARGE FIGURE AT THE BASIN DRAWING 1963
Charcoal on paper, 142 x 152 cm

Plate 24
NUDE AT BASIN *c.* 1963
Oil and tempera on board, 129 x 121.5 cm

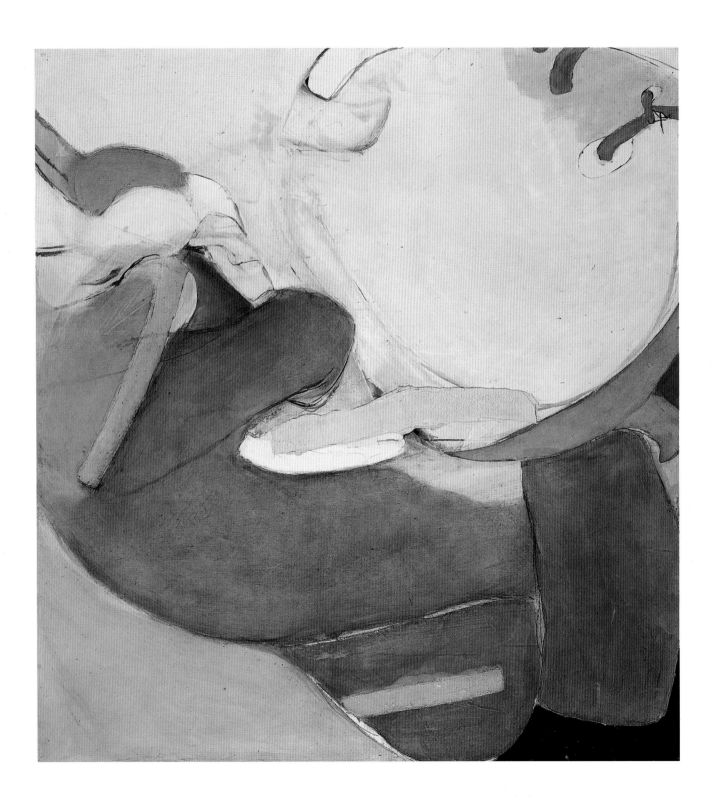

Plate 25
WOMAN IN BATH 1963
Pencil and charcoal on paper, 54.8 x 77 cm

Plate 26
WOMAN IN A BATH 1964
Oil, charcoal, tempera, material and collage on board, 146.8 x 120.2 cm

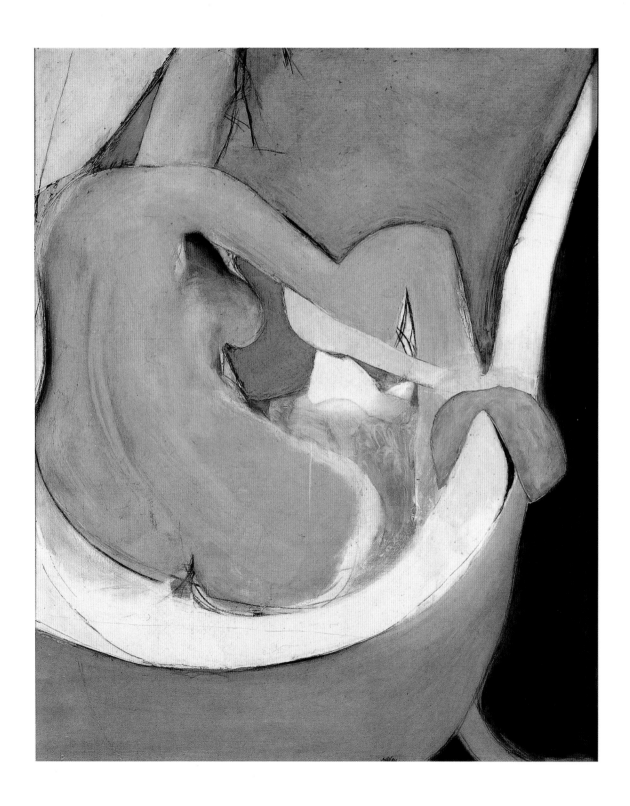

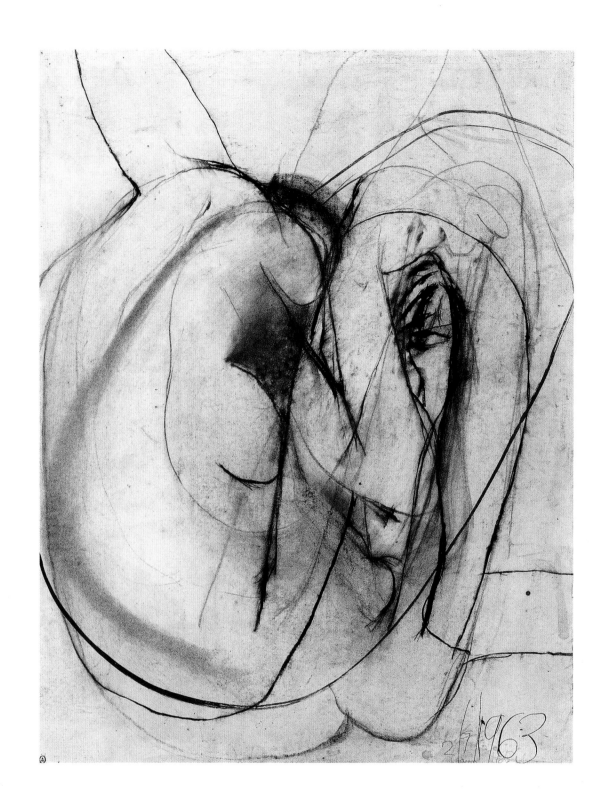

Plate 27
BATHROOM DRAWING 1963
Charcoal, brush and ink on paper, 75 x 57.5 cm

Plate 30
WOMAN IN THE BATH II 1963
Oil, tempera and collage of canvas strips on canvas, 182.9 x 188 cm

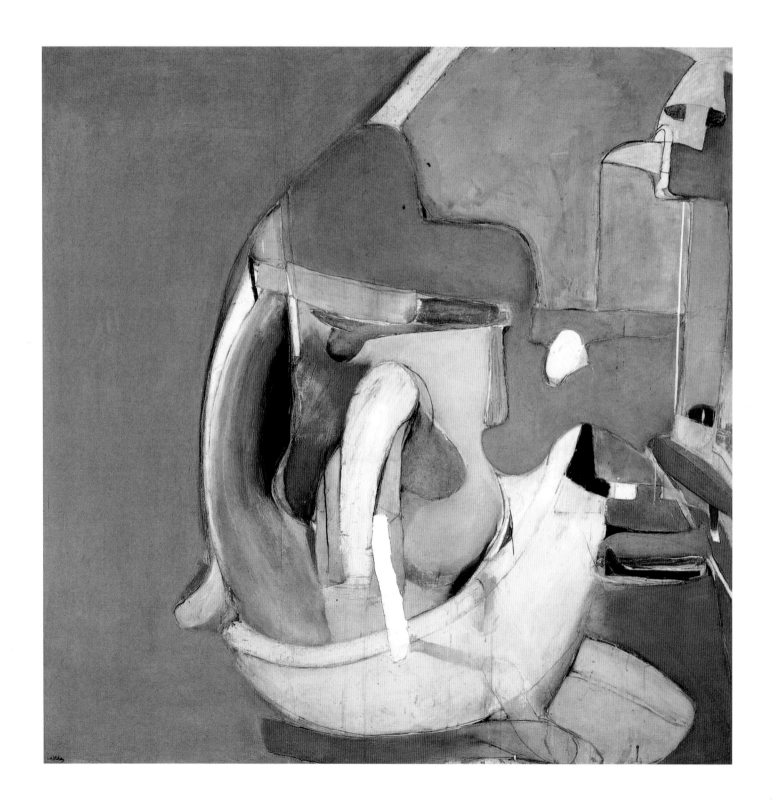

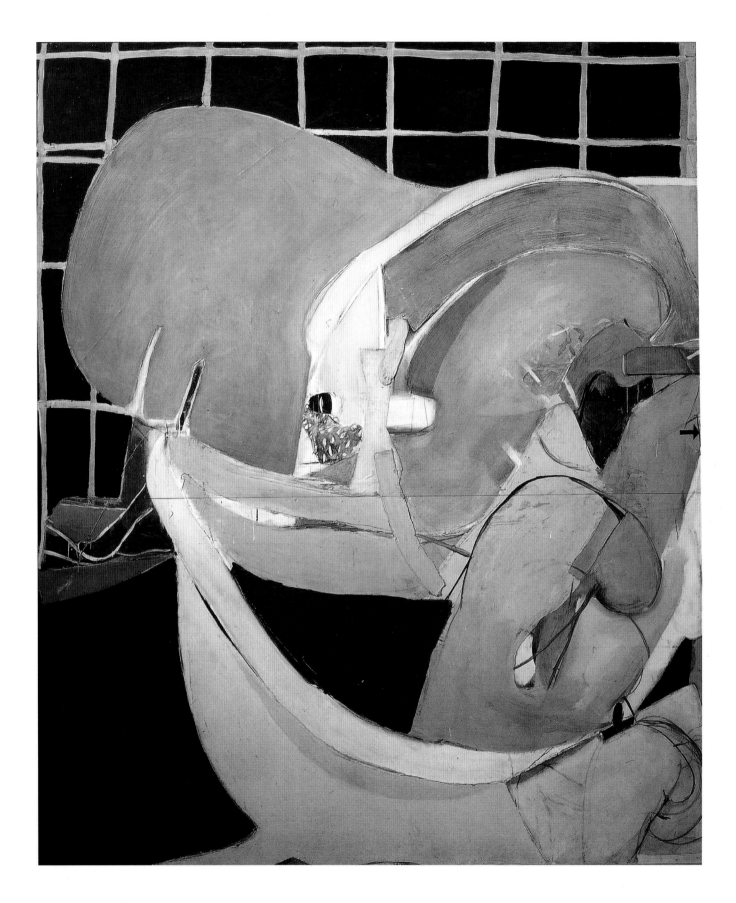

Plate 31
WOMAN IN THE BATH 5 1963–64
Oil and tempera on board, 188 x 183

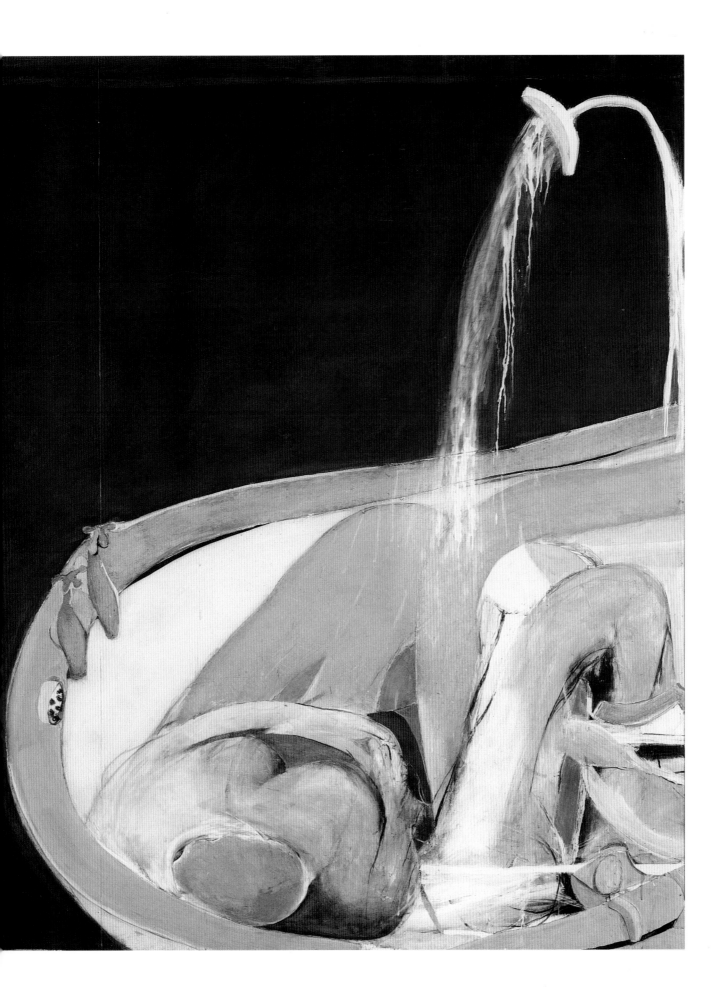

Christie & Zoo Series

When the Whiteleys arrived in London at the end of 1960 they moved to an apartment building in Ladbroke Grove, which was then a working-class district where other Australian and British artists lived and worked. There Whiteley became fascinated with a milieu of London violence that was buried away, festering behind closed doors. He lived not far from Rillington Place, where the necrophile murderer John Christie had murdered several women, mainly prostitutes, during the 1940s and early 1950s. Posing as a doctor, Christie had lured his victims on the pretext of curing their ailments with a special balsamic inhalant. After gassing them he ravished their bodies and hid them in the walls of his house.

The research that Whiteley did for this series of paintings and drawings, exhibited in 1965 at Marlborough New London Gallery, especially in contrast with his previous works on the bathroom theme, reflects his preoccupation with duality. Moving away almost entirely from the soft-focus ambience of abstraction, he now examined with sharp explicitness the evil side of the sexual drive within the human condition. His artistic mentor was Francis Bacon; unlike the British painter, however, Whiteley invested his nudes with a sensuality underlining a new-found command of figure draughtsmanship. Equally significant, the Christie series was a means for the artist to come to terms with his father's death in 1963, an event that throughout his life he would never adequately come to terms with.

Painted and exhibited at the same time were the London Zoo pictures. These were an essential complement to the Christie series, particularly in relation to Bacon's caged figures. Whiteley's spirited paintings and drawings of giraffes, monkeys and lions may also be appreciated in the context of his ongoing feeling of connection to the animal and bird kingdoms.

Plate 33
HEAD OF CHRISTIE 1964
Oil on board, 65.9 x 60.9 cm

Plate 34
CHRISTIE 1965
Oil, pen, ink, gouache, charcoal, wash and collage on paper, 78.8 x 57.3 cm

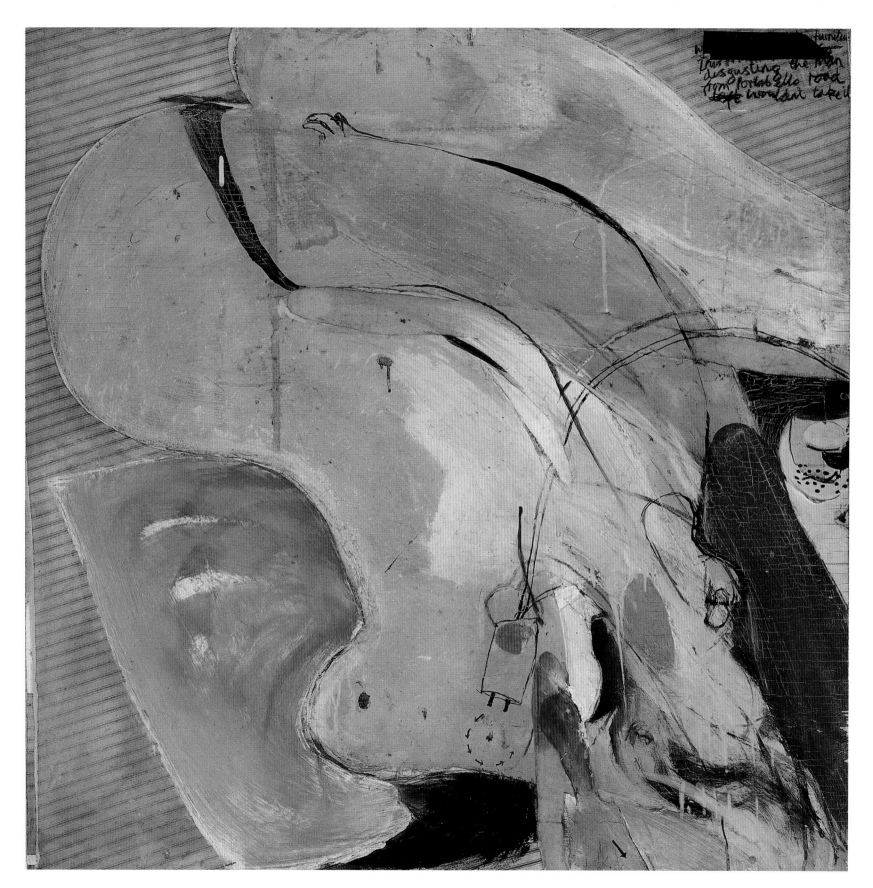

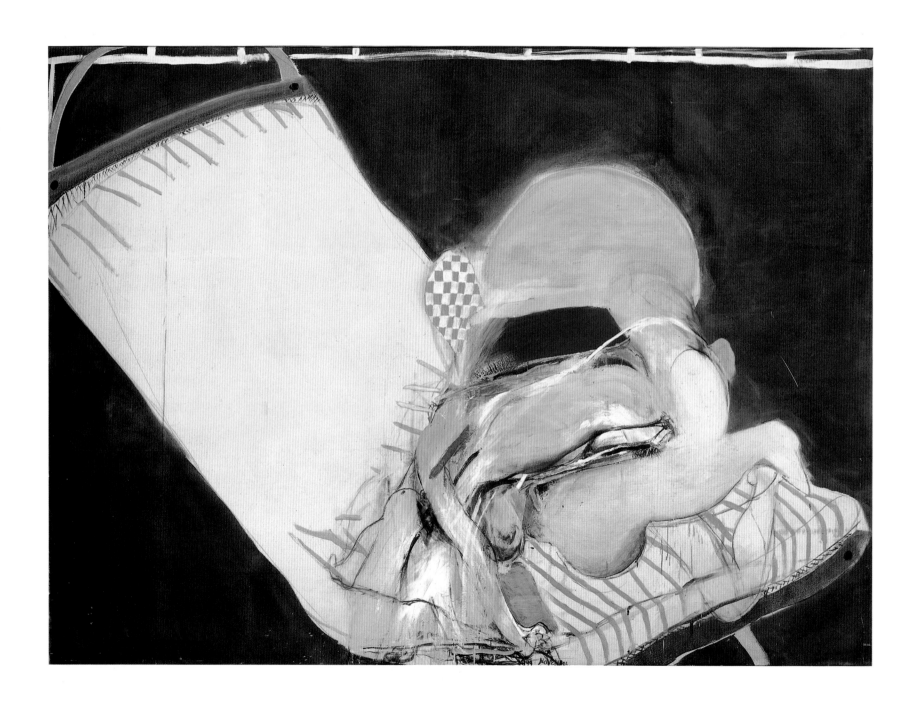

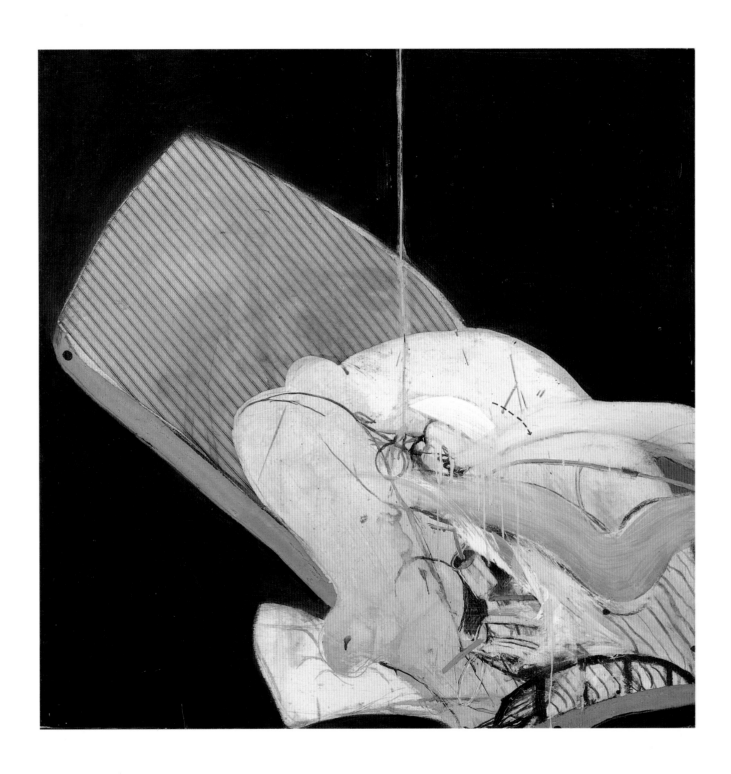

Plate 37
SMALL CHRISTIE PAINTING NO. 1 1965
Oil, tempera, collage and wax on plywood, 86.2 x 86.2 cm

Plate 38

PRELIMINARY SKETCH FOR CHRISTIE MURDER SERIES AND KATHLEEN MALONEY 1965
Charcoal, ink, wash and linseed oil on paper mounted on card, 55.3 x 76.8 cm

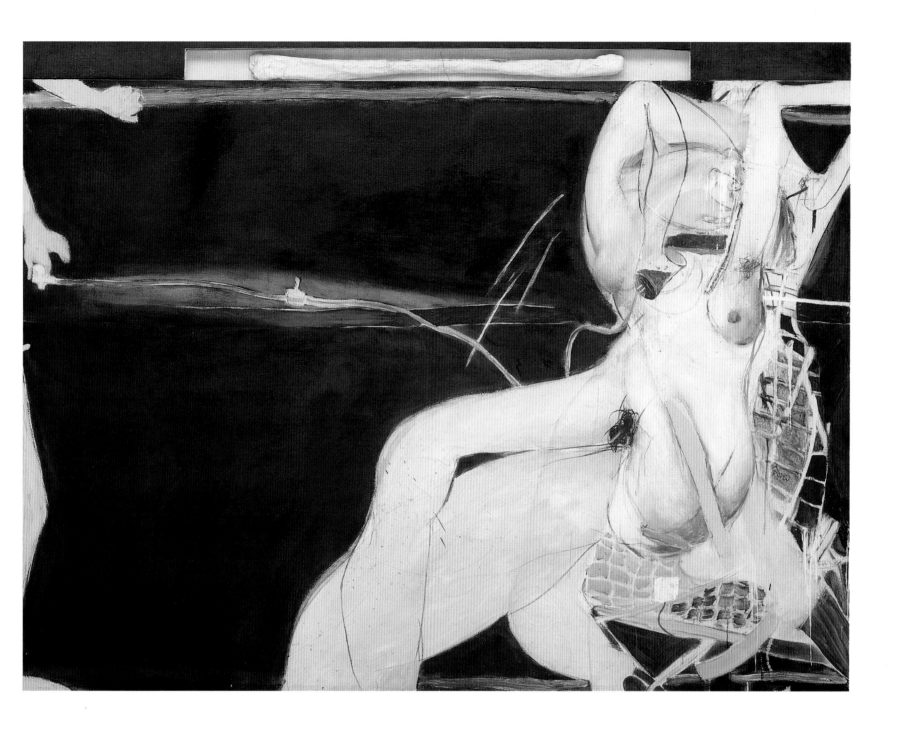

Plate 39
CHRISTIE WITH HECTORINA MCLENNAN 1964
Oil, wax, charcoal, collage, painted wood and cloth perspex object on canvas, 162.5 x 214 cm

Plate 40
CHRISTIE DRAWING (KATHLEEN MALONEY) 1964
Charcoal on paper, 56.6 x 76.7 cm

Plate 41
CHRISTIE AND KATHLEEN MALONEY 1964
Charcoal and paper on board, 160 x 152.4 cm

Plate 42
DON'T READ THIS *c.* 1964
Charcoal, oil, gouache, ink and linseed oil on canvas, 198.2 x 145 cm

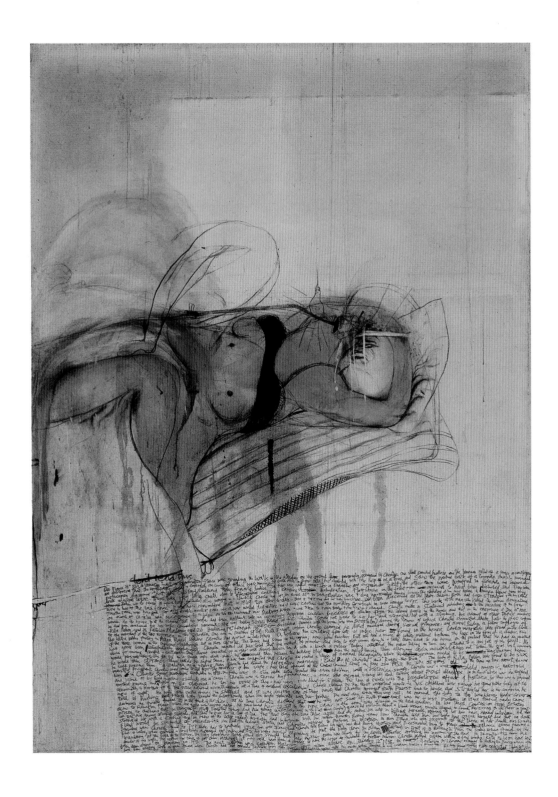

Plate 43
CHEETAH IN RILLINGTON PLACE 1964
Oil on board, 205.7 x 182.9 cm

Plate 44
TWO GIRAFFES NO. 1 1965
Oil and plaster on board, 183.5 x 244 x 5 cm

Plate 45
GIRAFFE NO. 1 *c.* 1965
Brass, mangrove wood, marble and oil, 243.8 x 30.5 x 30.5 cm

Plate 46
TWO INDONESIAN GIRAFFES 1964
Oil on board, 162.3 x 143.5 cm

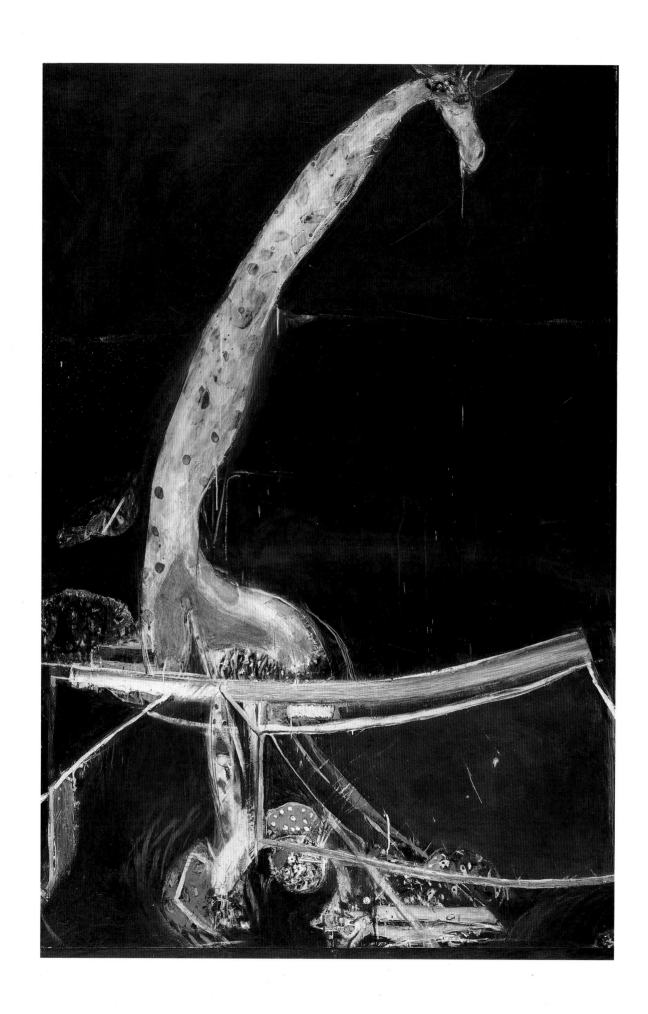

Plate 47
GIRAFFE (BLACK) 1965
Oil on board, 185.4 x 121.9 cm

Plate 48
CHIMPANZEE 1965
Oil, charcoal, perspex, material, plaster and varnish on board, 183.7 x 206 cm

Plate 49
WHITE SACRED BABOON 1965
Carved wood, wax and marble, 137.2 x 40.6 x 40.6 cm

Plate 52
PLATYPUS 1965
Perspex, platypus, encaustic, wax, wood and oil, 95.2 x 45.7 x 19 cm

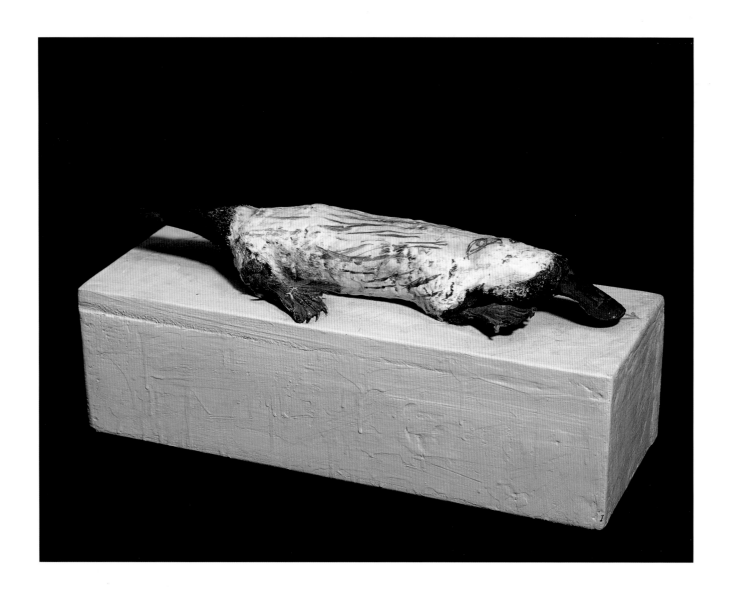

Plate 53
THE BOXING MATCH 1965
Oil on canvas, 214.6 x 240.1 cm

Plate 54
DRAWING 1965...(A SPLIT SECOND) 1965
Pencil, charcoal, collage, linseed oil and wash on paper on board, 126 x 122 cm

Plate 55
THE CRICKET MATCH 1964
Oil, charcoal, material, PVA and string on canvas, 212.3 x 234.6 cm

Nudes & Beaches

Whiteley began drawing the nude early in his career, at various night classes and sketch clubs in Sydney in 1956. This was also the year he met Wendy Julius, his future wife, who posed for him in his glasshouse studio in Longueville. Figure drawing from life, however, was not one of his strengths until the bathroom series in 1963, even though he had used nude female forms in his early abstractions. Following the bathroom paintings and drawings, Whiteley sharpened his attention more explicitly on the nude in the Christie works of 1964, albeit to shocking purpose.

It was not until Whiteley visited Australia for several months during 1965–66 that he discovered the more expressive possibilities of the female nude, giving it a natural setting and recording the pleasures that its curves and contours brought to his draughtsman's eye. Although the female nude became one of his most celebrated subjects, he worked incessantly to achieve the sense of ease with which he rendered it on the clean, dazzling beaches of Australia.

From this time on, nudes, principally inspired by Wendy, appeared consistently in Whiteley's work for the next three decades – in notebooks, easel drawings and large-scale paintings – culminating in an exhibition devoted to the subject in Sydney in 1981. In it he paid homage to Matisse and Picasso, placing the nude in the interiors as well as on the sand, although his interpretations could be more frankly erotic, and on occasions more brutal in distortion, than either of the two masters. Whiteley also made a number of drawing studies for nude sculpture, executing them mainly in wood and making use of the natural erotic forms of tree trunks and branches.

Plate 56
THE BEACH 1966
Oil, tempera, enamel, cloth, ink, PVA, shell, sand, collage, Australian currency one-pound note, pencil and photographs on board, 195.6 x 243.8 cm

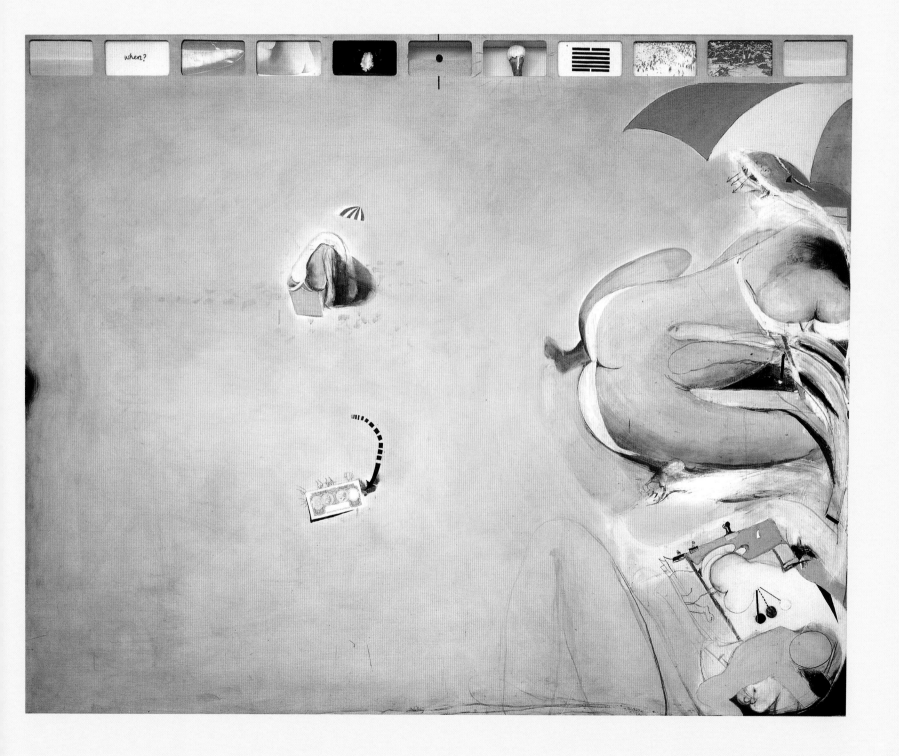

Plate 57
WENDY 1965
Charcoal on paper, 56 x 76.4 cm

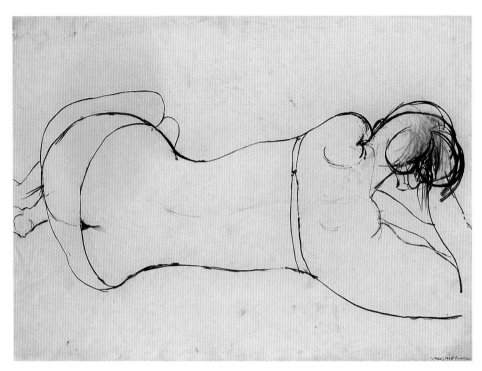

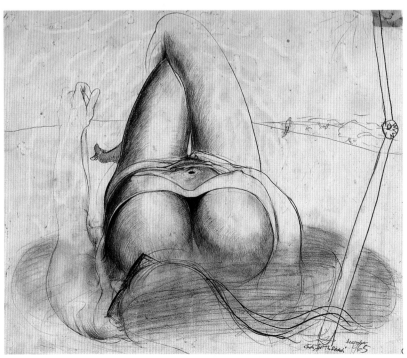

Plate 58
STUDY FOR THE BEACH 1965
Pencil on paper, 45.5 x 54 cm

Plate 59
HEADACHE 1965–66
Oil, collage of 'Bex' packets, rear-view mirror, ink, material, PVA,
sand, plaster and linseed oil on board, 95.3 x 76.2 x 12.7 cm

Plate 60
THE BEACH II 1966
Oil, collage, ink, plaster, hessian, Australian currency one-pound note,
'Bex' packets, cotton t-shirt on board, 141 x 106 cm

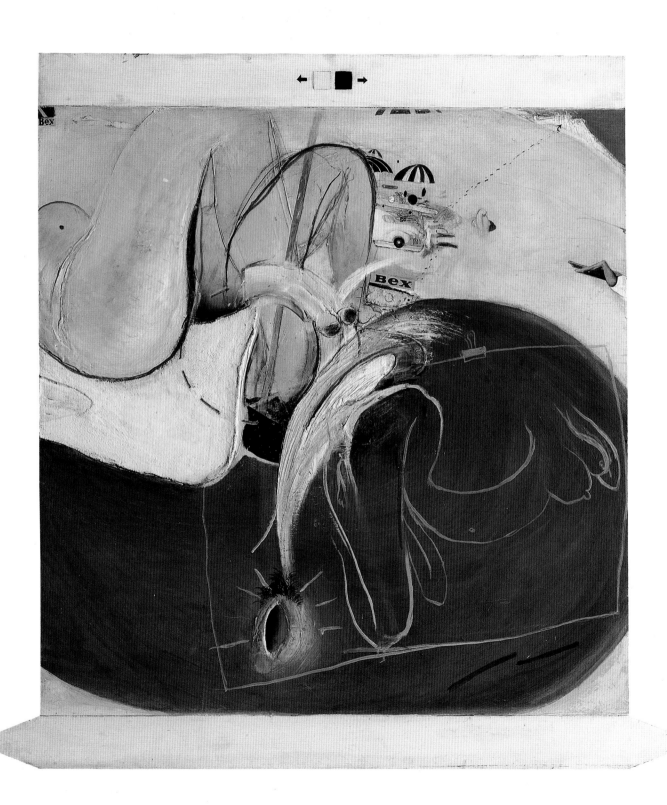

Plate 61
SHARK (FEMALE) 1965
Fibreglass, plaster, maplewood,
chrome and shark's teeth,
86.4 x 177.8 cm

SHARK (MALE) 1966
Fibreglass, plaster, copper and
maplewood, 193.1 x 71.1 cm

Plate 62
BONDI BEACH 1983
(Triptych) Oil and tempera with electricity on ply, 214 x 588 cm

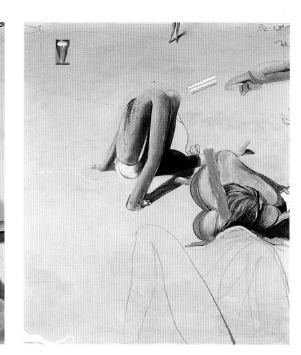

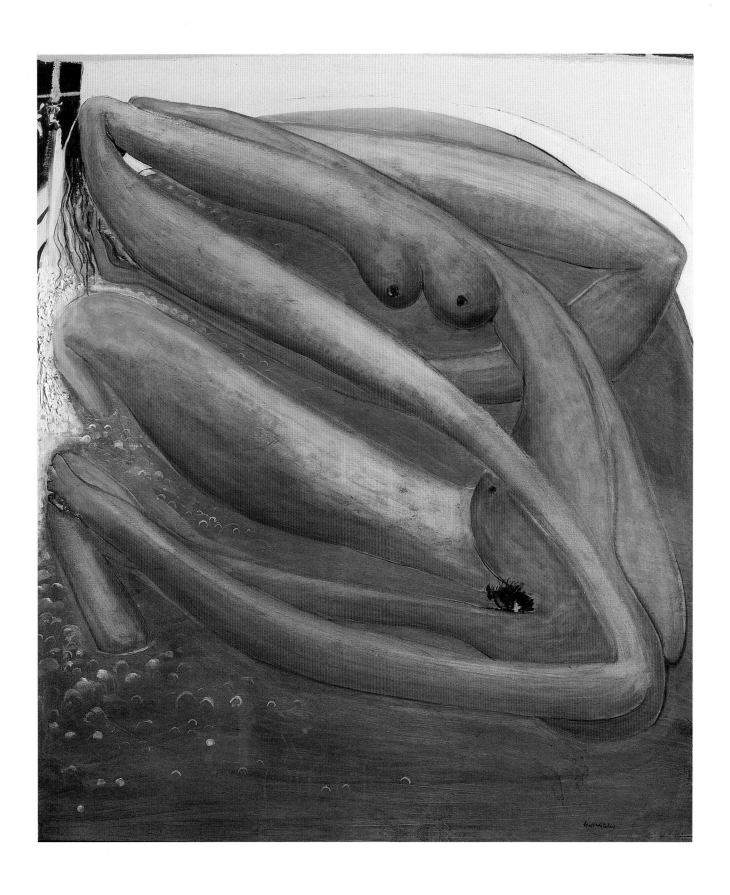

Plate 63
THE BATHER 1981
Oil on canvas, 106 x 91.4 cm

Plate 64
BATHER ON THE SAND 1976
Oil on canvas, 120 x 90 cm

Plate 65
AFTER THE SWIM TANGIER 1983–87
Oil, ink, glass eye, sunglasses and cotton t-shirt on board, 152 x 122 cm

Plate 66
HER (5) 1978
Ink, oil, felt-tipped pen and collage on paper, 61.5 x 51 cm

Plate 67
FOUR STUDIES OF HER 1975–80
Mangrove wood, marble, french polish, charcoal and oil

Plate 68*
HER 1975
Mangrove wood and
marble, 213.3 cm high

HER 1975
Mangrove wood and
marble, 274.3 cm high

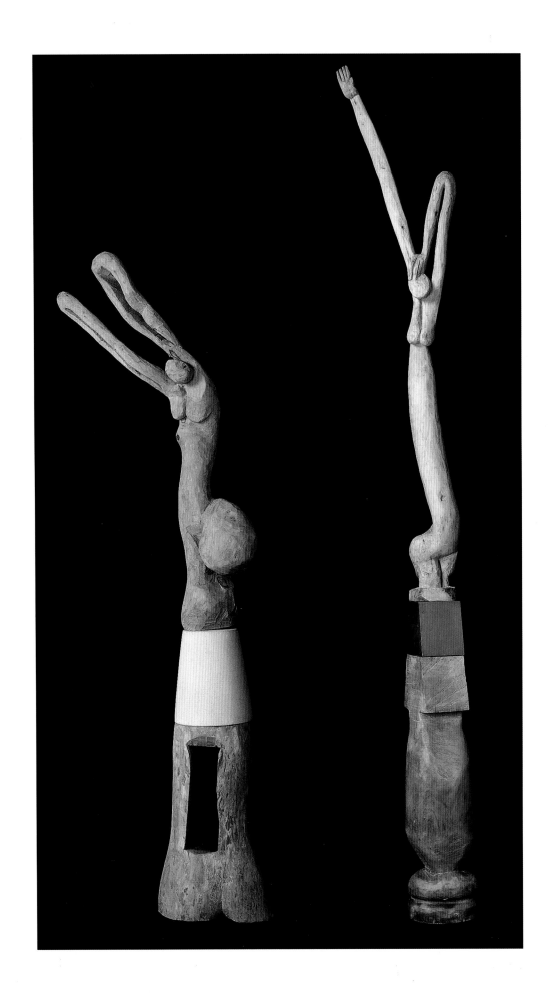

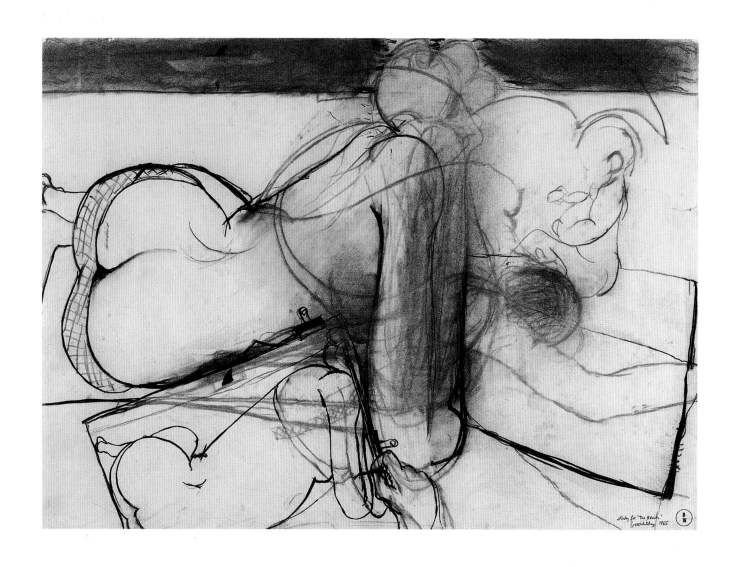

Plate 69
STUDY FOR THE BEACH II 1965
Charcoal and wash on paper, 56 x 76.4 cm

Plate 70
NUDE, STUDY FOR LARGE WOOD CARVING 1975
Wash, collage and charcoal on paper on board, 162 x 90 cm

Plate 71
THE ORANGE NUDE 1981
Oil on canvas, 182 x 151.5 cm

Travels Beyond Europe

After the birth of their daughter, Arkie, in 1964 in London, the Whiteleys decided to visit Australia in anticipation of two exhibitions arranged there for 1966. They arrived in Sydney at the beginning of summer of 1965, and soon after Whiteley began to think of Australia in terms of its relationship to its non-European neighbours rather than its Anglo-Celtic colonial beginnings. After about six months they travelled back to England via Calcutta. Whiteley's shock at the disjunction there between an impoverished material world and the spiritual aspirations of Eastern and Western cultures was reflected in the works he later exhibited in London. During a two-month stay in Morocco, he also made studies that underlined a growing fascination for the mystical 'otherness' of Eastern cultures.

Whiteley later visited Fiji, Africa and Bali in his attempt to glimpse the unsullied states of paradise envisaged by Baudelaire and Gauguin. Before those travels, however, he had become attracted to the hybrid energy of New York, which seemed to encapsulate the insanity of Western civilization at its most violent while projecting the possibilities of immense creative energy. It was there, during his two-year stay on a Harkness Fellowship from 1967 to 1969, that Whiteley embarked on one of his most ambitious painting projects: the massive eighteen-panel *The American Dream*. This was the largest work ever executed by Whiteley, and its sheer scale may have been prompted by the contact he made with American painters at that time. For example, he visited the studio of James Rosenquist, where he witnessed in process a painting measuring some twenty-four metres, similar in size to *The American Dream*.

With its mood of violence and despair, this magnum opus is essentially an expression of Whiteley's disappointment with America. But it also contains the anguish of a personal crisis which touched his life at that time. At the edges of the composition are glimpses of the Australasian – Pacific Edens to which he would soon return.

Plate 72
FIDGETING WITH INFINITY 1966–67
Oil, collage, pencil, photographs and fibreglass on board, 244 x 382 cm

Plate 73
ACHMID GETTING STONED *c.* 1964
Charcoal and ink on paper, 62.8 x 56.2 cm

Plate 74
ARAB 1964
Charcoal, ink, oil and linseed oil on paper, 52.2 x 28 cm

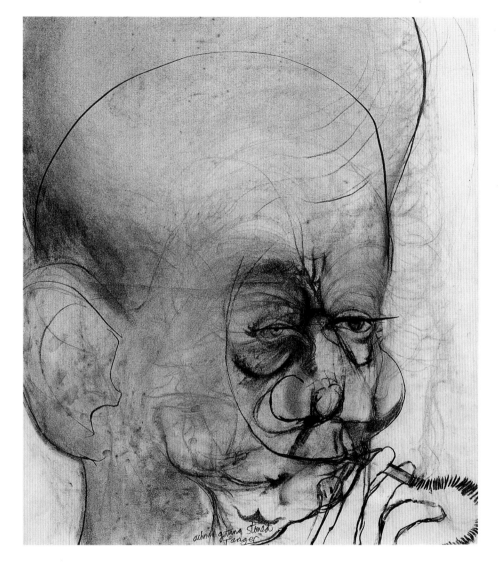

Plate 75
CALCUTTA 1966
(Triptych) Oil, collage, photographs, glass, gesso, pencil, cloth and plaster with detachable sculptural piece on board, 198 x 260 x 125 cm

Plate 76
TANGIER POSTCARD 1967
Gouache, ink, charcoal and collage on paper, 50.9 x 75.5 cm

Plate 77
THE DEALER 1967
Oil, gouache, watercolour, ink, pencil, collage and glass eye on paper, 55.8 x 76.2 cm

Plate 78
THE BUSH 1966
(Triptych) Oil, tempera, collage, hair, PVA, glass and plaster on board, 175 x 240 cm

Plate 79
NEW YORK 2 (FIRST SENSATION OF NEW YORK CITY) 1968
Oil, collage, charcoal, ink, US currency coin and electric light on board, 70 x 90.6 cm

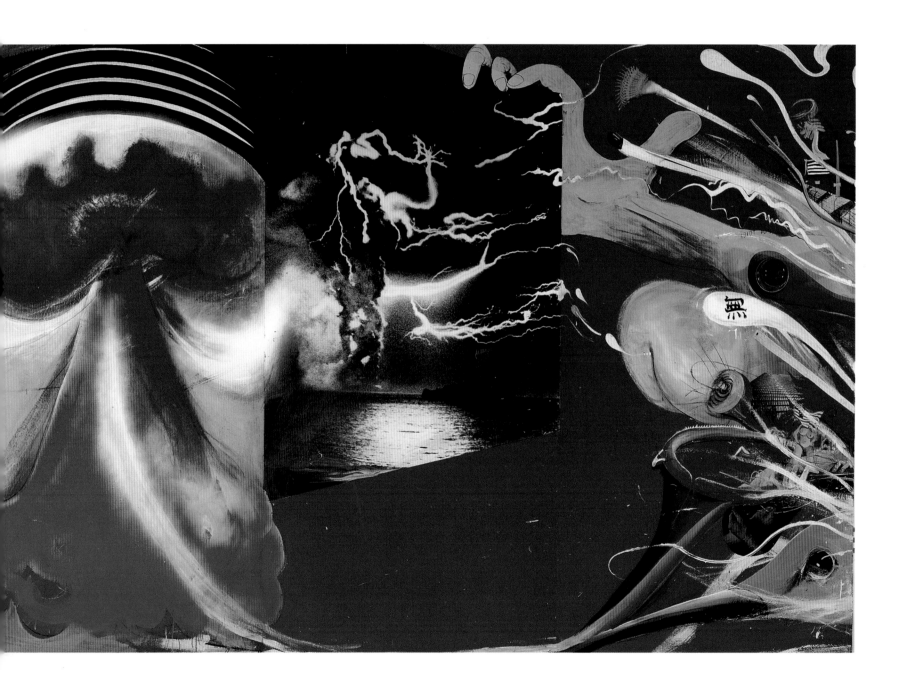

Plate 80c, d

THE AMERICAN DREAM 1968–69
Oil, tempera, collage, photography and objects on eighteen wood panels, 244 x 2196 cm

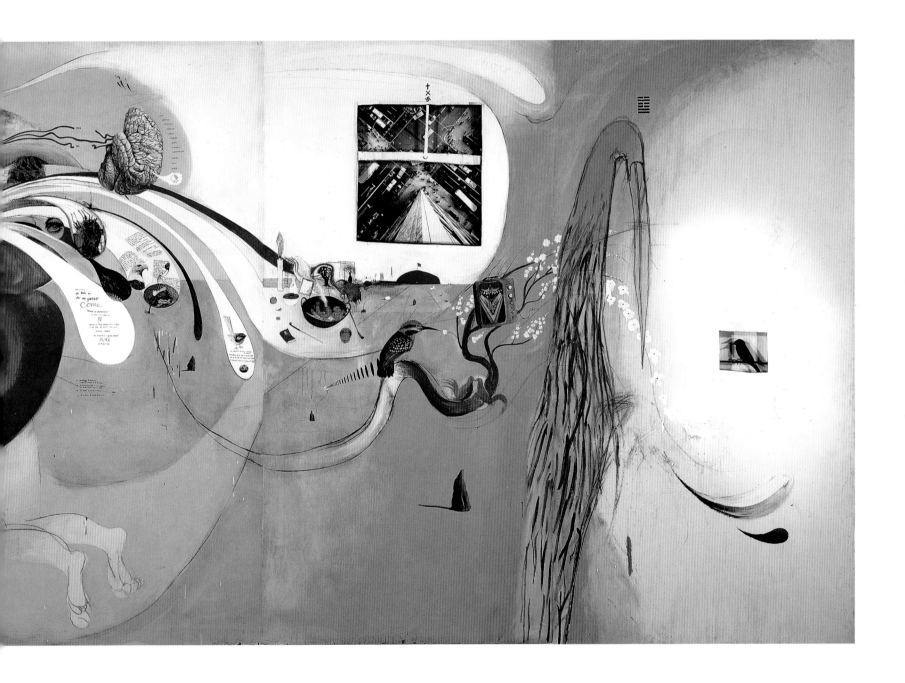

Plate 81
GAUGUIN 1968
Oil, photograph and poison on board, 152.4 x 264.1 x 5.1 cm

Plate 83
THE GREEN MOUNTAIN (FIJI) 1969
Oil and collage on board, 137 x 122 cm

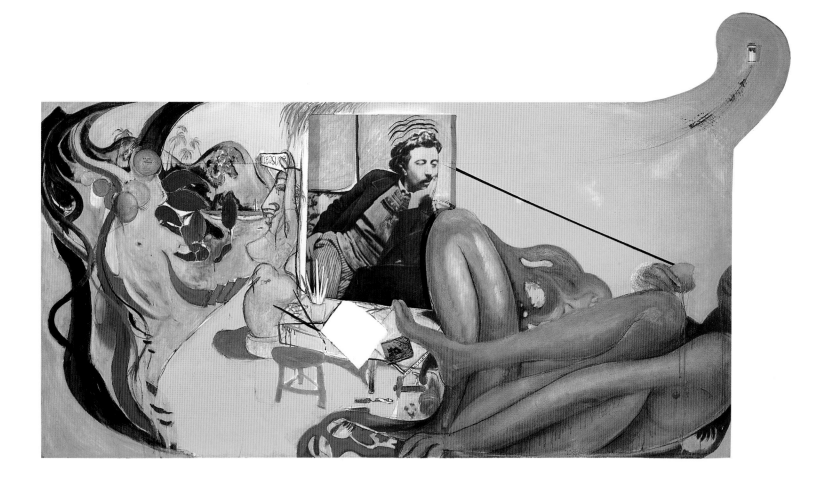

Plate 82
FIJI HEAD – TO A CREOLE LADY 1969
Charcoal, pen and ink and collage on paper,
56.5 x 44.3 cm

Return to Sydney: Lavender Bay

In July 1969 Whiteley flew to Fiji, seeking the refuge of a world far removed from the chaos and stress of his life in New York. He was joined shortly after by Wendy and Arkie, and for a few months he enjoyed the kind of tranquillity he had experienced in Sigean seven years earlier. Unfortunately, the period in Fiji was short-lived, and by November the Whiteleys were back in Sydney, with mixed feelings about remaining in Australia for very long. One factor that did pursuade them to stay was the house in Lavender Bay, which they found through the architect Rollin Schlicht, an Australian friend who had been in London at the same time as the Whiteleys and who was living with his family in the house's upper floor. The combination of the ambience of the house, which the Whiteleys purchased a few years later, and Sydney Harbour, whose large liquid presence was a perfect vehicle for Whiteley's gift at composing works with large, empty spaces, evoked in the artist the strong feeling that at last he had come home.

Inspired mainly by Matisse – particularly his masterpiece *The Red Studio* – Whiteley produced basically three kinds of Lavender Bay subjects during the 1970s: interiors, harbour views and table-top still lifes. These works exude an equilibrium and the sumptuous ecstasy of living. Unlike the vision of Matisse which eradicated the ego and its dark side, however, there are small hints that not all was perfect in paradise. In several paintings, harbour glimpses appear to be escape routes from enclosures, and there are subtle manifestations of a restlessness that became more explicit in Whiteley's portraits during this time and into the 1980s.

Plate 84
THE JACARANDA TREE (ON SYDNEY HARBOUR) 1977
Oil on canvas, 208 x 456 cm

Plate 85
BIG ORANGE (SUNSET) 1974
Oil on board, 244 x 305.5 cm

Plate 86
THE BALCONY 2 1975
Oil on canvas, 203.5 x 364.5 cm

Plate 87
GREY HARBOUR *c.* 1978
Oil and charcoal on canvas, 86.5 x 85.5cm

Plate 88
LAVENDER BAY IN THE RAIN 1981
Oil, PVA and perspex on canvas on board, 89.5 x 89 cm

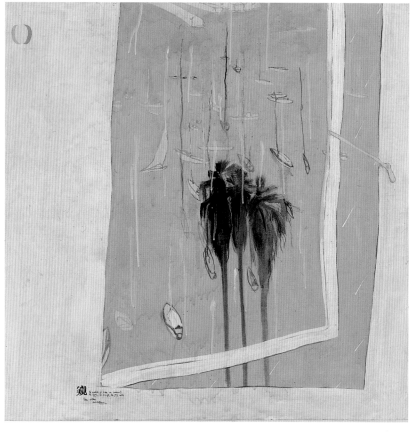

Plate 89
LAVENDER BAY IN THE RAIN 1974
Oil on perspex, string, wax on board, and perspex, 120.5 x 95 cm

Plate 90
BLUE NAKED STUDIO 1981
(Diptych) Oil, collage, hair, glass eye, charcoal and ink on board, 190.9 x 490.4 cm

Plate 91
STILL LIFE WITH THREE LEMONS 1976
Oil on canvas, 51 x 61 cm

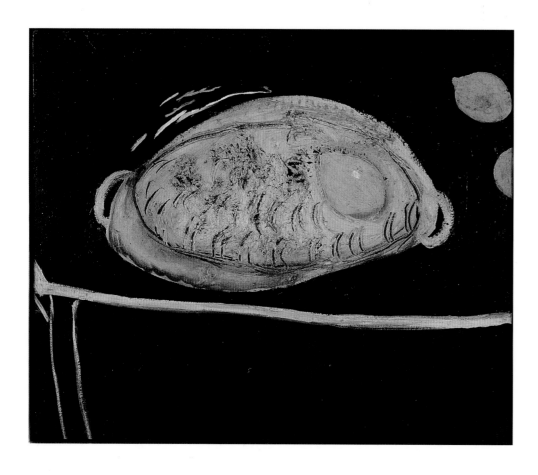

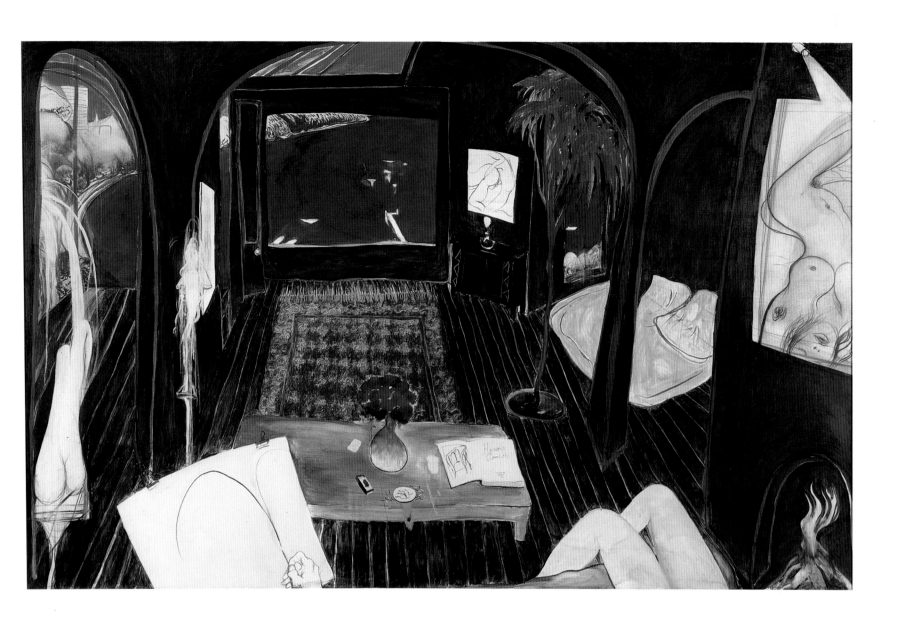

Plate 92
HENRI'S ARMCHAIR 1974–75
Oil, ink and charcoal on canvas, 195 x 302 cm

Plate 93
INTERIOR WITH TIME PAST 1976
Oil, charcoal and ink on canvas, 182 x 200 cm

Plate 94
CERAMICS *c.* 1979
Three works thrown by John Kimpton Dellow and two works thrown by Derek Smith

Plate 95
STILL LIFE WITH MEAT 1975–76
Synthetic polymer paint, shell, bone and artificial eye on board, 130.2 x 207.7 cm

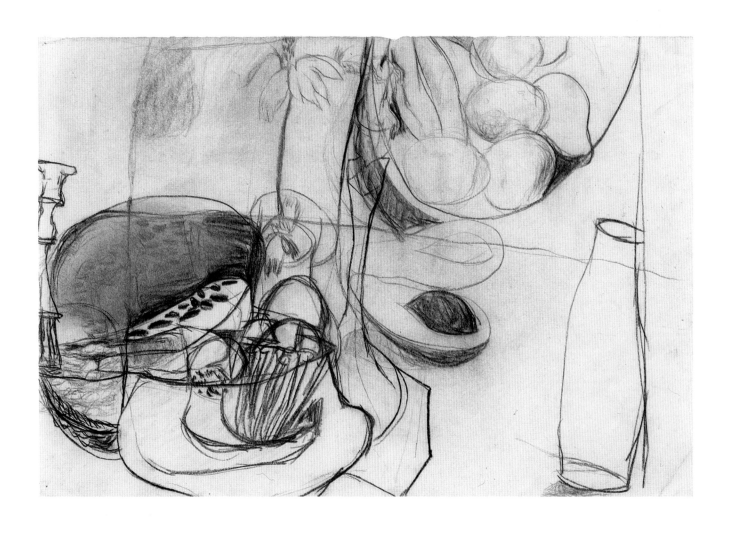

Plate 96
STILL LIFE DRAWING WITH MILK BOTTLE AND AVOCADO *c.* 1960
Charcoal on paper, 37.8 x 55.7 cm

Plate 97
STILL LIFE WITH PEE-WEE'S EGG 1976
Oil on canvas, 88 x 61cm

Plate 98
STILL LIFE WITH MAGNOLIA 1980–82
Oil and collage on canvas, 120 x 164 cm

Plate 99
STILL LIFE WITH CHERRIES 1975–76
Oil on board, 45 x 57 cm

Plate 100
MAGNOLIA 1977–78
Oil on board, 76.2 x 121.9 cm

Plate 101
PURITY AS A PROBLEM (IN RELATION TO STILL LIFE PAINTING) 1977–78
Oil on canvas, 124 x 225 cm

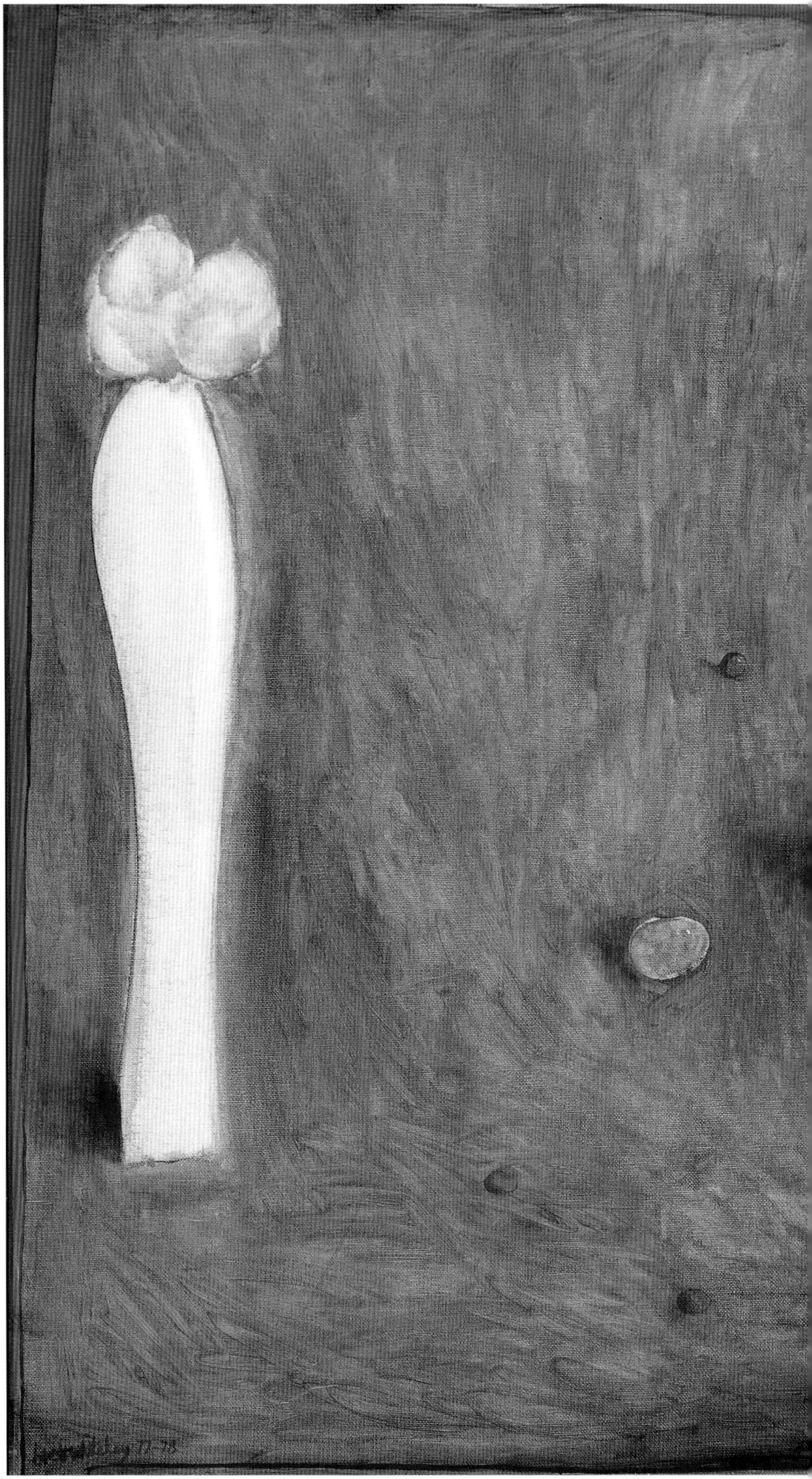

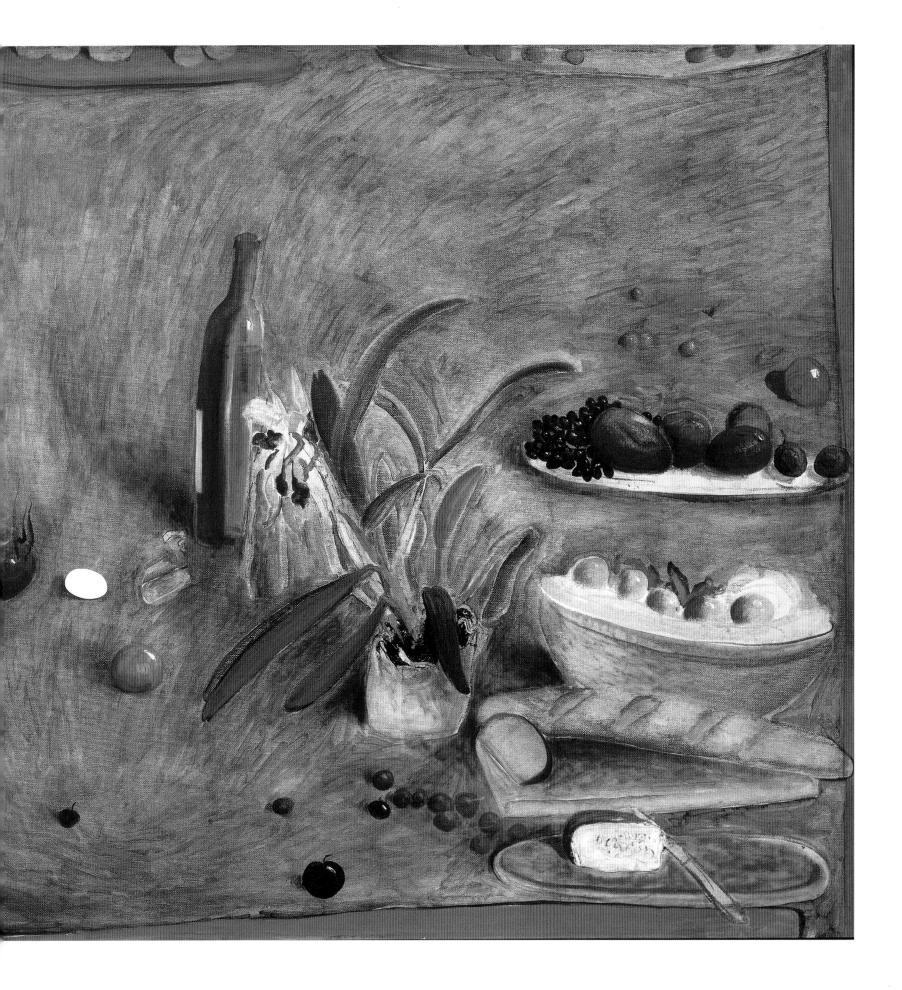

Plate 102
SKETCH FOR THE RED AND GREEN OF THE SUBURBS 1979
Oil on board, 30 x 30 cm

Plate 103
RED ROOFS WITH PALM TREE *c.* 1980
Oil on canvas mounted on board, 40 x 50 cm

Plate 104
SOUTH COAST AFTER THE RAIN 1984
Oil and collage on canvas, 137 x 122 cm

Self-Portraits & Other Intimacies

During the decade after Whiteley's return to Australia at the end of 1969, he produced many works covering a spectrum of moods – from the startling imagery of *Alchemy*, to the calm ecstasy of landscape and harbour views, to the implied violence of his van Gogh paintings. The contrasts of these moods, which often existed side by side, reflected Whiteley's interest in dual states and to a certain extent – in his figurative work – schizophrenia. It is unlikely that Whiteley suffered from such a condition in strict medical terms, but he was certainly possessed with it, and it is a useful concept with which to approach his portraits. Whiteley followed the writings of British psychiatrist R.D. Laing, who created self-induced states of madness and schizophrenia in order to analyse these disturbing aspects of the human condition.

From the mid-1960s, therefore, many of Whiteley's portraits can be seen not so much as optical studies as explorations of the psyche, whether his own or that of others with whom he identified. A number of self-portraits show Whiteley's image split into multiples, perhaps of himself, or other identities, and indeed such projections into alternative states can be read into the face of a weeping woman, or even the birds and animals that inhabit the artist's landscapes.

Perhaps the first portraits in Australian art that dealt with emotional or psychological archetypes were painted by Arthur Boyd and Albert Tucker in Melbourne during the 1940s. Whiteley added to this legacy with his Christie images in 1964. In the subsequent two decades Whiteley produced spectacular portraits of his heroes – van Gogh, Gauguin, Dylan, Baudelaire, Rimbaud and Bacon – focusing with particular fascination on those who had, as he perceived in himself, addictive personalities. His most ambitious self-portrait, however, was undoubtedly *Alchemy*, which was painted in 1972–73.

From its flashing sun against a gold sky representing the death vision of Japanese writer Yukio Mishima, through the straw-coloured landscape of western New South Wales, to the sexual turbulence of surrealist forms derived from Bosch, *Alchemy* represents everything that Whiteley called his 'inner paddock': an attempt to marry the seen with the unseen of his life.

Plate 105
SELF-PORTRAIT IN THE STUDIO 1976
Oil, collage and hair on canvas, 200.5 x 259 cm

Plate 107
NOT I – ME 1967
Oil and mixed media on board with detachable sculptural arm, 185.4 x 152.4 x 119.4 cm

Plate 108
SELF-PORTRAIT AFTER 3 BOTTLES OF WINE 1971
Oil and ink on board, 203.5 x 76 cm

Plate 109
PAGE OF SELF-PORTRAITS 1971
Pen and ink on rice paper, 31.5 x 30 cm

Plate 111
SELF-PORTRAIT DRAWING CALLIGRAPHICALLY 1975
Brush and ink on brown paper, 80.5 x 53.5 cm

Plate 112
TASMANIAN DEVIL 1984
Pen and ink and gouache on paper, 41.5 x 59.5 cm

Plate 113
SACRED BABOON 1975
Ink, woodstain, watercolour and collage on cardboard, 81 x 67 cm

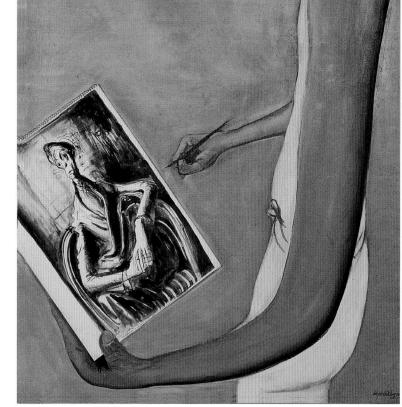

Plate 114
ART, LIFE AND THE OTHER THING 1978
(Triptych) Oil, glass eye, hair, pen and ink on cardboard, plaster, photography, oil, dried PVA,
cigarette butts, hypodermic syringe on board, 90.4 x 77.2, 230 x 122, 31.1 x 31.1 cm

Plate 115
GETTING QUITE CLOSE 1982
Colour photograph, oil, collage,
masking tape and card on board,
163 x 121 cm

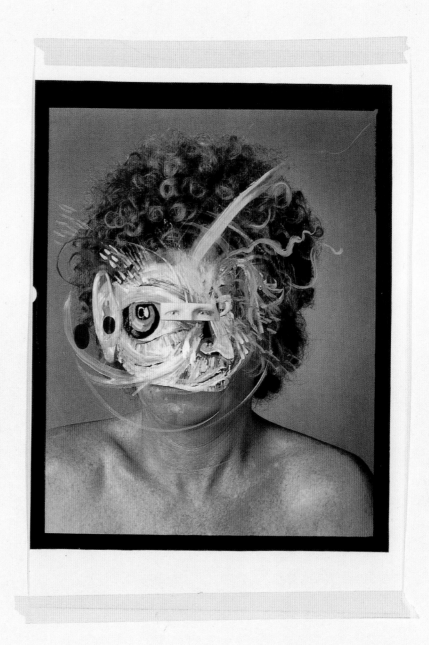

Plate 116
VINCENT 1968
Oil, ink, mirror and razor on board, 220.9 x 164.4 x 38.1 cm

Plate 117
REMBRANDT 1971–92
Oil and fibreglass on board, 136 x 125 x 11 cm

Plate 118
SELF-PORTRAIT AFTER HAIRCUT 1976
Pen and ink and hair on paper, 100 x 76 cm

Plate 119
THE BLOSSOM TREE 1971-82
Oil, silk flowers, branch, wood, canvas, nails and electricity on board, 186 x 194.5 x 26.6 cm

Plate 120
THE NIGHT CAFE 1972
Oil on board, 121.5 x 143.5 cm

Plate 121
THEBE'S REVENGE 1973–82
Oil and collage on board, 203 x 122 cm

Plate 122
PORTRAIT OF ARTHUR RIMBAUD 1970–71
Oil, gold leaf, synthetic polymer paint, mummified lacquered cat's head and
collage on six wooden panels, 203.3 x 518.1 cm

Plate 123
PORTRAIT OF BAUDELAIRE 1970
Oil, paper collage, plastic plum, twig, taxidermied bird, sand and polyfilla
on five wood door panels, 203 x 478 cm

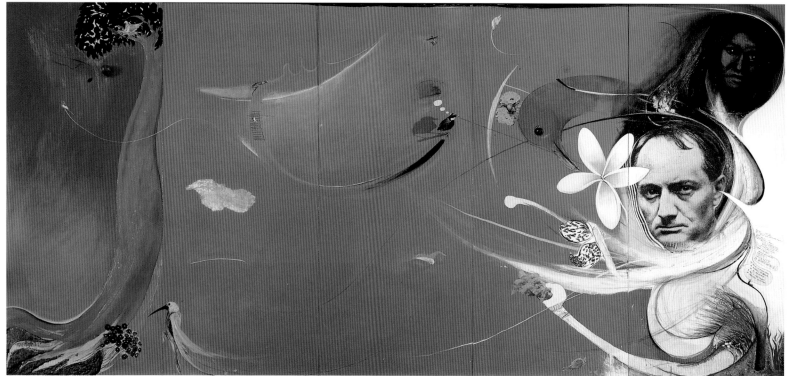

Plate 124
SAINT FRANCIS 1971
Ink on rice paper mounted on silk scroll on board, 162.5 x 80 cm

Plate 125a, b
ALCHEMY 1972–73
Oil, gold leaf, ink, collage, rock, perspex, electricity, pencil, PVA, varnish, brain, earth, twig, taxidermied bird,
nest, egg, feathers, cicada, bone, dentures, rubber and metal sink plug, pins, shell and glass eye on eighteen wood panels, 203 x 1615 x 9 cm

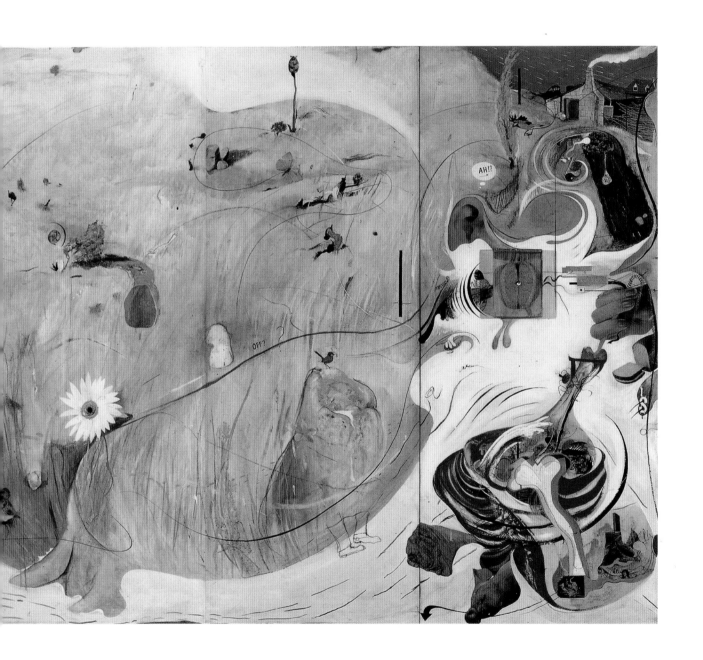

Plate 125c, d

ALCHEMY 1972–73

Oil, gold leaf, ink, collage, rock, perspex, electricity, pencil, PVA, varnish, brain, earth, twig, taxidermied bird,
nest, egg, feathers, cicada, bone, dentures, rubber and metal sink plug, pins, shell and glass eye on eighteen wood panels, 203 x 1615 x 9 cm

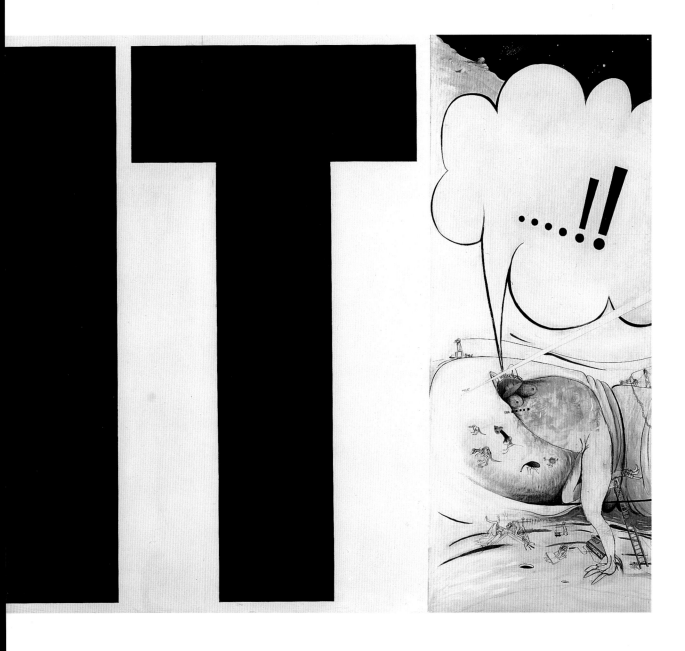

Plate 125e, f
ALCHEMY 1972–73
Oil, gold leaf, ink, collage, rock, perspex, electricity, pencil, PVA, varnish, brain, earth, twig, taxidermied bird,
nest, egg, feathers, cicada, bone, dentures, rubber and metal sink plug, pins, shell and glass eye on eighteen wood panels, 203 x 1615 x 9 cm

Plate 126
PORTRAIT OF WENDY 1984
Oil, material, pencil, charcoal, pen and ink on paper on canvas, 150 x 212 cm

Plate 127
WENDY DRUNK 11PM 1983
Brush and ink on paper, 74 x 103.4 cm

Plate 128
PORTRAIT OF JOEL ELENBERG 1980
Oil, collage, ink, charcoal and masking tape on canvas, 202 x 152 cm

Plate 129
THE LETTER (TO ANNA) 1980–81
Oil and pencil on canvas, 151.5 x 177.2 cm

Plate 130
'FATHER, FORGIVE THEM…' 1979
Charcoal and wash on paper, 246 x 131 cm

Plate 131
'MY GOD, MY GOD…WHY…' 1979–80
Oil, steel and gold leaf on board, 296.8 x 137.4 cm

Plate 132
THE GIVING UP 1979–80
Oil and steel on board, 264.4 x 122 cm

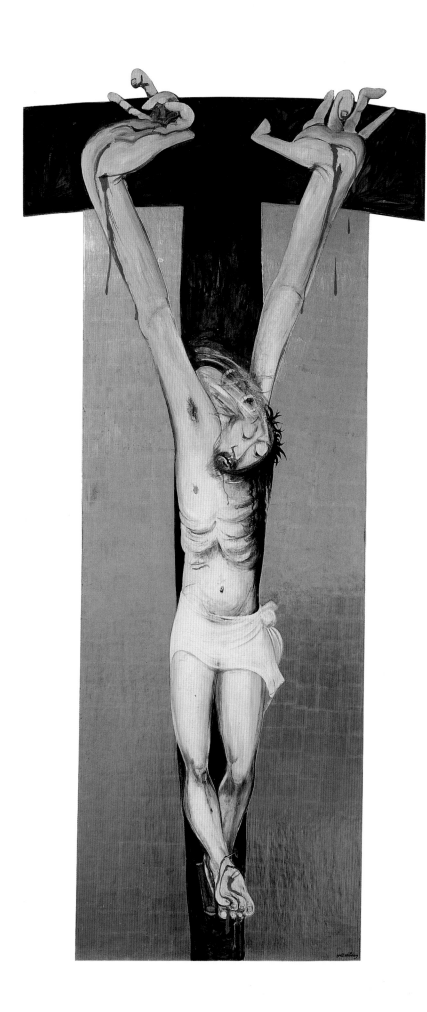
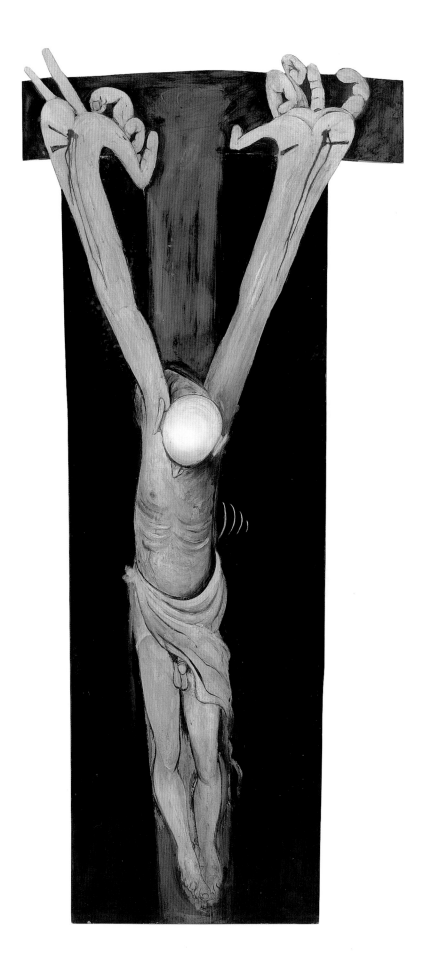

Plate 133
TRACY THE DEALER 1987
Oil, charcoal, teeth, plaster and collage on board, 28 x 27.5 cm

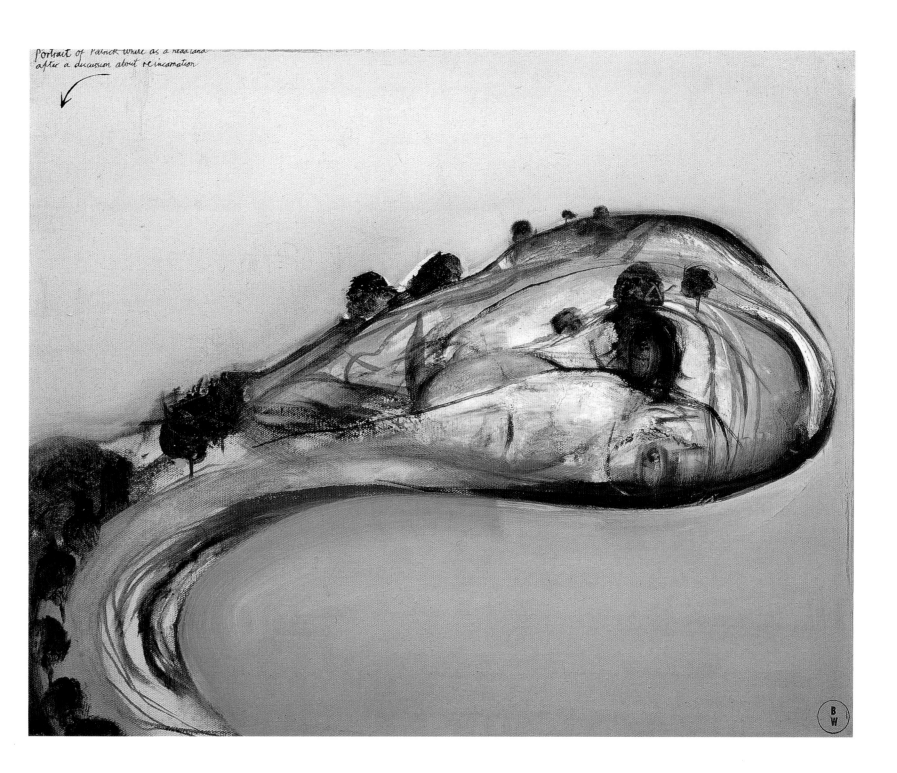

Portrait of Patrick White as a headland
after a discussion about reincarnation

Plate 134
PATRICK WHITE AS A HEADLAND *c.* 1981
Oil on canvas, 39.4 x 49.7 cm

Birds & Landscapes

Of all the subjects Whiteley painted in his career, landscape gave him the greatest sense of release. At school in Bathurst he set up his easel at the back of the classroom and drew the views through the window. The soft hills and fields of the surrounding countryside were indelibly embedded in his repertoire of images, and fed his imagination over many years. After leaving school he explored the edges of Sydney Harbour to emulate the visions of Lloyd Rees; he travelled to the old gold-mining towns of Sofala and Hill End in western New South Wales in the path of Russell Drysdale; and from the late 1970s, the influence of Japanese and Chinese art and Gauguin's painting *The Yellow Christ* reinforced his need to create landscape as a sanctuary. If in many of his other themes Whiteley confronted the difficult questions of his psyche, landscape provided a means of escape, an unencum-bered absorption into a painless, floating world.

He made paintings of central Australia as early as 1970. As he moved around the countryside of New South Wales – Oberon, Marulan, Carcoar, Bathurst – and the Glasshouse Mountains in Queensland, he depicted the landscape in all its seasons with a tendency he called 'Chinese'. Repetition of certain motifs symbolized states of mind: the arabesques of rivers echoed the flight paths of birds, which in turn represented the artist's relaxed journey through his own domain. Birds, rivers, trees, rocks, ponds, skidding insects, shy mammals, spaces alternately cluttered or uncluttered – such elements and passages were scattered throughout Whiteley's landscapes in different combinations, whether on the intimate level of small studies and sketches, or the elegiac majesty of his large-scale paintings.

Plate 135
THE OLGAS...SOON 1970
Tempera over gesso with enamel, gold paint, ink, paper collage, possum tail, jaw bone and wooden boomerang on four wooden panels, 203 x 325 cm

Plate 136

Plate 136
FRAGMENT OFF OLGA OR JAH! HOW BLACK CAN YOU GET 1974–75
Oil, collage, ink, plastic doll, modelling clay and plaster on board, 68.5 x 71 cm

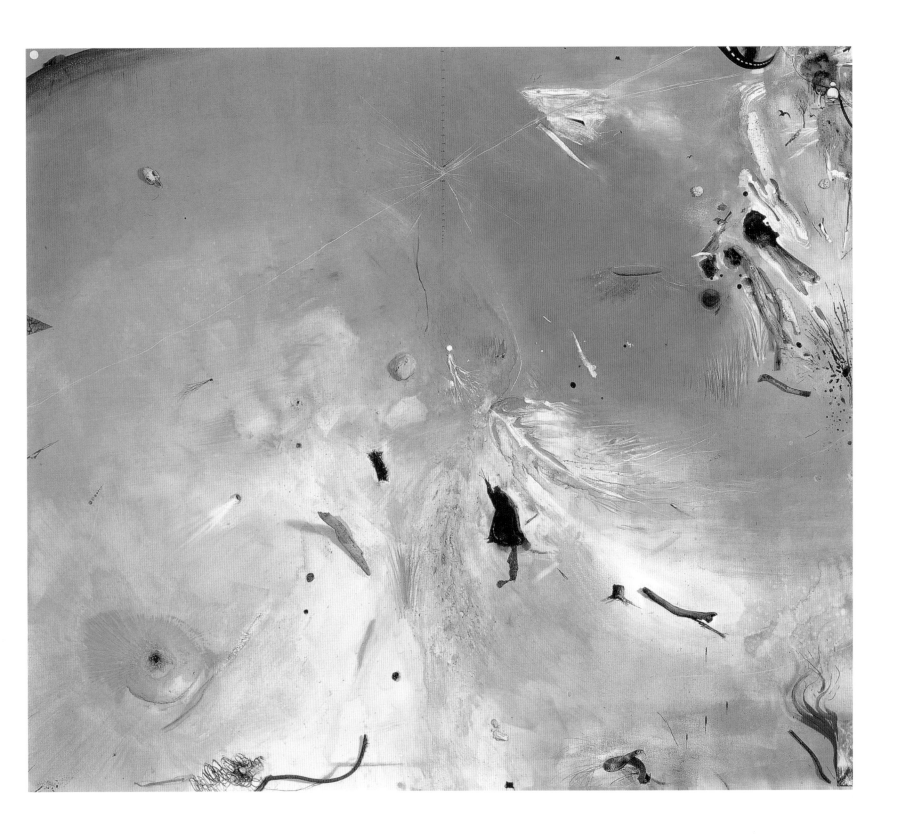

Plate 137
THE DROUGHT OF '83 I (COOTAMUNDRA NSW) 1983
Oil, tempera, sticks, bone, stone, earth and collage on board, 214 x 244 cm

Plate 138
BIRD SCULPTURES 1983–88
Bronze, plaster, wire, wood, metal, oil and glass eyes

Plate 139
THE DAY ASIA GOT BORN 1970
Oil, collage, branch, nest, egg, bird, cicada
and wood on board, 131.5 x 77.5 x 23.4 cm

Plate 140
BUTCHER BIRD WITH BAUDELAIRE'S EYES 1972
Pen, ink, gouache, brush, ink and collage on paper on board, 61 x 55.5 cm

Plate 141
CH'UAN *c.* 1978–79
Oil, branch, nest and egg on canvas, 91 x 91 x 13.5 cm

Plate 142
SHAO (RAIN SLANTED BY WIND) 1978–79
Oil, nest and bird's egg on board, 122 x 81 cm

Plate 143
TOTEM (WHITE FEMALE) 1978–88
Fibreglass, wood, marble, steel and oil, 271.8 x 215.9 x 55.9 cm

TOTEM I (BLACK – THE GET LAID TOTEM) 1978–88
Fibreglass and wood, 284.5 x 170.2 x 61 cm

TOTEM II (TAN FEMALE) 1978–88
Fibreglass, wood, chrome and oil, 259.2 x 203.2 x 53.4 cm

Plate 144
ORANGE FRUIT DOVE FIJI 1969
Oil on board, 138 x 120 cm

Plate 145
WHITE DOVE IN AVOCADO TREE 1979
Oil, charcoal, plastic avocado, collage, nest and egg on board, 99.5 x 102.5 cm

Plate 146
THE ARRIVAL – A GLIMPSE IN THE BOTANIC GARDENS 1984
Oil, collage and charcoal on canvas, 106.4 x 96.4 cm

Plate 147
BOOT OWL 1985
Ping-pong balls, leather boot, steel and paint, 22.9 x 17.8 x 12.7 cm

Plate 148
THE LYREBIRD 1972–73
Oil, red earth, wood and cloth, lyrebird tail, ink and collage on canvas, 198 x 183.5 x 26 cm

Plate 149
THE BLUE RIVER 1978
Oil, collage and egg on two panels of canvas, 91.5 x 60.5 cm

Plate 150
BAUDELAIRE'S DRIVE 1975
Oil on canvas, 228.6 x 190.5 cm

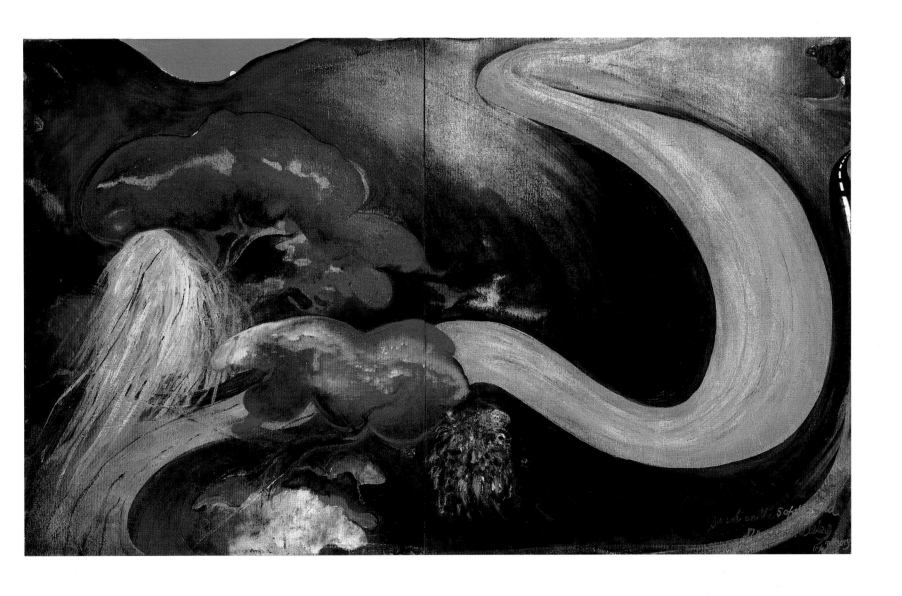

Plate 151
SUNSET ON THE SOFALA ROAD 1974
Oil on canvas on board, 81.2 x 134.6 cm

Plate 152
BLUE RIVER 1977
Oil, wax and collage on canvas, 59.5 x 59.5 cm

$E=mc^2$

Plate 153
THE RIVER AT MARULAN (...READING EINSTEIN'S GEOGRAPHY) 1976
Oil, electric light bulb and stones on board, 203.2 x 122 cm

Plate 154
TO YIRRAWALLA 1972
Oil, ink, collage, charcoal, wasp, stuffed platypus, stones, plaster, stick and plastic on board, 182 x 162.6 x 6 cm

Plate 155
SUMMER AT CARCOAR 1977
Oil, acrylic, paper, glue, rock and wood on chipboard, 244.5 x 199 cm

Plate 156
THE PADDOCK – LATE AFTERNOON 1979
Oil on canvas, 202 x 152 cm

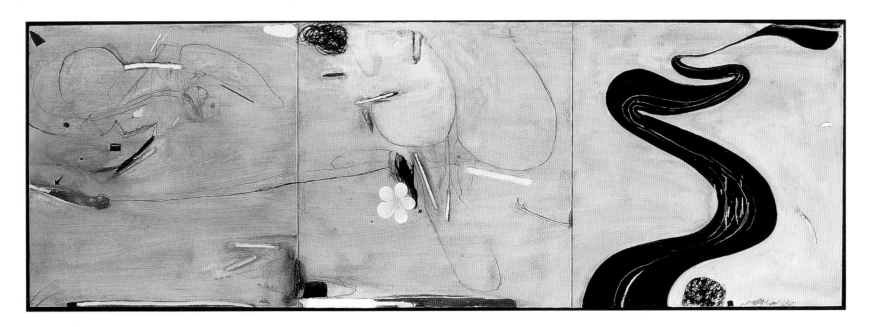

Plate 157
OBERON 1987
(Triptych) Oil and collage on canvas, 86 x 259 cm

Plate 158
THE RIVER 1976
Aubusson tapestry, 198 x 168 cm

Plate 159
AUTUMN (NEAR BATHURST) – JAPANESE AUTUMN 1987–88
Oil, tempera, ink, egg and photography on board, 285.4 x 411.5 cm

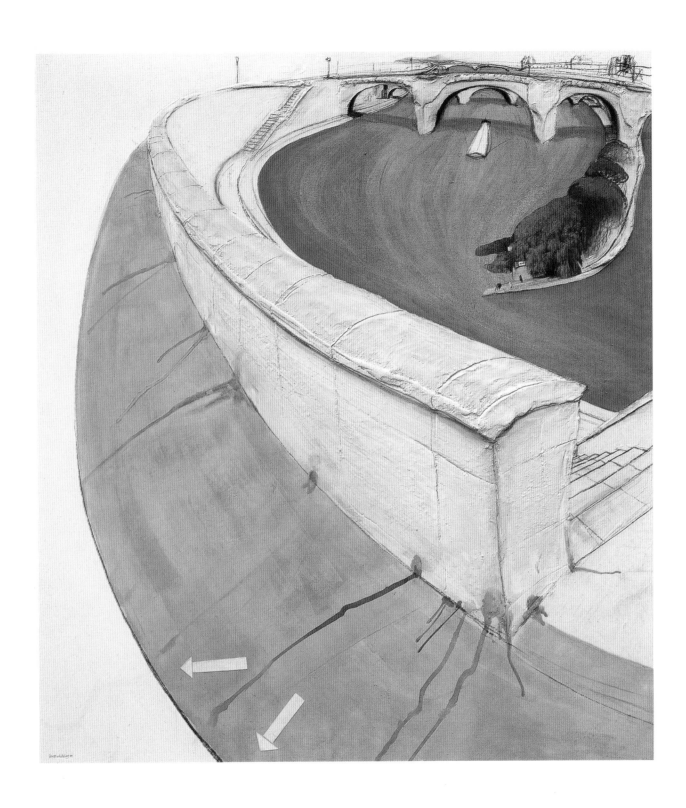

Plate 161
THE 15 GREAT DOG PISSES OF PARIS 1989
Oil, charcoal, plaster, collage and resin on canvas, 154 x 138.5 cm

Catalogue Entries

Figure 1
WENDY AND ARKIE AS A BABY 1964
Charcoal on paper, 56 × 76.2 cm; stamped with artist's monogram l.r. in black ink, dated l.r. in pencil '10/11/64'
Inscriptions: l.r. pencil 'with love'
Exhibited: The Artist's Studio, Circular Quay, Sydney, 1981, not catalogued, p.15 (illus). Robin Gibson Gallery, Sydney, 1985, Cat 85. 'Brett Whiteley–Lloyd Rees: On the Road to Berry', Museum of Modern Art at Heide and The Art Gallery of New South Wales, 1993, Cat 63
Collection: Private collection, Sydney

Figure 2
BATHROOM DRAWING 1963
Charcoal on paper, 54 x 76 cm; signed and dated l.r. in pencil 'brett Whiteley 63'
Collection: Robin Gibson Gallery

Figure 3
STUDY FOR SUMMER AT SIGEAN 1962
Charcoal, brown conté, paper collage and linseed oil on paper, 73.5 × 115 cm; signed and dated l.c. in pencil 'brett whiteley' and l.r. in ballpoint pen 'brett', dated in ballpoint l.r. '1962'
Inscriptions: in ballpoint l.r.
Exhibited: Robin Gibson Gallery, Sydney, 1985, Cat 122
Collection: Private collection, Sydney

Figure 4
STUDY FOR CHRISTIE c. 1964–5
Charcoal and brown conté on paper, 16.7 × 24.5 cm (image); stamped with artist's monogram l.r. in black ink, not dated
Collection: Robin Gibson Gallery, Sydney

Figure 5
FRANCIS BACON c. 1964–5
Charcoal on paper, 16.6 × 24.5 cm (image); stamped with artist's monogram l.r. in black ink
Collection: Robin Gibson Gallery, Sydney

Figure 6
RITA NELSON c. 1964–5
Charcoal, pen and ink, pencil, gouache and collage on paper, 16.7 × 24.5 cm; signed l.r. in black ink 'B.W.' and stamped with artist's monogram l.r. in black ink, not dated
Inscriptions: u.l. and u.r. in pencil 'RITA NELSON'
Collection: Robin Gibson Gallery, Sydney

Figure 7
VIEW (WHALE BEACH) 1966
Gouache, pencil, pen, brush and ink and collage on paper mounted on board, 57.2 × 69 cm; not signed, not dated
Inscriptions: verso in black ink 'By the single sun/this whole world is illumined/By its one knower/The Field is illumined BHAGAVD-GITA'
Exhibited: Robin Gibson Gallery, Sydney, 1985, Cat 1 (illus front cover). 'Brett Whiteley–Lloyd Rees: On the Road to Berry', Museum of Modern Art at Heide and The Art Gallery of New South Wales, 1993, Cat 47
Collection: Private collection, Sydney

Figure 8
CRAB c. 1964
Charcoal and wash on Ingres paper, 62.6 × 48 cm; not signed, not dated
Collection: Private collection, Sydney

Figure 9
SWINGING MONKEY c. 1964–5
Charcoal, ink and collage on paper, 76.2 × 54.4 cm; not signed, not dated
Collection: Private collection, Sydney

Figure 10
BATHROOM DRAWING 1962–63
Conté on paper, 54 × 70.5 cm (sight); signed and dated l.r. in charcoal 'Whiteley'
Inscriptions: on verso 'Exhibited Bonython Gallery, Sydney'
Provenance: Estate of artist Charles Bush
Collection: Castlemaine Art Gallery, Victoria

Figure 11
SELF PORTRAIT AT 16 (FIRST SELF PORTRAIT) 1955
Oil on board, 26.5 × 26 cm; signed and dated verso in black oil 'brett Whiteley/1955'
Inscriptions: verso in black oil 'Self portrait at 16 painted in/Fran's room at 18 Lucretia Ave, Longueville with/first oil painting set April 1955 given for my/birthday by Dad'. Further inscriptions in blue ink: 'cut down to this size "85"'
Collection: Private collection, Sydney

Figure 14
WENDY SLEEPING 1973
Pen, brush and brown ink on paper, 29.9 × 33.4 cm; not signed, not dated
Exhibited: Bonython Gallery, Sydney, 1974, Cat 74. 'Brett Whiteley–Lloyd Rees: On the Road to Berry', Museum of Modern Art at Heide and The Art Gallery of New South Wales, 1993, Cat 57
Literature: Art and Australia, Summer 1974, vol 11, no 3, illus, unpaginated
Collection: Private collection, Sydney

Figure 15
SIGEAN 1963
Charcoal on Annonay paper mounted on card, 65 × 50.5 cm (image); signed and dated l.r. in pencil on mount '1963 brett Whiteley'
Inscriptions: On mount l.r. in pencil 'Sigean'
Collection: Private collection, Sydney

Figure 16
BATHROOM DRAWING 1963
Charcoal on paper, 76.5 × 55.8 cm; not signed, not dated
Collection: Private collection, Sydney

Figure 17
AFTER CHRISTIE HAD FLED c. 1964
Charcoal on paper, 35.7 × 76.7 cm; stamped with artist's monogram l.r. in black ink, dated l.r. in pencil '65'
Inscriptions: l.l. in black ink 'After Christie had fled and was wandering around/London prior to his arrest, a spade workman/rendering 10 Rillington Place pulled back a piece/of pasted paper covering the pantry door in the/kitchen and found three bodies in this exact position'
Collection: Private collection, Sydney

Figure 18
WENDY ON CUSHIONS 1976
Also titled *Figure and Lavender Bay*
Charcoal on paper, 56 × 76 cm; stamped with artist's monogram l.r. in black ink, signed verso in charcoal 'Brett Whiteley', not dated
Exhibited: Australian Galleries, Melbourne, 1976, Cat 4. Artist's Studio, Circular Quay, 1981, not catalogued, p.15 (illus). 'Brett Whiteley–Lloyd Rees: On the Road to Berry' Museum of Modern Art at Heide and The Art Gallery of New South Wales, 1993, Cat 63

Literature: McGrath 1979, p.47 (illus)
Collection: Private collection, Melbourne

Figure 19
THE MAJESTIC HOTEL, TANGIER 1967
Also titled *Tangier Drawing, First Arab Image, Woman in Tangier*
Pen and ink and gouache, brush and ink, pencil on card, 160 × 85.5 cm; stamped with artist's monogram l.r. in black ink, dated l.r. in ink '1967'
Inscriptions: (with drawing) l.r. in black ink 'second image/on the beach at/Tangier. Guy with/sunglasses and/wife with black/bag on showing only/eyes./the Majestic Hotel/Tangier/1967/first Arab image, could be done in/white marble and black Belgium marble.'
Exhibited: Marlborough Gallery, New York, 1975, Cat 42
Collection: Private collection, Sydney

Figure 20
ALI AKBA KHAN PLAYING THE SAROD
Charcoal, brush and ink on rice paper, 55.8 × 73 cm; not signed, not dated
Collection: Private collection, Sydney

Figure 21
FRANCIS BACON AT 75 1984
(Triptych) Pen and ink and wash, oil, plaster, charcoal, ink on paper and board, 36 x 75.7 cm; signed l.r. in black ink 'brett whiteley', stamped with artist's monogram on each panel l.r. in black ink, signed and dated verso in pencil 'Brett Whiteley/1984'
Inscriptions: l.r. in black ink 'Francis Bacon at 75', verso in pencil 'FRANCIS BACON AT 75/SMALL TRIPTYCH/Brett Whiteley/London/1984'
Collection: Private collection, Sydney

Figure 22
WINTER SELF PORTRAIT 1971
Brush and ink on rice paper, 94 × 62.8 cm
Exhibited: Bonython Gallery, Sydney, 1972, Cat 32. Australian Galleries, Melbourne, 1972, Cat 32
Literature: McGrath 1979, p.224 (illus)
Collection: Unknown

Figure 23
THE MOST BEAUTIFUL MOUNTAIN 1969
Pen and ink and wash, 56.5 × 51 cm; signed and dated l.l in black ink '(Brett W./(Money [?])'
Inscriptions: l.l. centre in black ink '+ the most beautiful mountain/on globe earth green/slithering wet/[indecipherable]/like truth!'
Exhibited: 'Contemporary Australian Drawing', touring exhibition, Art Gallery of Western Australia, Queensland Art Gallery, The Art Gallery of New South Wales, 1978, Cat 93
Literature: Klepac 1978, p.108 (illus)
Provenance: Rudy Komon Gallery, Sydney, 1978
Collection: Private collection, Canberra

Figure 24
ETHIOPIAN IMAGE OF TIME 1974
Brush and ink and collage on paper, 64.9 × 50 cm; stamped with artist's monogram l.l. in black ink
Exhibited: Bonython Gallery, Sydney, 1973, Cat 81. Robin Gibson Gallery, Sydney, 1985, Cat 127.
Literature: McGrath 1979, p.167 (illus with title *Image of Ethiopia*)
Collection: Private collection, Sydney

Figure 25
SUNDAY 1973
Pencil and charcoal on paper, 49.5 × 45.3 cm (image); stamped with artist's monogram l.r. in black ink, not dated
Exhibited: Bonython Gallery, Sydney, 1974, Cat 54
Literature: McGrath 1979, p.172 (illus), also with incorrect title, p.229
Provenance: Rudy Komon Gallery, 'Australian and European Paintings', Geoff K. Gray, Sydney, 17 November 1986, lot 264
Collection: Ray Hughes, Sydney

Figure 26
STUDY EXTENSION TO THE DIVIDED UNITY
c. 1972–73
Pen and ink, pencil and wash on card, 76.3 × 44 cm; signed l.r. in pencil 'Brett Whiteley', not dated
Inscriptions: l.r. in pencil 'study extension to the Divided Unity'
Collection: Private collection, Sydney

Figure 27
PROVENCE LANDSCAPE 1982
Also titled *Nuclear Landscape with Dots*
Pen and ink, brush and ink, wash, collage, gouache and pencil on paper on linen on board, 182 × 120.5 cm; signed and dated l.l. in black ink '1982/brett whiteley', stamped with artist's monogram l.r. in red ink', artist's monogram adhered to linen u.l in red ink
Inscriptions: l.l. in black ink '(NUCLEAR VERSION OF)/Plain de la Crau/1888–1982/brett Whiteley from Vincent'
Exhibited: 'Another Way of Looking at Vincent Van Gogh 1888–1889 by Brett Whiteley 1968–1983', The Art Gallery of New South Wales, 1983. Greenhill Galleries, Perth, 1987, Cat 16 (illus)
Literature: Whiteley B. 1983
Collection: Private collection, Sydney

Figure 28
BULBUL'S NEST IN AVOCADO TREE 1976
Brush, pen and ink and wash on paper, 68 × 101 cm; signed and dated l.r. in black ink 'brett Whiteley 76'
Exhibited: 'Autumn Exhibition', Joseph Brown Gallery, Melbourne, 7–20 April, 1978, Cat 138. 'Four Australian Modern Masters: Arthur Boyd, Sidney Nolan, Brett Whiteley and Fred Williams', Savill Galleries, Sydney, 11 November–6 December 1988, Cat 45. ' Brett Whiteley–Lloyd Rees: On the Road to Berry', Museum of Modern Art at Heide and The Art Gallery of New South Wales, 1993, Cat 68
Provenance: Sotheby's Fine Australian Paintings, Sunday 24 July 1988, Melbourne, lot 233
Collection: Private collection, Sydney

Figure 29
EXPANDINGNESS 1983
Also titled *Glass house Mountains*
Ink and charcoal on paper, 74.5 × 104 cm; signed and dated l.c. in black ink 'brett whiteley July 2 83'
Inscriptions: l.c. in black ink ' 'Expandingness'/the Glass House Mountains/the foreground is known as Hitler's broccoli/meaningful scribble. Giacommetti would/love this landscape a little/like reverse surf'; l.r. in black ink 'one sees the most beautiful clouds/in the world in Queensland. The Queensland Tourist Bureau/should sell Queensland on its clouds.'
Exhibited: Greenhill Galleries, Perth, 1987, Cat 30. 'Brett Whiteley–Lloyd Rees: On the Road to Berry', Museum of Modern Art at Heide and The Art Gallery of New South Wales, 1993, Cat 77
Collection: Private collection, Sydney

Figure 30
THE BUSH 1970
Brush and ink on rice paper, 92 × 61 cm; signed and dated l.l. in pencil 'brett whiteley', stamped with artist's monogram in black ink, stamped in artist's monogram u.l. in red ink
Exhibited: Robin Gibson Gallery, Sydney, 1985, Cat 107
Literature: McGrath 1979 p.229 (illus)
Collection: Private collection, Sydney

Figure 31
RUE DE FROMAGE 1989
Gouache, collage and pencil, 56 × 76 cm; stamped with artist's monogram l.r. in black ink, dated l.r. in charcoal '18/7/81'
Inscriptions: l.r. in charcoal 'rue/de Fromage'

Exhibited: 'Paris: Regard de Côté', The Art Gallery of New South Wales, 1990, Cat 51 (illus). Australian Galleries, Melbourne, 1992, Cat 51 (illus)
Literature: Whiteley 1990
Collection: Private collection, Sydney

Figure 32
STANDING NUDE *c.* 1959
Charcoal on paper, 53.4 × 31 cm; not signed, not dated
Collection: Private collection, London

Figure 33
SHANKAR 1966
Charcoal and ink on paper, 213 × 203.2 cm; signed and dated l.r. in black ink '1966/Brett Whiteley'
Inscriptions: l.r. in black ink 'To Ravi Shankar – sublime purposelessness'
Exhibited: Marlborough New London Gallery, London, Cat 8 (illus). Marlborough–Gerson Gallery, New York, 1968, Cat 1. Bonython Gallery, Sydney, 1972. Australian Galleries, Melbourne, 1972, Cat 20
Literature: McGrath 1979, p.77 (illus)
Provenance: 'Australian Paintings' Christie's, Sydney, 5–6 October 1971, lot 359
Collection: The Art Gallery of New South Wales, Gift of Mrs Graham Ducker 1971

Figure 34
BUDDHISM 1969–70
Pen and ink, collage, oil and leaf on paper on board, 58.2 × 73.3 cm; stamped with artist's monogram l.l. in black ink, not dated
Exhibited: Bonython Art Gallery, Sydney, 1974 Cat 62. Robin Gibson Gallery, Sydney, 1985, Cat 47. 'Brett Whiteley–Lloyd Rees: On the Road to Berry', Museum of Modern Art at Heide and The Art Gallery of New South Wales, 1993, Cat 48
Literature: McGrath 1979, p.222 (illus)
Collection: Private collection, Sydney

Figure 35
BUDDHA *c.* 1972
Ink on canvas, 75 × 70.5 cm; not signed, not dated
Inscriptions: stamped l.r. in red ink with 2 Chinese stamps
Collection: Private collection, Sydney

Figure 36
INTERIOR, LAVENDER BAY 1976
Pen and ink on paper, 76.2 × 57.2 cm; stamped with artist's monogram u.r. in red ink, dated u.r. in pencil '22/Nov/76'
Exhibited: Fischer Fine Art, London, 1977, Cat 55. 'Brett Whiteley–Lloyd Rees: On the Road to Berry', Museum of Modern Art at Heide and The Art Gallery of New South Wales, 1993, Cat 63
Inscriptions: u.r. in black ink 'all lines lead to other lines/how the wrist twists/like doing a line for someone!/you draw water from the well you draw/something out (to DRAW delicious extraction)/its a discipline … get in line with an out line/line up!/listen linear LLL in ear/lean line.'
Literature: McGrath 1979, p.224
Collection: Private collection, Melbourne

Figure 37
STUDY FOR GAUGUIN 1968
Pencil, ink, collage and adhesive tape on paper, 35.3 × 55.7 cm; signed and dated l.r. in pencil 'Brett Whiteley 1968'
Inscriptions: l.r. in pencil 'study for Gauguin 1968 NY'
Collection: Private collection, Sydney

Figure 38
PORTRAIT OF JOEL ELENBERG 1980
Charcoal on paper, 39.5 × 37.9 cm; stamped u.r. in black ink with artist's monogram, signed and dated verso in ballpoint pen 'brett Whiteley'
Inscriptions: on wooden support verso in ball point pen '"Joel"' 1980
Exhibited: David Reid's Gallery, Sydney, 1980,

Cat 51. Robin Gibson Gallery, 1985, Cat 4
Collection: Private collection, Sydney

Figure 39
SENSORENO 1977
Ink and collage on paper, 20.3 × 25.4 cm; not signed, not dated
Exhibited: Robin Gibson Gallery, Sydney, 1985, Cat 77 (illus)
Literature: McGrath 1979, p.14 (illus)
Collection: Private collection, London

Figure 40
THE WILLOW TREE 1978
Charcoal on paper, 222 × 125 cm; signed and dated l.l.c. in pencil 'brett Whiteley/9–19/4/78', stamped with artists monogram l.r.c. in red ink
Inscriptions: l.l.c. in pencil 'the willow tree/brett Whiteley/9–19/4/78'
Exhibited: Australian Galleries, Melbourne, 1978, Cat 10
Collection: Private collection, Sydney

Plate 1
CHARLOTTE LANE 1957
Oil on cardboard, 20.3 × 26.5 cm; not signed,
not dated
Literature: McGrath 1979, p.22 (illus)
Collection: Private collection, Sydney

Plate 2
THE SOUP KITCHEN 1958
Oil on canvas, 76.2 × 63.7 cm; signed and dated l.r.
in brown oil 'Brett Whiteley 58'
Inscriptions: verso in charcoal 'THE SOUP KITCHEN
1958/BRETT WHITELEY/OIL ON CANVAS'
Exhibited: Bonython Art Gallery, Sydney, 1970, not
catalogued. 'Recent Acquisitions', Joseph Brown
Gallery, Melbourne, 14–30 October 1975, Cat 54.
'Dreams, Fears and Desires: Aspects of Australian
Figurative Painting 1942–1962', S. H. Ervin Gallery,
6 April–14 June 1984, Cat 44
Literature: McGrath 1979, p.21 (illus) Smith and
Dixon 1984 p.47 (illus)
Collection: Private collection, Sydney

Plate 3
MAN CONTEMPLATING *c.* 1959
Oil on board, 90 × 59.5 cm; signed verso in blue
pen 'WHITELEY BRETT', not dated
Collection: The Art Gallery of New South Wales,
Gift of the Rudy Komon Memorial Fund 1985

Plate 4
SOFALA 1958
Oil on canvas on board, 65.8 × 85.4 cm; signed
with initials and dated l.r. in pink oil
'B.W. 1958'
Exhibited: McRoberts and Tunnard Gallery,
London, 1960, Cat 28. Orange Regional Gallery,
Orange NSW, 1990, Cat 1
Literature: McGrath 1979, p.24–26 (illus)
Collection: New South Wales Government

Plate 5
DIXON STREET 1959
Oil on board, 81.5 × 119.8 cm; not signed,
not dated
Inscriptions: verso in white chalk 'DIXON STREET'
Exhibited: 'Italian Government Travelling Art
Scholarship', The Art Gallery of New South Wales,
1960, Cat 48
Collection: Private collection, Sydney

Plate 6
SOMEWHERE IN SUMMER 1961
Oil, tempera, collage, string and canvas on board,
183 × 213.5 cm; signed u.l. 'Brett Whiteley', signed
and dated verso in black oil '1961/Brett Whiteley'
Inscriptions: verso in black oil 'Somewhere in
Summer 1961/72" × 84'; label adhered verso 'John
Moores Liverpool/ Exhibition/1963/Junior
section/ oil + tempera £450/ No.347'
Exhibited: Matthiesen Gallery, London, 1962,
Cat 1. John Moores Liverpool Exhibition, 1963,
junior section, Cat 347
Collection: Private collection, London

Plate 7
THE KITCHEN 1960
Also titled *Untitled Gouache*
Pencil and gouache on board, 35.8 × 51.2 cm;
signed and dated verso in pen and ink 'Brett
Whiteley 60'
Inscription: verso in pen and ink 'Untitled
Gouache', in chalk '171 + 727 RB/ Mar 1–68',
stencilled in black paint '727RB'
Exhibited: 'Winter Exhibition', Joseph Brown
Gallery, Melbourne, 4–14 July 1977, Cat 119
Provenance: 'Australian Paintings', Leonard Joel,
Melbourne, 1–3 November 1978 Cat 476.
'Australian and International Paintings',
Australian Art Auctions, Sydney, 8–10 March
1980, Cat 112
Collection: Private collection, Sydney

Plate 8
GOLD MINING 1960
Originally titled *Gold Fields*
Oil, pencil and PVA on paper on board, 35 × 53 cm;
signed verso in black ink 'Whiteley 60'
Inscriptions: verso in black ink 'gold mining'
Collection: Private collection, Sydney

Plate 9
**PRELIMINARY STUDY FOR UNTITLED RED
PAINTING** 1960 [dated 1961]
Oil, charcoal and collage on canvas, 69.5 × 62.5
cm; signed and dated l.r. in black ink 'Brett
Whiteley 1961'
Inscriptions: l.r. in black ink 'preliminary for
Untitled/Red Tate Gallery London'
Collection: Private collection, Sydney

Plate 10
UNTITLED RED PAINTING 1960
Oil and collage on canvas, 132.7 × 186.1 cm; signed
and dated verso in black oil 'Brett Whiteley 60'
Inscriptions: verso in black oil 'Brett Whiteley/Top'
with arrows
Exhibited: Whitechapel Art Gallery, London, 1961,
Cat 108
Literature: Rothenstein 1962, p.262. Pringle 1963,
p.88. Alley 1981 pp.762–3
Collection: Tate Gallery, London

Plate 11
UNTITLED PAINTING 1961
Oil, tempera and collage on board, 153.4 × 152.3
cm; signed and dated verso in black oil 'Brett
Whiteley 61'
Inscriptions: verso u.r. in black oil 'Untitled/
Painting/60' × 60'/Brett/Whiteley/Matthiesen
Gallery/142 New Bond Street London W1' u.l.
'Untitled Painting 1961/Brett Whiteley 61/ 60' ×
60'/oil, tempera/and collage'
Exhibited: Matthiesen Gallery, London, 1962, Cat
5. 'Peter Stuyvesant Collection', Adelaide Festival
of Arts, Art Gallery of South Australia, 1963, Cat 24.
'Australian Art: Colonial to Modern', Deutscher
Fine Art, Perth, 20–25 August, Sydney, 5–13
September 1986
Literature: Spencer 1963, p.21 (illus)
Collection: Private collection, Melbourne

Plate 12
UNTITLED ABSTRACT *c.* 1960
Oil and charcoal on canvas, 86.5 × 115 cm; not
signed, not dated
Collection: Private collection, Sydney

Plate 13
UNTITLED PAINTING II 1961
Oil, pencil and collage of cotton and sandpaper on
board, 152.7 × 122 cm; signed and dated verso in
black oil 'Brett Whiteley 61'
Inscriptions: verso in black oil 'Brett Whiteley 61/
oil and mixed media/cat. no. 2/Untitled painting
2', (adhered verso) Matthiesen Gallery label
'cat. no.4'
Exhibited: Matthiesen Gallery, London, 1962, Cat
4. 'Young Australian Painters', Tokyo and Kyoto,
Japan 1965. 'Canadian Pacific Airlines Convention
Exhibition', Vancouver Art Gallery, 1969.
Collection: The Art Gallery of New South Wales

Plate 14
UNTITLED PAINTING 1962
Oil and mixed media on board, 122 × 127.7 cm;
signed and dated verso in black oil 'Brett
Whiteley/ 1962'
Inscriptions: verso in black oil 'Brett Whiteley/
1962/painted/in the summer at Sigean/France/
'Untitled Painting'/ 48" × 50 1/4'/OIL TEMPERA +
COLLAGE/figure bending over/comes from the
vineyard/worker picking grapes', (adhered verso)
Fischer Fine Art Limited label and New Metropole
Arts Centre label
Collection: Private collection, Melbourne

Plate 15
UNTITLED RED PAINTING I 1961
Oil, newspaper, charcoal and resin on board, 152.4
× 152.4 cm; signed and date, verso in black oil
'Brett Whiteley 1961'
Inscriptions: verso in black oil ' UNTITLED RED/OIL
AND COLLAGE/ON BOARD,/Brett Whiteley 1961/
MATTHIESEN/LONDON/SOLD/CAT NO 3'
Exhibited: The Matthiesen Gallery, London, 1962,
Cat 3. 'Selected Australian Works of Art', Lauraine
Diggins Gallery, Melbourne, June 1986.
Collection: Private collection, Melbourne

Plate 16
SUMMER FIELD PAINTING III 1962
Oil, tempera and collage on board, 122 × 127.5 cm;
signed l.c. in black oil 'Brett Whiteley', signed and
dated verso in black oil 'Brett Whiteley 1962'
Inscriptions: verso in black oil 'painted in
Sigean, France'
Exhibited: Rudy Komon Gallery, Sydney,
1963, Cat 1. 'Modern Australian Paintings',
Bridget Mcdonnell Gallery, Melbourne, 2–23
February 1994
Provenance: 'Australian and European Paintings'
Geoff K. Gray, Sydney, 17 November 1986, lot 91
Collection: Private collection, courtesy of Bridget
Mcdonnell Gallery, Melbourne

Plate 17
UNTITLED WHITE PAINTING II 1962
Tempera, ink, gouache, charcoal and collage on
paper, 74.6 × 67 cm; not signed, not dated
Exhibited: Matthiesen Gallery, London,
1962, Cat 22
Provenance: 'Australian Painting', Christie's,
Sydney, 5–6 October 1971, lot 374
Collection: The University of Queensland
Art Gallery

Plate 18
UNTITLED DARK PAINTING 1962
Oil, charcoal, material, string and wax on
canvas, 133 x 186.2 cm; signed and dated verso
in charcoal 'Brett Whiteley/1961'
Inscriptions: verso in charcoal 'UNTITLED/DARK/
PAINTING 1961/TEMPERA /+ MIXED MEDIA'
Literature: Millen 1963, p.187 (illus)

Plate 19
WHITE PAINTING WITH COLLAGE 1961
Oil, collage, pencil, canvas, charcoal, newspaper
and wax on board, 123.5 × 123.5 cm; signed and
dated verso in black oil 'Brett Whiteley'
Inscriptions: verso in black oil 'WHITE PAINTING WITH
COLLAGE/1961'
Exhibited: Rudy Komon Gallery, Sydney, 1963, Cat
2. 'Australian Painting Today', touring exhibition
of Australia and Europe funded by Australian state
Galleries and the Commonwealth Advisory Board,
1963–1965, Cat 76
Literature: Cormack 1962, p.9. Hughes 1970,
p.296 (illus)
Provenance: 'Australian Painting', Christie's,
Melbourne, 14 March 1972, Cat 84
Collection: Private collection, Sydney

Plate 20
TO ARRIVE AT A POINT OF 'CUBELESSISM' 1961
Also titled *Untitled Painting with Headline*
Charcoal, pencil, pen and ink, collage, material, oil
and gouache and paper on card, 70.7 × 71 cm;
signed and dated l.r. in charcoal 'Whiteley 61',
stamped with artist's monogram l.r. in black ink
Inscriptions: l.r. in black ink 'To arrive at a point
of cublessism'.
Exhibited: Matthiesen Gallery, London, 1962,
Cat 25
Literature: Reichardt 1962, pp.72–73 (illus)
Collection: Private collection, Sydney

Plate 21
TWO MILES TO GET THE LETTERS 1962–65

Charcoal, material, oil and linseed oil on board, 122 × 101.7 cm; signed and dated verso in black oil '1962–65/Brett Whiteley'
Inscriptions: verso in black oil 'TWO MILES TO GET THE LETTERS' 1962–65/Brett Whiteley/OIL, TEMPERA AND COLLAGE/48' × 40 1/4'/painted at Sigean, summer 1962/slightly reworked Oct, 1965/London'
Collection: Private collection, Sydney

Plate 22
SUMMER AT SIGEAN 1962–63
(Triptych) Synthetic polymer medium, oil, charcoal, pencil, tempera on hessian and cotton gauze on composition board, 198 × 456 cm; signed l.c. middle panel in pencil 'Brett Whiteley', dated verso in black oil '1962–63'
Inscriptions: on each panel verso centre in black oil 'SUMMER AT SIGEAN/1962–63/Panel No 1 [Panel No 2, No 3],TEMPERA COLLAGE AND OIL/PANEL SIZE/78" × 68"/Brett Whiteley'
Literature: McGrath 1979, p.36–37 (illus). Harris 1964, p.229 (illus)
Collection: National Gallery of Australia, Canberra

Plate 23
LARGE FIGURE AT THE BASIN DRAWING 1963
Also titled *Bathroom with Heater*
Charcoal on paper, 142 × 152 cm; signed and dated l.r. in black 'whiteley 1963'
Inscriptions: verso in black ink 'LARGE/FIGURE AT THE BASIN/DRAWING'/CHARCOAL ON PAPER/56' × 60'/1963'
Collection: Private collection, Sydney

Plate 24
NUDE AT BASIN *c.* 1963
Oil and tempera on board, 129 × 121.5 cm
Exhibited: Marlborough New London Gallery, London, 1964, Cat 24. Peter Gant Fine Art Exhibition, Melbourne, 17 May–14 June 1988, Cat 56
Collection: Private collection, Melbourne

Plate 25
WOMAN IN BATH 1963
Pencil and charcoal on paper, 54.8 × 77 cm; stamped with artist's monogram l.r. in black ink, dated l.r. in black ink '1963'
Inscriptions: l.r. in black ink 'Woman in the bath'
Exhibited: Marlborough New London Gallery, London, 1964, Cat 11
Literature: McGrath 1979, p.38 (illus).
Provenance: 'Fine Australian Paintings', Sotheby's, Melbourne, Monday 14 August 1989, lot 227
Collection: Private collection, Sydney

Plate 26
WOMAN IN A BATH 1964
Also titled *Woman in a Bath 3*
Oil, charcoal, tempera, material and collage on board, 146.8 × 120.2 cm; signed l.c. in black oil 'Whiteley'
Inscriptions: verso in white oil ' "WOMAN IN A BATH" 4/1963/OIL + TEMPERA/BRETT WHITELEY', in chalk 'SD/286', label adhered verso in black ink in artist's hand ' "WOMAN IN THE BATH"/58 1/2 × 48"/OIL + TEMPERA 1963/BRETT WHITELEY'
Exhibited: Marlborough New London Gallery, London, 1964, Cat 14
Literature: Spencer 1964, p.108 (illus)
Collection: Private collection, Melbourne

Plate 27
BATHROOM DRAWING 1963
Charcoal, brush and ink on paper, 75 × 57.5 cm; stamped with artist's monogram l.l. in black ink, dated l.r. in black ink '2/7/1963', dated l.r. in pencil '1965'
Inscriptions: l.r. in pencil 'bathroom'
Collection: Private collection, Sydney

Plate 28
WASHER PARTIALLY COVERING BATHER'S HEAD 1963
Oil, tempera and material on board, 60 × 55.5 cm;

signed l.r. in black ink 'Whiteley', not dated
Exhibited: Marlborough New London Gallery, London, 1964, Cat 7
Literature: Spencer 1964, p.108 (illus)
Collection: Private collection, Melbourne

Plate 29
WOMAN, BASIN AND MIRROR 1963
Oil, charcoal, material, cardboard, string and tempera on board, 96.5 × 91.2 cm; signed l.r. in charcoal 'Whiteley', not dated
Exhibited: Marlborough New London Gallery, London, 1964, Cat 9
Literature: McGrath 1979, p.39 (illus in reverse)
Collection: Private collection, Sydney

Plate 30
WOMAN IN THE BATH II 1963
Oil, tempera and collage of canvas strips on canvas, 182.9 × 188 cm; signed l.l. 'whiteley', signed and dated verso '1963/BRETT WHITELEY'
Inscriptions: verso 'WOMAN IN A BATH II 1963/BRETT WHITELEY/OIL TEMPERA AND COLLAGE/72" × 74"/HIGH WIDE'
Exhibited: Marlborough New London Gallery, London, 1964, Cat 3
Literature: Hughes 1970, plate f. (illus). Hoff 1978, p.176 (illus)
Collection: Tate Gallery, London

Plate 31
WOMAN IN THE BATH 5 1963–64
Also titled *Woman in a Bath*
Oil and tempera on board, 188 × 183 cm (sight)
Exhibited: Marlborough New London Gallery, London, 1964, not catalogued. Whitechapel Gallery, London, 1964, Cat 45
Collection: Private collection, Melbourne

Plate 32
WOMAN IN BATH 1964
Also titled (*Woman in Bath 4– from Marlborough Gallery, 1964*)
Oil, collage, tempera and polyvinyl acetate emulsion on board, 183.1 × 218.7 cm; signed l.l. 'Whiteley'
Exhibited: Marlborough New London Gallery, London, 1964, Cat 16. 'The Australian Painters', touring exhibition of the United States 1967–1970, Cat 75. 'Australian Paintings of the 1960s: Selections from the Mertz Collection', Huntington Art Gallery, The University of Texas at Austin, Austin, Texas, USA, 30 May–2 August 1984. 'Australian Paintings from the Mertz Collection', Huntington Art Gallery, The University of Texas at Austin, Austin, Texas, USA, 1 June–12 August 1990
Literature: Luck 1966, p.66 (illus)
Collection: Art Gallery of New South Wales, Purchased with funds provided by the Art Gallery Society of New South Wales 2000

Plate 33
HEAD OF CHRISTIE 1964
Oil on board, 65.9 × 60.9 cm
Exhibited: Marlborough New London Gallery, London 1965, Cat 23. Bonython Gallery, Adelaide and Sydney, 1966, Cat 14. Australian Galleries, Melbourne, 1966, Cat 12. 'The Australian Painters', touring exhibition of the United States 1967–1970, Cat 79. 'Australian Paintings of the 1960s: Selections from the Mertz Collection', Huntington Art Gallery, The University of Texas at Austin, Austin, Texas, USA, 30 May–2 August 1984. 'Australian Paintings from the Mertz Collection', Huntington Art Gallery, The University of Texas at Austin, Austin, Texas, USA, 1 June–12 August 1990
Literature: Wolfrom 1965, p.14. Hughes 1965, p.40 (illus). Spencer 1965, p.210. Luck 1966, p.68 (illus). Art and Australia, 1969, vol 7, no 2, p.182. Luck 1969, p.53 (illus)
Collection: Archer M. Huntington Art Gallery, The University of Texas at Austin. Gift of The Mertz Art Fund, 1972

Plate 34
CHRISTIE 1965
Oil, pen, ink, gouache, charcoal, wash and collage on paper, 78.8 × 57.3 cm; stamped in artist's monogram l.l. in black ink, dated l.l. in pencil '1965'
Literature: McGrath 1979, pp.59 and p.229 (illus)
Collection: Private collection, Sydney

Plate 35
SMALL CHRISTIE PAINTING NO. 2 1965
Oil, tempera, rubber tubing, metal and wood on board, 86.3 × 86.3 cm; not signed, dated verso '1965'
Inscriptions: label adhered verso, Marlborough Fine Art
Exhibited: Marlborough Fine Art London, London, 1965, Cat 36
Collection: Private collection, London

Plate 36
CHRISTIE AND KATHLEEN MALONEY 1964
Oil and collage on canvas, 177.8 × 243.8 cm; signed and dated verso l.r. in black oil '1964 Brett Whiteley'
Inscriptions: l.c. in black oil '1949 NOVEMBER', inscribed verso in black oil 'CHRISTIE/AND/KATHLEEN MALONEY'
Exhibited: Marlborough New London Gallery, London, 1965, Cat 28. Bonython Art Gallery, Adelaide and Sydney, 1966, Cat 16. Australian Galleries, Melbourne, 1966, Cat 9
Literature: McGrath 1979, p.53 (illus). *Time* magazine, 'The Young Londoners', 9 October 1964, p.34 (illus)
Collection: National Gallery of Australia, Canberra.

Plate 37
SMALL CHRISTIE PAINTING NO 1 1965
Oil, tempera, collage and wax on plywood, 86.2 × 86.2 cm; signed and dated verso c. in black oil 'Brett Whiteley '65'
Exhibited: Marlborough New London Gallery, London, 1965, Cat 35
Collection: National Gallery of Australia, Canberra

Plate 38
PRELIMINARY SKETCH FOR CHRISTIE MURDER SERIES AND KATHLEEN MALONEY 1965
Charcoal, ink, wash and linseed oil on paper mounted on card, 55.3 × 76.8 cm; stamped with artist's monogram l.l., dated l.r. in black ink '1965'
Inscriptions: l.r. in black ink 'Preliminary sketch for Christie Murder Series and Kathleen Maloney'
Literature: McGrath 1979, p.60–61 and p.227 (illus)
Collection: Private collection, Sydney

Plate 39
CHRISTIE WITH HECTORINA MCLENNAN 1964
Oil, wax, charcoal, collage, painted wood and cloth perspex object on canvas, 162.5 × 214 cm; signed u.c. in black oil 'Brett Whiteley/1964 re-worked June 1965'
Exhibited: Marlborough New London Gallery, London, 1965, Cat 31. 'Autumn Exhibition', Joseph Brown Gallery, Melbourne, 1973, Cat 44
Literature: Millar 1974 (illus). Spencer 1965, p.215. McGrath 1979, pp.56–57 (illus). Russell (2)1965 , pp.125–131. Hughes 1965. Melville (2) 1965, pp.445–7 (illus). Hughes 1970, p.297 and cover (illus). Thomas 1988, p.195 (illus). Hunter 1991, p.445–7 (illus)
Collection: National Gallery of Australia, Canberra

Plate 40
CHRISTIE DRAWING (KATHLEEN MALONEY) 1964
Charcoal on paper, 56.6 × 76.7 cm; signed verso in black ink 'Brett Whiteley'
Inscriptions: verso in black ink ' "CHRISTIE DRAWING"/22 × 30/1964/(REWORKED 1965 ON GLASS)'
Exhibited: Marlborough New London Gallery, London, 1965, Cat 27. Bonython Art Gallery,

Adelaide and Sydney, 1966, Cat 21. 'The Boxer Collection' University Art Gallery, University of Melbourne 1974, Cat 28. 'The Boxer *Collection: The Sydney Alternative*' The Nolan Gallery, Tharwa ACT, 1982, Cat 16
Literature: Gordon 1966, p.38 (illus)
Collection: Alan Boxer, Canberra

Plate 41
CHRISTIE AND KATHLEEN MALONEY 1964
Charcoal and paper on board, 160 × 152.4 cm; signed l.r. 'Whiteley'
Exhibited: 'The Australian Painters', touring exhibition of the United States 1967–70, Cat 76. 'Australian Paintings of the 1960s: Selections from the Mertz Collection', Huntington Art Gallery, The University of Texas at Austin, Austin, Texas, USA, 30 May–2 August 1984. 'Australian Paintings from the Mertz Collection', Huntington Art Gallery, The University of Texas at Austin, Austin, Texas, USA, 1 June–12 August 1990.
Literature: Luck 1966, p.67 (illus)
Collection: Archer M Huntington Art Gallery at the University of Texas, Austin. Gift of the Mertz Art Fund, 1972.

Plate 42
DON'T READ THIS *c.* 1964
Charcoal, oil, gouache, ink and linseed oil on canvas, 198.2 × 145 cm; not signed, not dated
Inscriptions: l.l.c. in charcoal 'don't read this' l.l.c. in ink '/On March 24th 1953, a Jamacan [sic] tenant of 10 Rillington Place was sounding the walls in the kitchen on the ground floor previously occupied by Christie. One wall sounded hollow and the Jamacan [sic] pulled off a corner of wall paper/He discovered that the wallpaper covered a cupboard, one corner of which was missing. He was able to peer into the cupboard with the help of a torch and saw the naked back of a woman. Hastily summoned/policemen discovered that the cupboard contained three female bodies. The first was naked except for a brassiere and suspender belt; the other two were wrapped in blankets and secured/with electric wire. There was very little smell due to atmospheric conditions causing dehydration. Floorboards in the front room appeared to have been disturbed and they were/taken up to reveal a fourth body (Mrs Christie) also wrapped in a blanket. Christie had left on March 20th. The back garden was dug up, + revealed human bones – the skeletons of two more bodies. A human femur was being/used to hold up the back fence. It was now remembered that in 1949 two other bodies – those of Mrs Evans and her baby Geraldine had been discovered at the same address. Both had been strangled + the husband/Timothy Evans was hanged for the double murder. Evans was a near mental defective and it seems certian [sic] that the murders for which he was hanged were the work of the man who killed the women downstairs./On March 31st Christie was recognised by P.c.Ledger on the embankment near Putney Bridge + was taken to Putney Bridge Station + charged. Christie made a statement admitting to the murders of the four/women in the house. In it he claimed that his wife had been getting into an increasingly nervous condition because of attacks from the coloured people in the house and that on the morning of Dec 14th 1952/he had been awakened by his wife [sic] convulsive movements; she was having some kind of fit: Christie 'could not bear to see her,' and strangled her with a stocking. His account of [the] other three murders/– Rita Nelson aged 25, Kathleen Maloney aged 26, Hectorina McLennan aged 26 – discribed [sic] quarrels with the women (who were prostutes) [sic] during the course of which Christie strangled them. Later he also confessed /to the murders of the two women in

the garden. One was an Austrian girl, Ruth Fuerst whom Christie claimed he had murdered during sexual intercourse; and Muriel Eady, a fellow employee of/the Ultra Radio Factory in Park Royal. Where Christie had worked in late 1944. A tobacco tin containg [sic] four lots of pubic hair was found in the house. Carbon monoxide was found in the blood/of the three women in the cupboard; although not in Mrs Christie. The three had semen in the vagina; none wore knickers but all had a piece of white material between the legs in the form of a diaper. This/has never been satisfactorily [sic] explained. Christie admitted at his trial that his method of murder had been to get women drunk + take them back to his house on the pretext that he had an excellent/device for curing coughs + cattarrh [sic] – this device consisted of a jar with Friar's Balson in it with a length of rubber tubing attached, this rubber tubing in turn was attacked [sic] to a gas jet of [sic] the wall. He/would persuade the girls to sit in a small rope deck chair, he would then release the bulldog clip from the rubber tubing thus allowing carbon monoxide to hiss out. When the girl lost consciousness/he would then strangle them while he raped them. It has been suggested that Christie had reached a stage of sexual incapacity where the women needed to be unconscious before/he could possess them. In Halifax, as a young man Christie had earned the derogatory nicknames 'Can't Do It Christie' and 'Reggie-No-Dick.' The body of Rita Nelson was found to be six/months pregnant. Christie was only tried for the murder of his wife; his trial opened at the Central Criminal Court on June 22nd 1953. He was 55 years old at the time of his arrest. He was/born in Chester Street Boothtown Yorkshire in 1898. The father was a stern man who treated his seven children with a Victorian severity. Christie was a weak child, myopic, introverted,/and jeered at by his fellow students as a 'cissy'. Christie was a chronic hypochondriac, a man who enjoyed being ill and talking about past illnesses. In the first world war he suffered /mustard gassing and was blown up. He claimed he lost his voice for three + half years + was blind for 5 months. The loss of voice was the psychological effect of hysteria, for there was no physical/abnormality to account for it. His voice returned spontaneously at a time of emotional excitement. Christie claimed one of the most important events in his childhood was seeing his grandfather's body at the/age of eight. His wife often visited friends in Sheffield and it was during one of these visits that Christie brought Ruth Fuerst back to the house and strangled her. In his confession he/told of hiding Ruth Fuerst's body under the floorboards when his wife returned with her brother. The next day when they were out, he moved the body to the wash house under cover of /darkness he finally buried it in the back garden. At his trial Christie declared that he was not sure if Ruth Fuerst was his first victim. In 1943 Muriel Eady came/alone to Rillington Place when his wife was away again, he persuaded her to sit in the rope chair + she soon was buried in the back garden. In his third confession from Brixton/prison he declares that in August 1949 Timothy Evans and his young wife (who lived in the flat above Christie) quarrelled violently about a blond woman. Christie claimed he found Mrs Evans on the floor in front/of gas fire [sic], having attempted suicide, and that he gave her a cup of tea. The next day she was there again and she asked his help in killing herself, offering to let him have sexual intercourse. He/strangled her with a stocking and (in view of the later cases) probably had intercourse with her. when Timothy Evans came home Christie told him his wife had gassed herself and that no doubt/Evans would be suspected of murdering

her. Ludovic Kennedy states that Christie offered to preform[sic] an abortion on Mrs Evans who was pregnant at the time of her death. Mrs Evans/panicked when Christie tried to persude [sic] her to inhale gas and was strangled. Christie told Evans his wife had died during abortion, and persuaded him to keep silence. Evans panicked +/fled to Wales, where confused + completely distressed he 'confessed' to his wife's murder claiming he put the body down the drain (like this) in front of 10 Rillington Place. The bodies where [sic] found in the/washroom at the back of the house. The baby Geraldine was found also strangled with her mother. Evans was hung for the double murder protesting his innocence to the end. In December 1952 came the/murder of his wife. The motive for this is not clear, although it may well have been a desire to have the house to himself for further murders. Christie killed again within a few weeks Rita Nelson had last/been seen alive on January 2nd 1953. The next victim was Kathleen Maloney last seen alive on January 12 1953. On March 3rd Hectorina McLennan returned to Rillington Place where she/had been staying with a man friend whom Christie had met outside Ladbroke Grove Tube Station. He left the house after this murder, when arrested he was unshaven, shabby + pennyless [sic]. He was found guilty + was executed July 15th 1953'
Collection: Private collection, Sydney

Plate 43
CHEETAH IN RILLINGTON PLACE 1964
Oil on board, 205.7 × 182.9 cm; signed and dated verso in black oil '1964/BRETT WHITELEY'
Inscriptions: verso in black oil 'CHEETA IN RILLINGTON PLACE/1964/BRETT WHITELEY/OIL AND MIXED MEDIA ON PLYWOOD/81" × 72". Label adhered verso 'This painting started as a scene of the/backgarden of 10 Rillington Place/London W11, the tiny slum where/John Reginald Halliday Christie,/a multiple sex murderer + psychopathic/personality strangled seven women +/one child between 1944 + 1953./The painting originally was a device/picture showing simultaneously the/backgarden + also an ariel view/of Ladbroke Grove W11 implying the/streets, lanes + general confusion of/that part of London./After two months the painting underwent/a drastic change of conception./The cheetah creep [sic] in + a plan/view of the house showing where/the bodies were found was also added – mainly for formal reasons./The backgarden became more like/pubic hair + the sinister element in/the painting was heightened. The/painting may still not be finished.
Exhibited: 'The Australian Painters', touring exhibition of the United States, 1967–70, Cat 78. 'Legends and Landscape in Australian Art', Sarah Campbell Blaffer Gallery, University of Houston, Texas, 7 November–19 December 1986. 'Australian Paintings from the Mertz Collection', Huntington Art Gallery, The University of Texas at Austin, Austin, Texas, 1 June–12 August 1990.
Literature: Luck 1966 p.68 (illus). Hughes 1986, p.22 (illus)
Collection: Archer M. Huntington Art Gallery, The University of Texas at Austin, Gift of the Mertz Fund, 1972.

Plate 44
TWO GIRAFFES NO. 1 1965
Oil and plaster on board, 183.5 × 244 × 5 cm; signed and dated verso in black oil 'brett whiteley 1965'
Inscriptions: verso in black oil 'Two Giraffes No 1'
Exhibited: Marlborough New London Gallery, London, 1965, Cat 7
Literature: Spencer 1965, p.214 (illus). Hughes 1965 (illus)
Collection: Private collection, London

Plate 45
GIRAFFE NO. 1 *c.* 1965
Brass, mangrove wood, marble and oil,
243.8 × 30.5 × 30.5 cm; not signed, not dated
Exhibited: Marlborough New London Gallery,
London, 1965, Cat 18
Literature: Gray 1986, p.223 (illus)
Collection: Private collection, Sydney

Plate 46
TWO INDONESIAN GIRAFFES 1964
Oil on board, 162.3 × 143.5 cm; signed and
dated l.r. in black oil 'Whiteley 64', signed and
dated verso
Inscriptions: inscribed verso in black oil 'TWO
INDONESIAN GIRAFFES 1964/The first oil on board,/63
1/2 × 56 1/2"/Lot 65/There are no Giraffes in
Indonesia if they got some they should look like this'
Exhibited: Marlborough New London Gallery,
London, 1965, Cat 10 (illus). Bonython Gallery,
Adelaide, and Sydney, Cat 2, 1966. Australian
Galleries, Melbourne, 1966, Cat 7
Collection: Private collection, Perth

Plate 47
GIRAFFE (BLACK) 1965
Oil on board, 185.4 × 121.9 cm
Exhibited: Marlborough New London Gallery,
London, 1965, Cat 8
Collection: Private collection, Melbourne

Plate 48
CHIMPANZEE 1965
Oil, charcoal, perspex, material, plaster and
varnish on board, 183.7 × 206 cm; signed and
dated verso in black '1965 Brett Whiteley'
Inscriptions: verso in black oil '(reworked all
thru/1965). "Chimpanzee" (cage)/1965/Brett
Whiteley/OIL, TEMPERA AND COLLAGE/WITH GLASS/AND
HAIR/72" × 78"'
Exhibited: Marlborough New London Gallery,
London, 1965, Cat 2
Collection: Private collection, Sydney

Plate 49
WHITE SACRED BABOON 1965
Carved wood, encaustic on marble base,
62.5 × 55 × 63 cm (overall); not signed, not dated
Exhibited: Marlborough New London Gallery,
London, 1965, Cat 17. Bonython Gallery, Adelaide
and Sydney, 1966, Cat 7. Australian Galleries,
Melbourne, 1966, Cat 4
Literature: Thomas 1989, Plate 332. Hughes 1965.
McGrath 1967, p.517 (illus)
Collection: National Gallery of Victoria, The Joseph
Brown Collection. Presented through the NGV
Foundation by Dr Joseph Brown AO OBE,
Honorary Life Benefactor, 2004

Plate 50
DRAWING OF AN APE 1965
Paint, pencil, charcoal on paper, perspex on
board, 121.4 × 104.6 cm; signed and dated verso in
black oil '1965/Brett Whiteley'
Inscriptions: inscribed verso in black paint
'DRAWING OF AN APE' 1965/48" × 42"/Charcoal on
paper/with perspex/Brett Whiteley/NB/Please be
careful/whilst [illeg] cleaning/perspex not/to
touch arrow/painted on the outside'
Exhibited: Marlborough New London Gallery,
London, 1965, Cat 4. Bonython Art Gallery,
Adelaide and Sydney, 1966, Cat 4. Australian
Galleries, Melbourne, 1966, Cat 2
Literature: Luck 1969, p.52. Smith B. with Smith, T.
1991, p.390 (illus)
Collection: National Gallery of Victoria

Plate 51
ART STUDENT DOING A DRAWING OF A LION
1965
Oil, tempera, collage and wire on board, 214 × 183
cm; signed and dated verso in black oil '1965
Brett Whiteley'
Inscriptions: inscribed verso in black oil '"ART
STUDENT/DOING A DRAWING/OF A LION"(wish you'd
seen it)/78" × 72"/OIL AND TEMPERA ON/BOARD.'
Exhibited: Marlborough New London Gallery,
London, 1965, Cat 12. Bonython Art Gallery,
Adelaide and Sydney, 1966, Cat 3. Australian
Galleries, Melbourne, 1966, Cat 1
Literature: Hughes 1965 (illus). Hayes and Hersey,
Australian Style, Sydney: Paul Hamlyn, 1970,
p.37 (illus)
Collection: Private collection, Melbourne

Plate 52
PLATYPUS 1965
Perspex, platypus, encaustic, wax, wood and oil,
95.2 × 45.7 × 19 cm; not signed, not dated
Exhibited: Marlborough New London Gallery,
London, 1965, Cat 16
Collection: Private collection, Sydney

Plate 53
THE BOXING MATCH 1965
Oil on canvas, 214.6 × 240.1 cm
Exhibited: Marlborough New London Gallery,
London, 1965 (illus on cover but not catalogued).
'The Australian Painters', touring exhibition of the
United States 1967–1970, Cat 77. 'Australian
Paintings of the 1960s: Selections from the Mertz
collection' Huntington Art Gallery, The University
of Texas at Austin, Austin, Texas, USA, 30 May–21
August 1984. 'Legends and Landscapes in
Australian Art', Sarah Campbell Blaffer Gallery,
The University of Houston, Texas, USA
Literature: Luck 1966, p.67 (illus)
Collection: Archer M. Huntington Art Gallery,
The University of Texas at Austin, Gift of the Mertz
Art Fund 1972

Plate 54
DRAWING 1965 … (A SPLIT SECOND) 1965
Also titled *The Boxing Match*
Pencil, charcoal, collage, linseed oil, wash on
paper on board, 126 × 122 cm; signed and dated
l.c. in ink Whiteley/1–5/Aug–65'/, signed verso in
charcoal 'Brett Whiteley'
Inscriptions: l.c. in black ink 'Sugar Ray Robinson +
Randy Turpin – 10:25pm July 10th 1951 Earls court
London'. Inscribed verso in charcoal 'DRAWING
1965' … (A SPLIT SECOND)/charcoal on paper,/50" ×
48"/lent by MARLBOROUGH FINE ART LIMITED'
Collection: Private collection, Sydney

Plate 55
THE CRICKET MATCH 1964
Oil, charcoal, material, PVA, string on canvas,
212.3 × 234.6 cm; signed l.l in charcoal
'whiteley'/signed and dated verso
Inscriptions: verso in charcoal '"THE CRICKET
MATCH"' 1964/84 1/2" × 94"/OIL, TEMPERA +
COLLAGE/Brett Whiteley'
Exhibited: Bonython Gallery, Adelaide and Sydney,
1966, Cat 23
Literature: Lynn 1966. McGrath 1979, pp.16–17.
Terry 1984
Provenance: Sandra McGrath Collection.
'Australian, European and American Painters
etc.', William S. Ellenden Art Auctioneers,
November 1975
Collection: Private collection, Sydney

Plate 56
THE BEACH 1966
Oil, tempera, enamel, cloth, ink, PVA, shell, sand,
collage, Australian currency one pound note,
pencil and photographs on board, 195.6 × 243.8
cm; signed l.c. in black oil 'Whiteley', not dated
Exhibited: Australian Galleries, Melbourne, 1966,
Cat 19. Bonython Gallery, Sydney, 1968, Cat 6.
NSW House London, 1977. 'The Boxer *Collection:*
The Sydney Alternative', Nolan Gallery, Tharwa,
ACT, 1982, Cat 15
Literature: McGrath 1967, p.369 (illus). Horton
1969, p.236. Thomas 1977, p.39. McGrath 1979,
p.70. Sturgeon 1987, p.47 (illus)

Collection: Alan Boxer, Canberra

Plate 57
WENDY 1965
Charcoal on paper, 56 × 76.4 cm; signed and dated
l.r. in pencil '1965 brett Whiteley'
Inscriptions: l.r. in pencil 'wendy'
Collection: Private collection, Sydney

Plate 58
STUDY FOR THE BEACH 1965
Pencil on paper, 45.5 × 54 cm; stamped with
artist's monogram l.r. in black ink, dated l.r. in
black ink 'December/1965'
Inscriptions: l.r. in black ink: 'study for "The
Beach"/December/1965'
Exhibited: Bonython Art Gallery, Sydney, 1974, Cat
13. Marlborough Prints and Drawings Gallery,
New York, 1975, Cat 26. Robin Gibson Gallery,
Sydney, 1985, Cat 15. Artist's Studio, Circular
Quay, Sydney, 1981, not catalogued, p.15 (illus)
Literature: McGrath 1979, p.42 (illus)
Collection: Private collection, Sydney

Plate 59
HEADACHE 1965–66
Oil, collage, 'Bex' packets, rear-view mirror, ink,
material, PVA, sand, plaster and linseed oil on
board, 95.3 × 76.2 × 12.7 cm; signed and dated
verso in black oil '1965–66/Brett Whiteley'
Inscriptions: verso in black oil ''HEADACHE'/
1965–66/37 1/4" × 30 1/4"/OIL, TEMPERA/BEX/
MIRROR/Brett Whiteley'
Exhibited: Australian Galleries, Melbourne, 1966,
Cat 14. Bonython Gallery, Sydney, 1968, Cat 1
Literature: Art and Australia1966, p.177 (illus)
Collection: Robin Gibson Gallery

Plate 60
THE BEACH II 1966
Oil, collage, ink, plaster, hessian, Australian
currency one-pound note, 'Bex' packets, cotton
t-shirt on board, 141 × 106 cm; signed and dated
verso in black oil 'brett whiteley 1966'
Inscriptions: verso in black oil '(SPLIT DAY DREAM)
"THE BEACH"/II/1966/Whale Beach/oil, tempera,
collage + photography/on ply/brett whiteley',
inscribed in charcoal verso 'found under the
house/at 31 Bent St Lindfield/Wendy's mother's
place/painting discarded in 1966/on return
to London'
Collection: Private collection, Sydney

Plate 61 (a)
SHARK (FEMALE) 1965
Fibreglass, plaster, maplewood, chrome and
shark's teeth, 86.4 × 177.8 cm; not signed,
not dated
Exhibited: Australian Galleries, Melbourne, 1966,
Cat 22. Bonython Art Gallery, Sydney, 1966, Cat 8
Literature: McGrath 1967, p.371 (illus). McGrath
1979, p.74 (illus). Gray 1986, p.223 (illus)
Collection: Private collection, Sydney

Plate 61 (b)
SHARK (MALE) 1966
Fibreglass, plaster, copper and maplewood, 193.1
× 71.1 cm; not signed, not dated
Exhibited: Australian Galleries, Melbourne, 1966,
Cat 21. Bonython Art Gallery, Sydney, 1966, Cat 7
Literature: McGrath 1979, p.74 (illus). Gray 1986,
p.223 (illus)
Collection: Private collection, Sydney

Plate 62
BONDI BEACH 1983
(Triptych) Oil and tempera with electricity on ply,
214 × 588 cm; signed and dated l.r. in black
'1983/brett whiteley'
Inscriptions: l.r. in black '"Bondi" 1983/brett
whiteley'
Exhibited: Australian Galleries, Melbourne,
1984, Cat 31
Collection: Private collection, Perth

Plate 63
THE BATHER 1981
Oil on canvas, 106 × 91.4 cm; signed l.r. in blue oil 'brett whiteley', not dated
Exhibited: The Artist's Studio, Circular Quay, Sydney, 1981, Cat 27.
Collection: Private collection, Sydney

Plate 64
BATHER ON THE SAND 1976
Oil on canvas, 120 × 90 cm; signed and dated l.l. in black oil 'Brett Whiteley 76'
Exhibited: Australian Galleries, Melbourne, 1976, Cat 30. The Artist's Studio, Circular Quay, Sydney, 1981, Cat 44. Australian Galleries, Melbourne, 1984, Cat 33
Literature: McGrath 1979, p.73.
Collection: Private collection, Melbourne.

Plate 65
AFTER THE SWIM TANGIER 1983–87
Oil, ink, glass eye, sunglasses and cotton t-shirt on board, 152 × 122 cm; signed and dated l.r. in black ink 'brett whiteley 86–87'
Inscriptions: l.r. in black ink 'After the swim Tangier'
Exhibited: 'Beaches', Museum of Modern Art at Heide, Heide, 1994–95
Collection: Private collection, Sydney

Plate 66
HER (5) 1978
Ink, oil, felt-tipped pen and collage on paper, 61.5 × 51 cm; signed and dated l.r. in pencil 'brett whiteley – 1978', stamped with artist's monogram l.r. in black ink
Exhibited: The Artist's Studio, Circular Quay, Sydney, 1981, Cat 31
Collection: Private collection, Sydney

Plate 67 (a)
HER 1975
Also titled *Bather I*
Mangrove wood and french polish, 243 cm high; not signed, not dated
Exhibited: Bonython Art Gallery, Sydney, 1975, Cat 33. Australian Galleries, Melbourne, 1976, Cat 25. Artist's Studio, Circular Quay, Sydney, 1981, Cat 12
Literature: McGrath 1979, p.211 (illus). Gray 1986, p.223 (illus)
Collection: Private collection, Sydney

Plate 67 (b)
HER 1975
Also titled *Arkie's Torso*
Mangrove wood and marble, 90 cm high; not signed, not dated
Exhibited: Bonython Art Gallery, Sydney, 1975, Cat 33. Australian Galleries, Melbourne, 1976, Cat 26. Artist's Studio, Circular Quay, Sydney, 1981, Cat 13
Literature: McGrath 1979, p.211 (illus). Gray 1986, p.223 (illus).
Collection: Private collection, Sydney

Plate 67 (c)
HER *c.* 1980
Also titled *Bather II*
Mangrove wood, charcoal, marble and oil, 225.6 cm high; not signed, not dated
Collection: Private collection, Sydney

Plate 67 (d)
HER *c.* 1980
Also titled *Bather*
Wood, 155.7 cm high; not signed, not dated
Collection: Private collection, Sydney

Plate 68 (a)
HER 1975
Mangrove wood and brass, 274.3 cm high; not signed, not dated
Exhibited: Bonython Art Gallery, Sydney, 1975, Cat 33. Australian Galleries, Melbourne, 1976, Cat

25. Artist's Studio, Circular Quay, Sydney, 1981, Cat 15
Literature: McGrath 1979, p.211 (illus)
Collection: Private collection, Melbourne

Plate 68 (b)
HER 1975
Mangrove wood and marble, 213.3 cm; not signed, not dated
Exhibited: Bonython Art Gallery, Sydney, 1975, Cat 33. Australian Galleries, Melbourne, 1976, Cat 25. Artist's Studio, Circular Quay, Sydney, 1981, Cat 14
Literature: McGrath 1979, p.211 (illus)
Collection: Private collection, Melbourne

Plate 69
STUDY FOR THE BEACH II 1965
Also titled *Preliminary Sketch for The Beach*
Charcoal and wash on paper, 56 × 76.4 cm; signed and dated l.r. in black ink 'brett whiteley 1965', stamped with artist's monogram l.r. in black ink
Inscriptions: l.r. in black ink 'study for "The Beach"'
Exhibited: Robin Gibson Gallery, Sydney 1985, Cat 34 (illus). 'Brett Whiteley–Lloyd Rees: On the Road to Berry', Museum of Modern Art at Heide and The Art Gallery of New South Wales, 1993, Cat 46
Collection: Private collection, Sydney

Plate 70
NUDE STUDY FOR LARGE WOOD CARVING 1975
Also titled *Preliminary Study for Wood Sculpture, Study and Large Wood Carving*
Wash, collage, charcoal on paper on board, 162 × 90 cm; signed and dated l.r. in black ink '5/75./Brett Whiteley', stamped with artist's monogram at l.r. in black ink.
Inscriptions: l.r. in black ink 'study for large wood carving/mangrove wood 60" high'
Exhibited: Bonython Art Gallery, Sydney, 1975, Cat 32. Australian Galleries, Melbourne, 1976, Cat 27. 'Brett Whiteley–Lloyd Rees: On The Road to Berry', Museum of Modern Art at Heide and The Art Gallery of New South Wales, 1993, Cat 75
Collection: Private collection, Melbourne

Plate 71
THE ORANGE NUDE 1981
Oil on canvas, 182 × 151.5 cm; signed l.l.c. in green 'brett whiteley', dated l.r. in white '81'
Exhibited: The Artist's Studio, Circular Quay, Sydney, 1981, Cat 37
Collection: Private collection, Sydney

Plate 72
FIDGETING WITH INFINITY 1966–67
Oil, collage, pencil, photographs and fibreglass on board, 244 × 382 cm; not signed, not dated
Inscriptions: label adhered verso 'Brett Whiteley (b 1939)/Fidgeting with Infinity/(triptych) for Piero/oils and mixed media on plywood/96 × 150 inches/Date 1966–67/,inscribed u.r. in black ink: '*Jesus said to them*/When you make the two one, and when you make the inner as the outer and the outer/as the inner and the above as the below and when you make the male and the female into/a single one so that the male will not be male and the female no the female, when you/make eyes in the place of an eye, and a hand in the place of a hand, and a foot in a/place of a foot, and an image in the place of an image, then shall you/enter the/kingdom./The Gospel according to Thomas'
Exhibited: Marlborough New London Gallery, London, 1967, Cat 16
Literature: McGrath 1979, pp.76–79. Harrisop 1967, p.154–6
Collection: Philip Bacon, Brisbane

Plate 73
ACHMID GETTING STONED *c.* 1964
Charcoal and ink on paper 62.8 × 56.2 cm; not

signed, not dated
Inscriptions: l.c. in black ink 'achmid getting stoned'/in pencil 'Tanger'
Collection: Private collection, Sydney

Plate 74
ARAB 1964
Charcoal, ink, oil and linseed oil on paper, 52.2 × 28 cm
Exhibited: Robin Gibson Gallery, Sydney, 1985, Cat 161
Collection: Private collection, Sydney

Plate 75
CALCUTTA 1966
(Triptych) Oil, collage, photographs, glass, gesso, pencil, cloth and plaster with detachable sculptural piece on board, 198 × 260 × 125 cm; signed and dated verso in black ink '1966/BRETT WHITELEY'
Inscriptions: verso in black ink 'CALCUTTA 1966/TRIPTYCH/78" × 102" × 50"
Exhibited: Marlborough New London Gallery, London, 1967, Cat 7. Gallery Ad Libitum, Belgium (date unknown)
Literature: McGrath 1979, pp.76–78
Provenance: 'Fine Australian Paintings', Sotheby's, Melbourne, 22–23 August 1994, Cat 155
Collection: Private collection, Brussels

Plate 76
TANGIER POSTCARD 1967
Gouache, ink, charcoal and collage on paper, 50.9 × 75.5 cm; not signed, not dated
Exhibited: Marlborough New London Gallery, London, 1967, Cat 4. Bonython Art Gallery, Sydney, 1968, Cat 11–16. 'Modern Australian Paintings', Bridget McDonnell Gallery, Melbourne, 1986, Cat 29
Literature: McGrath 1979, p.78 (illus)
Collection: Private collection, Melbourne

Plate 77
THE DEALER 1967
Oil, gouache, watercolour, ink, pencil, paper collage and glass eye on paper, 55.8 × 76.2 cm; not signed, not dated
Inscriptions: l.l. 'The Dealer'
Exhibited: Marlborough New London Gallery, London, 1967, Cat 4. Bonython Art Gallery, Sydney, 1968, Cat 11–16
Literature: McGrath 1979, p.79 (illus)
Collection: The Art Gallery of New South Wales

Plate 78
THE BUSH 1966
(Triptych) Oil, tempera, collage, hair, PVA, glass and plaster on board, 175 × 240 cm; signed verso in white paint 'Brett whiteley' (1st panel), dated verso '1966'
Inscriptions: u.r. (3rd panel) in black ink 'what perfumes, what evils, be below all this green/ singing ringing lazy: unpredictable unshaved shrapnel seen;/but go well beneath – beyond any death adder scheme/– There! Stillness? Seething complete/divided + kindled on uranium heat, that can't/ask reason gently to kiss flesh to cheat.' Inscribed verso in white paint 'THE BUSH/1966/ TRIPTYCH/69" × 95"/Brett Whiteley
Exhibited: Australian Galleries, Melbourne, 1966, Cat 75. Bonython Gallery, Sydney, 1968, Cat 2
Literature: McGrath 1967, p.368–73 (illus)
Collection: New South Wales Government

Plate 79
NEW YORK 2 (FIRST SENSATION OF NEW YORK CITY) 1968
Oil, collage, charcoal, ink, US currency coin and electric light on board, 70 × 90.6 cm (sight); signed (later) l.c. in pencil 'brett', dated l.r. in ink 'Jan 68'
Inscriptions: l.r. in ink 'First Sensation of New York City'
Exhibited: Marlborough–Gerson Gallery, New

York, 1968, Cat 9. 'America As We See It', Hogarth Gallery, Sydney, June 1976
Collection: Private collection, Sydney

Plate 80 a–f
THE AMERICAN DREAM 1968–69
Oil, tempera, collage, photography and objects on 18 wood panels, 244 × 2196 cm; signed, dated and inscribed on statement concerning the work:
'Oil, tempera, photography and objects on eighteen plywood panels, ninety-six by 864 inches. Painted between July 1968 and June, 1969 in New York City.
'Statement concerning the work: 'Arrived in New York, November 1967 for a two-year Harkness Fellowship. The first year was spent producing an exhibition of easel paintings for Marlborough Fine Art Ltd. By the second year I determined myself to produce a monumental work of art that would summarise the sensation of impending the necessity for America to own up, analyse and straighten out the immense and immediately seeable madness that seemed to run through most facets of American life – of little use for continuing. There appeared in much behaviour, a stark sort of unnecessary cerebral violence, to which I was completely unaccustomed, and which I held in considerable fear.
'As the work began I still considered myself an outsider, a white Asian staying in America for a short time, capable of being able to objectify the separation I felt from needing to behave as most Americans did. But as the work progressed I realised that anyone who steps foot off a plane in New York instantly becomes an American and cannot remain indifferent or aloof by presuming he belongs elsewhere.
'The existential experiment was so hungry that one quickly became possessed with a struggle to reconcile the forces of good and evil just as possessively as most Americans were doing. They said it was no use talking about the abstraction of a whole nation, everyone had to do it on their own. So as the work progressed it developed into a struggle within myself to own up, analyse and straighten out . . .
'But the further I went the more difficult it became. The more American I felt the more painful and dual nature of everything became. All hope of peace seemed to break apart with the evening television news. There seemed no sign of reconciliation between old and young, black and white, hip and square, etc. And the eyes of the riot squads bespoke of everything one had ever ima-gined of human collapse. Day after day the ache and panic edged up a little – for the Madness was now itself upon me, and I, who had benignly dared to point to America that she was sick and getting everyone else sick, had fallen quick victim without even so much as a misty vision for any solution beyond dreaming of nature and a simpler life.
'So I drank more and smoked more, hoping that if I felt Hell and could report it up, that would be of benefit, and turn something of the tide . . . But alas I just got unhappier and unhealthier until physical and mental fatigue forced me in July 1969 to abandon the work and fly to Fiji to live.
'This painting is a record of a struggle and my inability to resolve it; it is an admittance of failure. 'Of course romantics are only ever concerned with Beauty.'
Exhibited: Bonython Art Gallery, Sydney, 1970. 'Australian Painting 1955–1970', Art Gallery of Western Australia, 2–27 March 1977. 'Opening Exhibition–works from the permanent collection', Art Gallery of Western Australia, 2 October–January 1980. 'Acquisitions 1977–80', Art Gallery of Western Australia, 31 January–15 March 1981. 'Regions, Beaches Interiors', Art Gallery of Western Australia, 16 November–16 March, 1986

Literature: McGrath 1979, pp.85–93 (illus). Fry 1984, p.58–63 (illus). Broinowski 1992, p.116 (illus)
Collection: Art Gallery of Western Australia

Plate 81
GAUGUIN 1968
Oil, photograph and poison on board, 152.4 × 264.1 × 5.1 cm; signed and dated l.r. in black ink 'Brett Whiteley 1968. N.Y.'
Inscriptions: l.r. in black ink 'portrait of Paul Gauguin on the eve of his attempted suicide. Tahiti.'
Exhibited: Marlborough–Gerson Gallery, 1968, Cat 4
Literature: McGrath 1979, p.86
Collection: Private collection, New York

Plate 82
FIJI HEAD – TO A CREOLE LADY 1969
Charcoal, pen and ink and collage on paper, 56.5 × 44.3 cm; not signed, not dated
Inscriptions: in ink l.c. 'To a Creole Lady/in that perfumed land fonded [sic] by the sun, I knew – beneath a canopy of trees aglow with crimson and palms from which languor/pours upon your eyes – a Creole lady whose charms are unknown to the world. Her complexion is pale + warm;/that dark enchantress has, in the poise of her head poses of aristocratic grace, tall + slender as she walks like a huntress, her/smile is peaceful her eyes assured. Should you go Lady, to the true home of fame, to the banks of the/Seine or of the Verdant Loire, your beauty might well grace some ancient manor-house,/and in many a shady arbour, you would inspire a thousand sonnets in the hearts of poets, whom your colde eyes/would make more submissive than your black slaves./1848 published 1845 c. Baudelaire translated F. Scarte./*To Vilimaina* Of course its you! a few miles + a whisper of history between spiritual faminilies is nothing/but maybe that is something you will never know, but please, please flower your promise./..Your reluctance.'
Exhibited: 'Contemporary Australian Drawing', Art Gallery of Western Australia, Queensland Art Gallery, The Art Gallery of New South Wales, 1978, Cat 93
Literature: Klepac 1978, p.109 (illus)
Collection: Artbank

Plate 83
THE GREEN MOUNTAIN (FIJI) 1969
Also titled *The Most Beautiful Mountain Fiji*
Oil and collage on board, 137 × 122 cm; signed and dated in black ink on a piece of paper '1969 Fiji/Brett Whiteley'
Inscriptions: verso in black ink on a piece of paper 'the green mountain/1969 Fiji/Brett Whiteley'
Exhibited: Bonython Art Gallery, Sydney, 1970. 'Three Years On: A Selection of Acquisitions 1978–81', exhibition cat. The Art Gallery of New South Wales, 15 October–1 December 1981, Cat 44
Literature: McGrath 1979, p.24. Hayes and Gervasoni 1992, p.4. Hawley 1993, p.44. Pearce 1989, p.144
Collection: The Art Gallery of New South Wales, gift of Patrick White, 1979.

Plate 84
THE JACARANDA TREE (ON SYDNEY HARBOUR) 1977
Oil on canvas, 208 × 456 cm; signed l.c. in white oil 'brett Whiteley 1977', not dated
Exhibited: 'Archibald, Wynne and Sulman' exhibition, The Art Gallery of New South Wales, 1977, awarded Wynne Prize. S. H. Ervin Gallery, Sydney, 'Touring Retrospective of Wynne Prize Winners', 1986–87. 'The Art Of Knitting', Westpac Galleries, Melbourne, 22 May–2 June 1991
Literature: Terry 1984, p.178
Provenance: 'A Major Auction of Australian and European Paintings', Geoff K Gray, Sydney, 8 March 1982, Cat 100

Collection: The Holmes à Court Collection, courtesy of Heytesbury Holdings

Plate 85
BIG ORANGE (SUNSET) 1974
Oil on board, 244 × 305.5 cm; not signed not dated
Exhibited: Australian Galleries, Melbourne, 1974, Cat 1. 'Sydney Harbour', S. H. Ervin Gallery, Sydney, 1979
Literature: Bonython and Lynn 1976. McGrath, 1979, p.171. McGrath *Sydney Harbour*, 1979, p.100
Collection: The Art Gallery of New South Wales, Gift of Patrick White, 1975

Plate 86
THE BALCONY 2 1975
Oil on canvas, 203.5 × 364.5 cm; signed and dated l.l. 'Brett Whiteley 1975'
Exhibited: Bonython Art Gallery, Sydney, 1975. The Art Gallery of New South Wales, 1981, Cat 45
Literature: Art and Australia, 1976, p.223. 'Three Years On: A Selection of Acquisitions 1978–1981', exhibition cat. The Art Gallery of New South Wales, 15 October–1 December 1981, p.25. Davenport and Rees 1991. Ash 1993, p.97
Provenance: Collection of Governor General Sir John Kerr 1975. Collection of George Grunhut 1980. Blue Boy Art Gallery, Melbourne, 1981
Collection: The Art Gallery of New South Wales

Plate 87
GREY HARBOUR *c.* 1978
Oil and charcoal on canvas, 86.5 × 85.5 cm; not signed, not dated
Collection: Private collection, Sydney

Plate 88
LAVENDER BAY IN THE RAIN 1981
Oil, PVA and perspex on canvas on board, 89.5 × 89 cm (sight); signed and dated l.l. in black ink 'brett whiteley 81'
Inscriptions: l.l. in black ink 'to watch or see in secret;/to spy, to peep, to pry into/the rain/Lavender Bay'
Collection: Private collection, Sydney

Plate 89
LAVENDER BAY IN THE RAIN 1974
Oil on perspex, string, wax on board, and perspex, 120.5 × 95 cm (sight); stamped with artist's monogram l.r. in black ink, signed and dated verso in pencil '1974' in black oil 'brett Whiteley'
Inscriptions: verso in pencil 'LAVENDER BAY IN THE RAIN' 1974/4' × 3'2'/OIL/' inscribed in oil 'brett whiteley'
Exhibited: Australian Galleries, Melbourne, 1974, Cat 18
Literature: McGrath 1979, p.173 (illus)
Collection: Private collection, Sydney. Courtesy of Martin Browne Fine Art

Plate 90
BLUE NAKED STUDIO 1981
(Diptych) Oil, collage, hair, glass eye, charcoal and ink on board, 190.9 × 490.4 cm; signed l.r. in white oil 'brett whiteley', dated l.c. in black ink '1981'
Inscriptions: inscribed l.l. in black ' "the naked studio" 1981/circular Quay Sydney'
Exhibited: The Artist's Studio, Circular Quay, 1981, Cat 1
Collection: Private collection, Sydney

Plate 91
STILL LIFE WITH THREE LEMONS 1976
Oil on canvas, 51 × 61 cm; not signed, not dated
Exhibited: Australian Galleries, Melbourne, 1976, Cat 6
Collection: Richard and Arija Austin, Queensland

Plate 92
HENRI'S ARMCHAIR 1974–75
Oil, ink and charcoal on canvas, 195 × 302 cm; signed and dated verso in black oil 'brett whiteley 12/March/75'
Inscriptions: verso in black oil ' "HENRI'S

ARMCHAIR"/(SEPT–OCT NOV–DEC) 1974/OIL ON CANVAS,/BRETT WHITELEY/TO Clive Evatt/(21 March) 75'
Exhibited: Bonython Art Gallery, Sydney, 1975, Cat 1
Literature: McGrath 1979, p.168–69 (illus)
Collection: Hogarth Galleries, Sydney

Plate 93
INTERIOR WITH TIME PAST 1976
Oil, charcoal and ink on canvas, 182 × 200 cm; signed and dated l.r. in blue oil 'Brett Whiteley '76'
Inscriptions: verso in charcoal ' "Interior with time past" 1976/Brett Whiteley/182 × 200 oil on canvas'. Inscribed l.r. in black ink 'GELEGEN-HEITSARBEIT/work performed as the occasion arose/constant curiousness, autographs the last end/of cannibalism/authentic magic no compass diviners/TRUTH AND PARODOX, to be ignorantly ironized, who/is perforce himself and can no more be another/than I can/E = MC^2/from now on space by itself, and time by itself/are destined to sink completely into shadows, and/only a kind of union of both to refrain an/independent existance [sic]. First do not try to/visualise four-dimensional space-time. It/is completely impossible. Not even Einstein/could do it/Euclids snake, breathless attention and/the Albino rainbow administered intravenously/six times a day are responsible for this painting. /no blame/Brett Whiteley 1976'
Exhibited: Australian Galleries, Melbourne, 1976, Cat 2. Fischer Fine Art, London, 1977, Cat 1
Literature: McGrath 1979, pp.178–79
Collection: National Gallery of Australia

Plate 94 (a)
CRUCIFIXION *c.* 1979
Ceramic vase, 45.8 cm high; not signed, not dated (thrown by Derek Smith)
Inscriptions: embossed on base 'D.S/DEREK SMITH/BACKFRIARS/POTTERY'
Exhibited: Artist's Studio, Circular Quay, Sydney, 1981, Cat 60
Collection: Private collection, Sydney

Plate 94 (b)
NUDE *c.* 1979
Ceramic plate, 34 cm diameter; not signed, not dated (thrown by John Kimpton Dellow)
Collection: Private collection, Sydney

Plate 94 (c)
BIG BLUE LEAVES *c.* 1979
Ceramic vase, 48 cm high; not signed, not dated (thrown by John Kimpton Dellow)
Collection: Private collection, Sydney

Plate 94 (d)
HIPPO *c.* 1979
Ceramic vase, 16.5 cm high; not signed, not dated (thrown by Derek Smith)
Exhibited: David Reid's Gallery, Sydney, 1981, Cat 71
Collection: Private collection, Sydney

Plate 94 (e)
MAGNOLIA *c.* 1979
Ceramic vase, 40 cm; not signed, not dated (thrown by John Kimpton Dellow)
Collection: Private collection, Sydney

Plate 95
STILL LIFE WITH MEAT 1975–76
Synthetic polymer paint, shell, bone, artificial eye on board, 130.2 × 207.7 cm; signed and dated l.r. in oil 'Brett Whiteley 75–76'
Inscriptions: verso u.c.r in thin black paint 'STILL LIFE WITH MEAT', inscribed l.c.r in black felt-tip upside down 'preliminary sketch/made in New York April/1975'. Inscribed l.r. in black felt-tip '1975/brett whiteley'. Inscribed l.r. in black felt-tip scored out with wash of thin black paint 'SCULPTURAL PORTRAIT OF/SUZI MENDERFARMAY/'
Collection: The Art Gallery of New South Wales

Plate 96
STILL LIFE DRAWING WITH MILK BOTTLE AND AVOCADO 1960s
Charcoal on paper, 37.8 × 55.7 cm; not signed, not dated
Collection: Private collection, Sydney

Plate 97
STILL LIFE WITH PEE-WEE'S EGG 1976
Oil on canvas, 88 × 61 cm; signed and dated l.r. in pen and ink 'Brett Whiteley/1976'
Inscriptions: l.r. in pen and ink 'Still Life with Pee Wee's Egg 1976'
Exhibited: Australian Galleries, Melbourne, 1976, Cat 11
Literature: McGrath 1979, p.203 (illus)
Collection: Private collection, Melbourne

Plate 98
STILL LIFE WITH MAGNOLIA 1980–82
Oil and collage on canvas, 120 × 164 cm; signed and dated l.l. 'brett whiteley 80–82'
Exhibited: '20th Century Australian and New Zealand Painting', Martin Brown Fine Art, Sydney, November, 1993, Cat 64
Collection: Private collection, Sydney

Plate 99
STILL LIFE WITH CHERRIES 1975–76
Oil on board, 45 × 57 cm
Literature: McGrath 1979, p.201 (illus)
Collection: Philip Bacon, Brisbane

Plate 100
MAGNOLIA 1977–78
Oil on board, 76.2 × 121.9 cm; signed and dated l.r. '1977–78 brett whiteley'
Literature: McGrath 1979, p.202 (illus)
Collection: Private collection, Sydney. Courtesy of Martin Browne Fine Art

Plate 101
PURITY AS A PROBLEM (IN RELATION TO STILL LIFE PAINTING) 1977–78
Oil on canvas, 124 × 225 cm; signed and dated l.l. in brown oil 'brett whiteley 77–78'
Inscriptions: u.l. 'Still life …' (rest of inscription obscured)
Collection: Private collection, Melbourne

Plate 102
SKETCH FOR THE RED AND GREEN OF THE SUBURBS 1979
Oil on board, 30 × 30 cm; signed and dated verso in black oil
Inscriptions: verso in black oil 'test to see if there/is any possibility of/exploring the half closed/eyes technique of De Stael'
Collection: Private collection, Sydney

Plate 103
RED ROOFS WITH PALM TREE *c.* 1980
Oil on canvas, mounted on board, 40 × 50 cm; signed verso in black 'brett whiteley', not dated
Inscriptions: verso in black ink 'RED ROOFS/WITH PALM TREE'
Collection: Private collection, Sydney

Plate 104
SOUTH COAST AFTER THE RAIN 1984
Oil and collage on canvas, 137 × 122 cm; signed u.l. in black ink 'Brett Whiteley'
Inscriptions: l.r. in black ink 'The South Coast, June 1984'
Exhibited: 'Archibald, Wynne and Sulman' exhibition, The Art Gallery of New South Wales, 1984, awarded Wynne Prize
Collection: Private collection, Melbourne

Plate 105
SELF PORTRAIT IN THE STUDIO 1976
Oil, collage, hair on canvas, 200.5 × 259 cm; signed and dated l.r. in black ink 'brett Whiteley/1975–76'
Inscriptions: verso l.r. of a painting within composition 'brett Whiteley/1975–76/Lavender Bay/Studio'. Inscribed verso u.c. in black felt-ti p "SELF PORTRAIT IN THE STUDIO"/(THE EASTER PURPOSE TRADITION)/brett Whiteley/1975–76/Lavender Bay/'
Exhibited: 'Archibald, Wynne and Sulman' exhibition, The Art Gallery of New South Wales, awarded Archibald Prize 1976. 'Archibald Retrospective Exhibition', S. H. Ervin Gallery, Sydney, 1985
Literature: McGrath 1979, pp.204–5 (illus). Terry 1984, p.177. Hergenhan 1992. McGrath 1992. Tesoriero and Nilson 1993, p.23. Alland and Darby 1991, p.8
Collection: The Art Gallery of New South Wales

Plate 106
REMEMBERING LAO TSE (SHAVING OFF A SECOND) 1967
Pencil, pen and ink on paper, 66.4 × 56.2 cm; not signed, dated u.l. in ink '7/4/67'
Inscriptions: u.l. in ink 'Remembering Laotse …/He who is to be made to dwindle (in power)/Must First be cause to expand/He who is to be weakened/must first be made strong/He who is to be laid low/Must first be exalted to power/He who is to be taken away from/must first be given/This is the subtle light./Gentleness overcomes strength/Fish should be left on the deep pool/and sharp weapons of state should/be left where none can see them!!!'
Exhibited: Marlborough New London Gallery, London, 1967, Cat 12. Bonython Gallery, Sydney, 1968, Cat 17
Literature: McGrath 1979, p.100 (illus)
Collection: Ballarat Fine Art Gallery, Gift of Jerry van Beek and Barry Stern, 1968

Plate 107
NOT I – ME 1967
Oil and mixed media on board with detachable sculptural arm, 185.4 × 152.4 × 119.4 cm; signed and dated verso in black oil '1967/Brett Whiteley'
Inscriptions: verso in black oil 'NOT I–ME'
Exhibited: Marlborough New London Gallery, London, 1967, Cat 13. Gallery Ad Libitum, Belgium
Literature: Burr 1967, pp.231–32 (illus). Harrisop 1967, pp.154–56
Collection: Private collection, Melbourne

Plate 108
SELF-PORTRAIT AFTER THREE BOTTLES OF WINE 1971
Oil and ink on board, 203.5 × 76 cm; not signed, dated l.r. in black ink '12/2/71'
Inscriptions: l.r. in black ink '17/2/71 '"Self portrait in exactly/the spirit in which/it was drawn"'. Inscribed l.r. with red Chinese calligraphy stamp in red ink and flower stamp l.r. in red ink
Exhibited: Bonython Art Gallery, Sydney, 1972, Cat 31. Australian Galleries, Melbourne, 1972, Cat 31. Bonython Gallery, Sydney, 1974, Cat 20. Robin Gibson Gallery, Sydney, 1985, Cat 50
Literature: McGrath 1979, pp.105 and 226 (illus) Krausmann 1975–76
Collection: New South Wales Government

Plate 109
PAGE OF SELF-PORTRAITS 1971
Pen and ink on rice paper, 31.5 × 30 cm (irregular); not signed, dated l.r. in black ink '28/7/71'
Exhibited: Marlborough Prints and Drawings Gallery, New York, 1975, Cat 8. Fischer Fine Art, London, 1977, Cat 17. 'Brett Whiteley–Lloyd Rees: On the Road to Berry', Museum of Modern Art at Heide and The Art Gallery of New South Wales, 1993, Cat 50
Collection: Private collection, Sydney

Plate 110
SELF-PORTRAIT WITH BEARD 1972
Brush and ink on rice paper on card, 88 × 62.5 cm (sight); signed and dated verso u.l. in black ink

'Brett Whiteley 1972', stamped with artist's monogram stamp l.r. in red ink and u.l. in black ink
Exhibited: Robin Gibson Gallery, 1985, Cat 65 'Brett Whiteley–Lloyd Rees: On the Road to Berry', Museum of Modern Art at Heide and The Art Gallery of New South Wales, 1993, Cat 53
Collection: Private collection, Sydney

Plate 111
SELF-PORTRAIT DRAWING CALLIGRAPHICALLY 1975
Brush and ink on brown paper, 80.5 × 53.5 cm; signed l.r. in pencil 'brett whiteley', stamped with artist's monogram u.r. and l.r. in red ink, dated u.r. in pencil '16/April/75'
Inscriptions: l.r. in black ink 'Self-portrait drawing calligraphically'
Exhibited: Australian Galleries, Melbourne, 1976, Cat 24. Fischer Fine Art, London, 1977, Cat 45
Literature: Broinowski 1992, p.149
Collection: Private collection, Sydney

Plate 112
TASMANIAN DEVIL 1984
Pen and ink and gouache on paper, 41.5 × 59.4 cm; signed and dated l.r. in pencil 'brett whiteley/28/11/84', stamped with artist's monogram l.r. in black ink
Inscriptions: u.l. in black ink 'every time I visited the zoo in the sixties there was/a cement enclosure with a box at the end of it/containing one Tasmanian devil, who never put in an appearance. Six visits to the zoo + never a/sighting. I even took to hurling two bob pieces/at the box hoping that irritating it, it might/appear. Suddenly on the seventh visit, this strange/little black pig-dog came waddling out of his box/walked down the cement walkway to where I was/standing in amazed fascination … stopped dead/in front of me; and let out the most bitter, twisted/tirade of resentment + swearing; like an/undertipped Egyptian taxi driver/curdling noises too; turned without/waiting for any sort of reply,/+ waddled back to his box/ill tempered + lonely./I remember that the/reds inside his mouth/were as vivid as/a Monet sunset/This is our little/south-sea hyena/one of the/damned!'
Exhibited: Robin Gibson Gallery, Sydney, 1985, Cat 58
Collection: Private collection, Sydney

Plate 113
SACRED BABOON 1975
Ink, woodstain, watercolour and collage on cardboard, 81 × 67 cm; not signed, not dated
Inscriptions: verso u.l. in pencil '33', u.r. '8', centre 'C', l.r. '19434'
Exhibited: Marlborough Prints and Drawings Gallery, New York, 1975, Cat 33. Fischer Fine Art, London, 1977, Cat 37. Australian Galleries, Melbourne, 1978, Cat 30
Literature: McGrath 1979, p.220 (illus)
Collection: National Gallery of Victoria

Plate 114
ART, LIFE AND THE OTHER THING 1978
(Triptych) Oil, glass eye, hair, pen and ink on cardboard, plaster, photography, dried PVA, cigarette butts, and hypodermic syringe on board, 90.4 × 77.2 cm, 230 × 122 cm, 31.1 × 31.1cm; signed and dated in black ink l.r. 'brett Whiteley 1978', signed verso in black oil on masking tape 'BRETT WHITELEY'
Inscriptions: u.r. in black ink 'rage/rage/against the dying of the light/DYLAN THOMAS'. Inscribed 2nd panel on verso on paper 'hanging instruction for Art Life and The Other Thing'
Exhibited: 'Archibald, Wynne and Sulman', The Art Gallery of New South Wales, 1978, awarded Archibald Prize. Greenhill Galleries, Perth, 1987, not catalogued

Literature: Waldmann 1982, pp.213–36. Hunt 1994.
Collection: New South Wales Government

Plate 115
GETTING QUITE CLOSE 1982
Colour photograph, oil, collage, masking tape and card on board, 163 × 121 cm; signed and dated l.r. in brown ink 'brett Whiteley 1982', stamped with artist's monogram on paper l.r. in red ink
Inscriptions: l.r. in brown ink 'Aries?/Vincents eyes at 13/brett whiteley 1982'
Exhibited: 'Another Way of Looking at Vincent Van Gogh', The Art Gallery of New South Wales, 1983
Literature: Whiteley 1983
Collection: Private collection, Sydney

Plate 116
VINCENT 1968
Oil, ink, mirror and razor on board, 220.9 × 164.4 × 38.1 cm; signed and dated l.r. in red oil 'Brett 68'
Exhibited: Marlborough–Gerson Gallery, New York, 1968 Cat 3. The Art Gallery of New South Wales, 1983, Cat 5
Literature: Whiteley 1983, (illus, unpaginated)
Provenance: 'Australian Paintings, Drawings Watercolours and Sculpture', Christie's Sydney, 6 and 7 December 1994
Collection: Marlborough Fine Art, London

Plate 117
REMBRANDT 1971–92
Alternatively titled 'Concerning whats Time and whats Real or all that stuff about Rembrandt being Lonely at the end is bullshit'
Oil and fibreglass on board, 136 × 125 × 11 cm; signed verso in charcoal 'brett whiteley'
Inscriptions: verso u.l. in pencil 'as I work on this/painting once a year/took photograph on Mar 6 1982/and discussed the/presentment of the/possibility of going/blind in right eye.' u.r. in pencil 'started 1971/have re worked/it every year since then'. u.r. in charcoal '(SELF PORTRAIT/declared finished/upon my death)'. u.r. in orange felt tip pen 'THIS PAINTING WAS/BEGUN IN 1971. IT/IS WORK IN PROGRESS/AS I GET OLDER I WILL CHANGE IT'. u.r. in charcoal 'TO DISCOVER THE SELF/THROUGH SOME ONE ELSE/EVERY YEAR OR FEW YEARS/AS I AGE I WILL AGE THIS/I HOPE TO DISCOVER WHO/REMBRANDT WAS BY THE/EXPERIENCE OF PROJECTION/BY THE EXPERIENCE OF/PAINTING THIS PICTURE/OFF + ON FOR THE REST/OF MY LIFE, I HOPE TO/DISCOVER WHO I AM/+ SHOW IT/brett whiteley'. u.l. in charcoal 'CONCERNING WHATS REAL,/AND WHATS TIME, PART, 3/1970/105" high 48 1/2 WIDE 4 1/2 DEEP/Brett Whiteley/alternate title …/All that stuff about Rembrandt being lonely/at the end, is bullshit./signed ../Brett Whiteley.'
Exhibited: Bonython Gallery, Sydney, 1972, Cat 7
Collection: Private collection, Sydney

Plate 118
SELF-PORTRAIT AFTER HAIRCUT 1976
Pen and ink and hair on paper, 100 × 76 cm; signed l.r. in pencil 'brett whiteley'
Inscriptions: l.r. in pencil 'Self portrait after a haircut at 36'
Exhibited: Australian Galleries, Melbourne, 1976, Cat 22
Literature: McGrath 1979, p.93 (illus). Lynn 1976
Collection: Private collection, Melbourne

Plate 119
THE BLOSSOM TREE 1971–82
Oil, silk flowers, branch, wood, canvas, nails and electricity on board, 186 × 194.5 × 25.6 cm; signed and dated verso in black oil '1970/Brett Whiteley'
Inscriptions: verso in black oil 'PLEASE HANDLE WITH EXTREME CARE/– MUCH OF THE PAINT SURFACE WILL TAKE/MONTHS TO THROUGHLY [sic] DRY/"CONCERNING WHATS REAL, AND WHATS TIME. PART ONE"/1970/72. 76" × 5"/Brett Whiteley/START/When Vincent/arrived in Arles/the blossoms/came out/IN CASES OF THIS/GLOBE BEING LOST/OR BROKEN REPLACE/WITH OSRAM 15a 240 – 260V

Exhibited: 'Another Way of Looking at Vincent Van Gogh', The Art Gallery of New South Wales, 1983. Australian Galleries, Melbourne, 1984, Cat 28 Greenhill Galleries, Perth, 1984, Cat 28. Greenhill Galleries, Perth, 1987, Cat 18.
Literature: Whiteley 1983, (illus, unpaginated)
Collection: Private collection, Sydney

Plate 120
THE NIGHT CAFE 1972
Oil on board, 121.5 × 143.5 cm; signed l.r. in red 'brett whiteley', signed verso in felt-tip pen 'brett whiteley'
Inscriptions: verso in felt-tip pen '"THE NIGHT CAFE/OR THE VIRUS INN"/1971–72/OIL ON PLY
Exhibited: 'Another Way of Looking at Vincent Van Gogh', The Art Gallery of New South Wales, 1983. Greenhill Galleries, Perth, 1987, Cat 20
Literature: Whiteley 1983 (illus, unpaginated)
Collection: New South Wales Government

Plate 121
THEBE'S REVENGE 1973–82
Oil and collage on board, 203 × 122 cm
Exhibited: Australian Galleries, Melbourne, 1973, Cat 10. Bonython Art Gallery, Sydney, 1974, Cat 90. 'Another Way of Looking at Vincent Van Gogh', The Art Gallery of New South Wales, 1983
Literature: McGrath 1979, p.150 (illus in reverse and before addition of moon). Whiteley 1983 (illus, unpaginated)
Provenance: 'Fine Australian Paintings', Sotheby's, Melbourne, 19 April 1993, lot 328
Collection: Private collection, Sydney

Plate 122
PORTRAIT OF ARTHUR RIMBAUD 1970–71
Oil, gold leaf, synthetic polymer paint, mummified lacquered cat's head and collage on six wooden panels, 203.3 × 518.1 cm; not signed, not dated
Exhibited: Bonython Gallery, Sydney, 1972, Cat 4. Australian Galleries, Melbourne, Cat 4
Literature: McGrath 1979, p.128–9 (illus). *Selected Works*, Queensland Art Gallery, Brisbane, 1982
Collection: Queensland Art Gallery

Plate 123
PORTRAIT OF BAUDELAIRE 1970
Oil, paper collage, plastic plum, twig, taxidermied bird, sand and polyfilla on five wood door panels, 203 × 432.5 cm; not signed, not dated
Inscriptions: c.r. in black ink 'THE SOARING MAD PLEASURE OF/OPIUM AND WINE – THE EMENSE [sic]/REMORSE./THE ACHING REGRET. THE EXCRUCIATING MISCALCULATION/ORIGINAL SIN?/DISGUST OF HUMAN WEAKNESS AND VICE./WRONG ACCUSATION OF OBSENITY [sic] AND IMMORTALITY/FOR BAUDELAIRE'S AIM – TO BRING MAN UP WITH A SHOCK IN FRONT/OF THEMSELVES. TO SEE THE REAL MOTIVES/IN THE HEART & SO THE RECOGNITION OF/THE UNEXPLAINED FORCE, EVIL/TO EXTRACT BEAUTY FROM EVIL./GREAT MEN ARE STUPID/the piercing soft, intelligibility to feel and fit rightness/to inevitability/INTENSITY/IS QUINTESSENCE!/NO DESIRE TO DEMONSTRATE/TO ASTONISH, TO AMUSE/OR TO PERSUADE/I TAKE IT UPON MYSELF/TO DENOUNCE IMITATIONS.'
Exhibited: Bonython Art Gallery, Sydney, 1970
Literature: McGrath 1979, pp.126–27 (illus). Lynn 1970, p.46. McCulloch 1970, pp.69–70 (illus)
Provenance: 'Fine Australian Paintings, Drawings and Watercolours', Sotheby's, 29 May, 1984, Melbourne, lot 157
Collection: Private collection, Melbourne

Plate 124
SAINT FRANCIS 1971
Ink on rice paper mounted on silk scroll on board, 93.5 × 63 cm (image) 162.5 × 80 cm (scroll); signed l.l. in black ink 'brett whiteley', stamped with artist's monogram l.l. in black ink
Exhibited: Bonython Art Gallery, Sydney, 1972. Australian Galleries, Melbourne, 1972, Cat 36
Collection: Private collection, Sydney

Plate 125 a-f
ALCHEMY 1972–73
Oil, gold leaf, ink, collage, rock, perspex, electricity, pencil, PVA, varnish, brain, earth, twig, taxidermied bird, nest, egg, feathers, cicada, bone, dentures, rubber and metal sink plug, pins, shell and glass eye on eighteen wood panels, 203 × 1615 cm; not signed, not dated
Inscriptions: c.in black ink (panel 1) 'For the poet is a light + winged and holy thing,/and there is no invention in him until he has been/inspired and is out of his senses, and the mind/is no longer in him; when he has not attained/to this state, he is powerless and is unable to/utter his oracles/Plato/1. The way that can be spoken of/Is not the constant way;/Alchemy/the Grand work/to bring together all the previous/TRANSMUTATION/or God?/A lot of the time the experience cannot be expressed by merely discribing [sic] one single absolute image,/for one image cannot hold it. Only by evoking a chain of images, as in a dream, does one/approximate the experience. A single flash of understanding with each grouping or 'chapter' of /forms, is what is expected from the viewer. This elliptical + heretic style of painting allows/for infinite freedom —— for both of us. But to lose the place, or stumble, all is lost, the/picture is meaningless. The thread is the Transmutation./The fine art of painting, which is the bastard of alchemy, always has been and always will be,/a game. The rules of the game are quite simple: in a given arena, on as many psychic/fronts as the talent allows, one must visually describe, the centre of the meaning of existense [sic]'
Exhibited: Bonython Art Gallery, Sydney, 1972–3, show not catalogued
Literature: Thomas (2) 1972. Adams 1973. Borlase 1973. Thomas 1973. Rawlinson 1973. Lynn 1976. McGrath 1978. McGrath 1979, pp.143–9 (illus)
Collection: New South Wales Government

Plate 126
PORTRAIT OF WENDY 1984
Oil, material, pencil, charcoal, pen and ink on paper on canvas, 150 × 212 cm; signed and dated l.l.c. in pencil 'Brett Whiteley 84', stamped l.l.c. with artist's monogram
Inscriptions: l.l.c. in pencil ' "Portrait of Wendy" Brett Whiteley 84'
Exhibited: Australian Galleries, Melbourne, 1984, Cat 16. Greenhill Galleries, Perth, 1984, Cat 19
Collection: Private collection, Melbourne

Plate 127
WENDY DRUNK 11PM 1983
Also titled *Drunk (Queensland)*
Brush and ink on paper, 74 × 103.4 cm; stamped with artist's monogram l.r. in red ink
Exhibited: Australian Galleries, Melbourne, 1984, Cat 19. Greenhill Galleries, Perth, 1984, Cat 19. Robin Gibson Gallery, Sydney, 1985, Cat 159. 'Brett Whiteley–Lloyd Rees: On the Road to Berry', Museum of Modern Art at Heide and The Art Gallery of New South Wales, 1993, Cat 76
Collection: Private collection, Sydney

Plate 128
PORTRAIT OF JOEL ELENBERG 1980
Oil, collage, ink, charcoal and masking tape on canvas, 202 × 152 cm; signed and dated l.r. in black ink 'brett whiteley 1980'
Exhibited: David Reid's Gallery, Sydney, 1980, Cat 50. Australian Galleries, Melbourne, 1983, Cat 5
Collection: New South Wales Government

Plate 129
THE LETTER (TO ANNA) 1980–81
Oil and pencil on canvas, 151.5 × 177.2 cm; signed l.l. in white 'brett whiteley', dated verso in white '80/81'
Inscriptions: verso in white paint ' "THE LETTER TO ANNA" 80/81'

Exhibited: The Artist's Studio, Circular Quay, Sydney, 1981, Cat 38
Collection: Private collection, Sydney

Plate 130
'FATHER, FORGIVE THEM…' 1979
Charcoal and wash on paper, 246 × 131 cm; signed and dated l.r. in pencil '1979/brett whiteley', stamped with artist's monogram stamp l.r. in black ink
Inscriptions: l.r. in pencil 'preliminary drawing for/crucifixion 1979/brett whiteley'. Inscribed l.r. in pencil 'gold/background/no/landscape/image'
Exhibited: David Reid's Gallery, Sydney, 1980, Cat 40
Collection: Private collection, Sydney

Plate 131
'MY GOD, MY GOD…WHY…' 1979–80
Oil, steel and gold leaf on board, 296.8 × 137.4 cm; signed l.r. 'brett whiteley'
Exhibited: David Reid's Gallery, Sydney, 1980, Cat 41. Australian Galleries, Melbourne, 1983, Cat 2
Literature: Art and Australia, Spring 1980, vol 18, no 1, p.1
Collection: Private collection, Sydney

Plate 132
THE GIVING UP 1979–80
Oil and steel on board, 264.4 × 122 cm; not signed, not dated
Exhibited: David Reid's Gallery, Sydney, 1980, Cat 42
Collection: Private collection, Sydney

Plate 133
TRACY THE DEALER 1987
Oil, charcoal, teeth, plaster, collage on board, 28 × 27.5 cm; signed verso in black ink 'Brett Whiteley'
Inscriptions: verso in black ink 'PORTRAIT OF TRACY THE DEALER'
Collection: Private collection, Sydney

Plate 134
PATRICK WHITE AS A HEADLAND *c.* 1981
Oil on canvas, 39.4 × 49.7 cm (sight); signed verso in charcoal 'brett whiteley' and stamped with artist's monogram l.r. in black ink
Inscriptions: u.l in ink 'Portrait of Patrick White as a headland/after a discussion about reincarnation'
Collection: Private collection, Sydney

Plate 135
THE OLGAS…SOON 1970
Tempera over gesso with enamel, gold paint, ink, paper collage, possum tail, jaw bone, wooden boomerang on four wooden panels, 203 × 325 cm; signed and dated verso u.l. '1970 Brett Whiteley'
Inscriptions: verso u.l. ' "THE OGLAS … SOON" 1970 Brett Whiteley'
Exhibited: Bonython Art Gallery, Sydney, 1970. 'The Australian Landscape', touring exhibition Australian state capitals 1972–73
Literature: Sturgeon 1987, p.37 (illus). McCulloch 1970, p.69–70 (illus). *Art and Australia*, vol 8 no 1, 1970 pp.6–7
Provenance: 'Australian Spring Sales', Christies, 1977, lot No 113
Collection: Art Gallery of South Australia

Plate 136
FRAGMENT OFF OLGA OR JAH! HOW BLACK CAN YOU GET 1974–75
Oil, collage, ink, plastic doll, plaster modelling clay on board, 68.5 × 71 cm; signed and dated verso in black oil '1974–75/Brett Whiteley'
Inscriptions: verso in black oil 'OR/TITLE: "FRAGMENT OFF OLGA OR JAH! HOW BLACK CAN YOU GET" 1974–75/Work in progress/Brett Whiteley'
Exhibited: 'Art in the Making', Art Gallery of New South Wales Travelling Art Exhibition 1979–80
Collection: Private collection, Sydney

Plate 137
THE DROUGHT OF '83 I (COOTAMUNDRA NSW) 1983
Oil, tempera, sticks, bone, stone, earth, collage on board, 214 × 244 cm
Exhibited: Australian Galleries, Melbourne, 1983, Cat 8
Collection: Private collection, Melbourne

Plate 138(a)
THE GREEN HERON 1983
Bronze and painted eye, 271.8 × 30.5 × 45.8 cm; not signed, not dated
Exhibited: Robin Gibson Gallery, Sydney, 1983, Cat 14. Australian Galleries, Melbourne, Cat 30. The Artist's Studio, Surry Hills, Sydney, 1988, Cat 56
Literature: Gray 1986, p.223 (illus)
Collection: Private collection, Sydney

Plate 138(b)
PELICAN II 1988
Bronze, 101.7 × 76.2 × 30.5 cm; not signed, not dated
Exhibited: The Artist's Studio, Surry Hills, Sydney, 1988, Cat 53
Collection: Private collection, Sydney

Plate 138(c)
WREN *c.* 1988
Plaster, metal, paint, glass eye and wood, 64 cm high; not signed, not dated
Collection: Private collection, Sydney

Plate 138(d)
WREN 1988
Bronze and glass eye, 33 × 22.8 × 5.1 cm; not signed, not dated
Exhibited: The Artist's Studio, Surry Hills, Sydney, 1988, Cat 54
Collection: Private collection, Sydney

Plate 138(e)
HUMMINGBIRD 1988
Bronze and glass eye, 55.9 × 36.4 × 5.1 cm; not signed, not dated
Exhibited: The Artist's Studio, Surry Hills, Sydney, 1988, Cat 52
Collection: Private collection, Sydney

Plate 138(f)
PELICAN I 1983
Painted bronze, 94 × 91.5 × 30.5 cm; not signed, not dated
Exhibited: Australian Galleries, Melbourne, 1984, Cat 8. The Artist's Studio, Surry Hills, Sydney, 1988, Cat 55
Literature: Gray 1986, p.223 (illus)
Collection: Private collection, Sydney

Plate 139
THE DAY ASIA GOT BORN 1970
Oil, collage, branch, nest, egg, bird, cicada and wood on board, 131.5 × 77.5 × 23.4 cm; signed and dated verso in charcoal 'Brett Whiteley 1970'
Inscriptions: verso in charcoal' "THE DAY ASIA GO BORN"/Brett Whiteley 1970'
Exhibited: Bonython Art Gallery, Sydney, 1970. 'Winter Exhibition', Joseph Brown Gallery, Melbourne, 15–31 July 1974, Cat 60. 'The Australian Landscape 1802–1975', exhibition to China, Peking, September 1975; Nanking, October 1975
Literature: McGrath 1979, p.227 (illus)
Collection: Private collection, Sydney

Plate 140
BUTCHER BIRD WITH BAUDELAIRE'S EYES 1972
Pen, ink, gouache, brush, ink and collage on paper on board, 61 × 55.5 cm; not signed, dated verso in black oil '1972'
Inscriptions: verso in black oil ' "THE BUTCHER/BIRD" PALM BEACH/1972/NOTE/(THE EYES OF CHARLES BAUDELAIRE)/THE BUTCHER BIRD/HAS THE

MOST/BEAUTIFUL SONG'
Collection: Private collection, Sydney

Plate 141
CH'UAN *c.* 1978–79
[1. Perfect 2. Complete; whole; total; intact; totally.
3. to keep 4. absolute; absolutely 5. a Chinese
family name]
Oil, branch, nest and egg on canvas, 91 × 91 × 13.5
cm; not signed, not dated
Exhibited: Robin Gibson Gallery, Sydney,
1979, Cat 3
Collection: Private collection, Sydney

Plate 142
SHAO (RAIN SLANTED BY WIND) 1978–79
Oil, nest and bird's egg on board, 122 × 81 cm;
signed l.c.l. in white 'brett whiteley', not dated
Exhibited: Robin Gibson Gallery, Sydney, 1979,
Cat 9. 'Major Modern Masters', Savill Galleries,
Sydney, 1992 (illus)
Literature: McQueen 1979, p.51 and cover (illus)
Collection: Private collection, Sydney

Plate 143(a)
TOTEM (WHITE FEMALE) 1978–88
Fibreglass, wood, marble, steel and oil, 271.8 ×
215.9 × 55.9 cm; not signed, not dated
Exhibited: The Artist's Studio, Surry Hills, Sydney,
1988, Cat 59
Collection: Private collection, Sydney

Plate 143(b)
TOTEM I (BLACK – THE GET LAID TOTEM)
1978–88
Fibreglass and wood, 284.5 × 170.2 × 61 cm; not
signed, not dated
Exhibited: Robin Gibson Gallery, Sydney, 1979, Cat
3. Australian Galleries, Melbourne, 1983, Cat 28b.
The Artist's Studio, Surry Hills, Sydney, 1988,
Cat 57
Literature: McQueen 1979, p.50 (illus). Gray 1986,
p.223 (illus)

Plate 143(c)
TOTEM II (TAN FEMALE) 1978–88
Fibreglass, wood, chrome and oil, 259.2 × 203.2 ×
53.4 cm; not signed, not dated
Exhibited: The Artist's Studio, Surry Hills, Sydney,
1988, Cat 58

Plate 144
ORANGE FRUIT DOVE FIJI 1969
Oil on board, 138 × 120 cm; not signed, not dated
Collection: Private collection, Brisbane

Plate 145
WHITE DOVE IN AVOCADO TREE 1979
Also titled *T'an*
Oil, charcoal, plastic avocado, collage, bird's nest
and egg on board, 99.5 × 102.5 cm; signed l.r. 'brett
whiteley'
Exhibited: Robin Gibson Galleries, Sydney,
1979, Cat 7
Literature: Gray 1986, p.216
Collection: Private collection, Sydney

Plate 146
**THE ARRIVAL – A GLIMPSE IN THE BOTANIC
GARDENS** 1984
Also titled *Sunset in Centennial Park*
Oil, collage and charcoal on canvas, 106.4 × 96.4
cm; signed l.r. 'brett whiteley' signed and dated
verso in charcoal '1984/brett whiteley'
Inscriptions: verso in charcoal 'THE ARRIVAL –
a/glimpse in the Botanical Gardens/1984/brett
whiteley'
Exhibited: Australian Galleries, Melbourne, 1984,
Cat 26. Greenhill Galleries, Perth, 1984, Cat 26
Literature: Pearce 1989, p.146 (illus)
Collection: Private collection, Sydney

Plate 147
BOOT OWL 1985
Ping-pong balls, leather boot, steel and paint,

22.9 × 17.8 × 12.7 cm; not signed, not dated
Exhibited: The Artist's Studio, Surry Hills, Sydney,
1988, Cat 62
Collection: Private collection, Sydney

Plate 148
THE LYREBIRD 1972–73
Oil, red earth, wood, cloth, lyre bird tail, ink and
collage on canvas, 198 × 183.5 × 26 cm; not signed,
not dated
Inscriptions: l.r.c. in white paint 'a pointless
painting needs looking at for a long time in order
to think about it'
Literature: McGrath, 1979, p.220 (illus)
Collection: Private collection, Sydney

Plate 149
THE BLUE RIVER 1978
Oil, collage, egg on 2 panels of canvas, 91.5 × 60.5
cm; not signed, not dated
Exhibited: David Reids Gallery, Sydney, 1980, not
catalogued
Collection: Private collection, Sydney

Plate 150
BAUDELAIRE'S DRIVE 1975
Oil on canvas, 228.6 × 190.5 cm
Exhibited: Bonython Art Gallery, Sydney, 1975, Cat
21. 'Winter Exhibition', Joseph Brown Gallery,
Melbourne, 7–18 June 1976, Cat 91. Robin Gibson
Gallery, Sydney, 1977, Cat 3
Collection: Private collection, Melbourne

Plate 151
SUNSET ON THE SOFALA ROAD 1974
Oil on canvas on board, 81.2 × 134.6 cm; signed
and dated in green oil l.r. 'Brett Whiteley/11/6/74'
Inscriptions: l.r. in green oil 'Sunset on the Sofala
Road/Brett Whiteley/memory/11/6/74'
Exhibited: 'Autumn Exhibition', Joseph Brown
Gallery, Melbourne, 1–12 March 1976, Cat 62
Collection: Private collection, Melbourne

Plate 152
BLUE RIVER 1977
Oil, wax, and collage on canvas, 59.5 × 59.5 cm;
signed and dated l.c. in brown ink 'brett
whiteley 77'
Literature: McGrath 1979, p.209 (illus). Walker
1988, p.144 (illus)
Collection: Private collection, Sydney

Plate 153
**THE RIVER AT MARULAN (…READING
EINSTEIN'S GEOGRAPHY)** 1976
Oil, electric light bulb and stones on board,
203.2 × 122 cm
Exhibited: Australian Galleries, Melbourne, 1976,
Cat 21. Robin Gibson Gallery, 1977, Cat 2. 'Selected
Australian Works of Art', Lauraine Diggins Gallery,
May, 1984
Literature: McGrath 1979, pp.206–210 (illus).
Walker 1988
Collection: Private collection, Melbourne

Plate 154
TO YIRRAWALLA 1972
Oil, ink, collage, charcoal, wasp, stuffed platypus,
stones, plaster, stick and plastic on board, 182 ×
162.6 × 6 cm; signed and dated l.r. in black ink
'Brett Whiteley/Aug/Sept/1972'
Inscriptions: l.r. in black ink 'To Yirrawalla/from
Brett Whiteley/Aug/Sept/1972', u.r. in black ink
'There is a rumour/which threatens to take on a
preportion [sic] of a myth that Yirrawalla/the
purest painter Australia has ever produced/can tell
the age of a small rock/by infinitely gently
touching it/with his index finger/and quite simply
../going back/in/down/time'
Exhibited: Robin Gibson Gallery, Sydney, 1977, Cat
10. Bonython Gallery, Sydney, 1975. Orange
Regional gallery, Orange NSW, 1990, Cat 2
Collection: New South Wales Government

Plate 155
SUMMER AT CARCOAR 1977
Oil, acrylic, paper, rock, glue and wood on
chipboard, 244.5 × 199 cm; signed l.r. in brown oil
paint 'brett whiteley 77', stamped with artist's
monogram l.r. in red ink
Inscriptions: l.r. in brown oil paint with 'brett
whiteley 77/for Bill Bowmore "Summer at
Carcoar"'
Exhibited: Robin Gibson Gallery, 1977, Cat 1
Literature: McGrath 1979, pp.206–8. Bonython
1980. Murray 1989, p.59
Collection: Newcastle Region Art Gallery, Gift of
William Bowmore OBE

Plate 156
THE PADDOCK – LATE AFTERNOON 1979
Oil on canvas, 202 × 152 cm; signed l.c. in orange
oil 'brett whiteley', not dated
Exhibited: David Reids Gallery, Sydney,
1980, Cat 36
Collection: Private collection, Sydney

Plate 157
OBERON 1987
(Triptych) Oil and collage on canvas, 86 × 259 cm
Exhibited: Artist's Studio, Surry Hills, 1988, Cat 21
Collection: Private collection, London

Plate 158
THE RIVER 1976
Aubusson tapestry, 198 × 168 cm; signed l.r. 'brett
whiteley', artist's monogram l.r.
Inscriptions: inscribed verso '1 of an edition of 6,
woven at Tapisserie D'Aubusson'
Exhibited: Robin Gibson Gallery, Sydney, 1977, Cat
18. 'Four Australian Modern Masters: Arthur Boyd,
Sidney Nolan, Brett Whiteley', Savill Galleries,
Sydney, 11 November–6 December 1988, Cat 47.
'Spring Exhibition', Sydney, 23 October–28
November 1987, Cat 51
Literature: McGrath 1979, p.206
Collection: Private collection, Sydney

Plate 159
**AUTUMN (NEAR BATHURST) – JAPANESE
AUTUMN** 1987–88
Oil, tempera, ink, egg and photography on board,
285.4 × 411.5 cm; signed l.r. in oil 'brett whiteley'
Inscription: l.l. in brown oil 'Landscape near
Bathurst'
Exhibited: Artist's Studio, Surry Hills, Cat 1
Collection: Private collection, Sydney

Plate 160
PARIS DRAWING *c.* 1984
Charcoal, pen, ink, collage and Chinese white on
paper, 50 × 65 cm; stamped l.r. in black ink, artist's
monogram l.r. in black ink, not dated
Collection: Private collection, Sydney

Plate 161
THE 15 GREAT DOG PISSES OF PARIS 1989
Oil, charcoal, plaster, collage and resin on canvas,
154 × 138.5 cm; signed and dated l.l. in black ink
'brett Whiteley 89' and verso in charcoal
'1989/brett whiteley'
Inscriptions: l.r. in black ink 'the 15 great dog
pisses of Paris' and verso '"THE 15 GREAT DOG/PISSES
ON PARIS"/1989/OIL ON PLASTER AND COLLAGE/ON
CANVAS,/MOUNTED ON PLY/61" × 55"/brett whiteley'
Exhibited: 'Regard de Côté', The Art Gallery of New
South Wales, 1 March–6 May 1990, Cat 65.
Australian Galleries, Melbourne, 1992, Cat 65
Literature: Whiteley1990 (illus)
Collection: Private collection, Sydney

Select Bibliography

Items in this bibliography are organized in chronological order.

NEWSPAPER AND JOURNAL ARTICLES

Reichardt 1962
Reichardt, J., 'Brett Whiteley at Matthiesen Gallery'. *Apollo Magazine* [London], vol.LXXVI (New Series), no.1, March 1962, pp.72–73.

Cormack 1962
Cormack, Robin, 'Brett Whiteley: Matthiesen Gallery', *The Arts Review* [London], vol. XIV, no.4, March 1962, p.9.

Hughes 1963
Hughes, Robert, 'Obsessions with the Flesh', *Nation* [Sydney], no.118, 4 May 1963, p.18.

Spencer 1963
Spencer, Charles S., 'The Peter Stuyvesant Collection: Paintings While You Work', *Studio* [London], January 1963, pp.18-21.

Millen 1963
Millen, Ronald, 'Paris Seen', *Art and Australia* [Sydney], vol.1, no.3, November 1963, pp.186–91.

Harris 1964
Harris, Max, 'Art Collections: Kym Bonython', *Art and Australia* [Sydney], vol.1, no.4, February 1964, p.229

Spencer 1964
Spencer, Charles S., 'Brett Whiteley: Classicism and Actuality', *Studio* [London], March 1964.

Gosling 1964
Gosling, Nigel, 'Art', *The Observer*, London, 3 May 1964.

Lynton 1964
Lynton, Norbert, 'Voyeurs', *New Statesman* [London], vol.LXVII, no.1730, 8 May 1964, p.739.

Rosenthal 1964
Rosenthal, T.G., 'Ancient and Modern', *The Listener* [London], vol. LXXI, no.1833, 4 May 1964, p.804.

'No Anguish Here', The Evening Standard, London, 11 May 1964.

Wallis 1964
Wallis, Neville, 'The Bride in the Bath', *The Spectator* [London], no.7090, 15 May 1964, p.664.

'The Young Londoners: Britannia's New Wave', *Time* [Australia], vol.84, no.15, 9 October 1964, p.34.

Wolfram 1965
Wolfram, Eddie, 'Zoo Story: Rillington Place', *Arts Review* [London], vol. XVII, no.20, 16 October 1965.

Russell 1965 London
Russell, John, 'Brain, Brawns and Blood', *Sunday Times*, London, 17 October 1965.

Russell 1965 New York (1)
Russell, John, 'The London Pornocrats', *Art in America* [New York], vol.53, no.5, October 1965, pp.125–31.

Russell 1965 New York (2)
Russell, John, 'London: From Imperium to Maniac', *Art News* [New York], vol.64, no.7, November 1965, pp.48–49.

Rosenthal 1965
Rosenthal, T.G., 'No Devil in the Flesh', *The Listener* [London], vol. LXXIV, no.1909, 28 October 1965, p.672.

Melville 1965 (1)
Melville, Robert, 'Last of the Decadents', *New Statesman* [London], vol. LXX, no.1807, 29 October 1965, p.668.

Melville 1965 (2)
Melville, Robert, 'Treasures from the Museums', *Architectural Review* [London], vol.CXXXVIII, no.826, December 1965, pp.445–47.

Robertson 1965
Robertson, Bryan, 'Innocence and Experience', *Spectator* [London], no.7167, 5 November 1965, p.586.

Whittet 1965
Whittet, G.S., 'Commonwealth Artists and Uncommon Luminists', *Studio International* [London], vol.170, no.871, November 1965, p.215.

Spencer 1965
Spencer, Charles S., 'First Commonwealth Arts Festival: Australian Artists in London', *Art and Australia* [Sydney], vol.3, no.3, December 1965, p.210–15.

Hughes 1965
Hughes, Robert, 'The Shirley Temple of Australian Art: Brett Whiteley's Splash at the Mainstream', *The Bulletin*, 18 December 1965.

Gordon 1966
Gordon, Alistair, 'Art in the Modern Manner', *The Connoisser* [London], vol. 161, January–April 1966, p.38.

Baro 1966
Baro, Gene, 'A Busy Vigorous Season', *Arts Magazine* [New York], vol.40, no.3, January 1966, pp.47–49.

Lynn 1966
Lynn, Elwyn, 'The Picture of Horror', *The Australian*, March 1966, p.9.

Art and Australia [Sydney], vol.4, no.3, 1966, p.177.

McGrath 1967
McGrath, Sandra, 'Profile: Brett Whiteley', *Art and Australia* [Sydney], vol.5, no.1, June 1967, pp. 368–73

Burr 1967
Burr, James, 'Originators and Imitators', *Apollo Magazine* [London], July 1967, pp.154–56.

'A Newsy Art', *The Times*, London, 16 October 1967.

Harrisop 1967
Harrisop, Charles, 'London', *Studio International* [London], vol.174, no.893, October 1967, pp.154–56.

Roberts 1967
Roberts, Keith, 'Current and Forthcoming Exhibitions', *Burlington Magazine* [London], vol.CIX, no.776, November 1967, p.659.

'Painting: Plaster Apocalypse', *Time* [Australia], vol.90, no.19, 10 November 1967, p.42.

Glesson 1968
Gleeson, James, 'A Landmark in Painting', *The Sun*, Sydney, 7 February 1968.

Brook 1968
Brook, Donald, 'A Huge Talent', *The Sydney Morning Herald*, 8 February 1968.

Lynn 1968
Lynn, Elwyn, 'Erotic Obsessions', *The Bulletin*, 17 February 1968.

'In the Galleries', *Arts Magazine* [New York], vol.42, no.8, June/Summer, p.62.

Art and Australia [Sydney], vol.7, no.2, September 1969, p.182.

'Pleasant Surprise in Old Bulk Store', *The Fiji Times*, Suva, 21 October 1969.

Read 1969
Read, Adrian, 'He Climbed Into His Own Picture', *The Australian*, 8 November 1969.

Thomas L. 1970
Thomas, Laurie, 'Passion and Power in Whiteley Exhibition', *The Australian*, 16 June 1970.

Brook 1970
Brook, Donald, 'Painters, Poets, Sages', *The Sydney Morning Herald*, 18 June 1970.

Thomas D. 1970
Thomas, Daniel, 'Whiteley's Paradise', Sunday Telegraph, Sydney, 21 June 1970.

Lynn 1970
Lynn, Elwyn, 'How Pilgrim in the Slough of Despond Sights Paradise', The Bulletin, 27 June 1970.

McCulloch 1970
McCulloch, Alan, 'Letter from Australia', *Art International* /London], October 1970, p.69–70.

Heathwood 1970
Heathwood, Gail, 'Brett Whiteley: Flying High', *Vogue Living*, [Australia], vol.3, no.4, 13 November 1970–12 February 1971, pp.100-3.

Read 1972
Read, Adrian, 'Painting at the Last Abyss', *The Australian*, 26 February 1972.

McGrath 1972
McGrath, Sandra, 'Deciphering the Mysteries of Flesh and Matters', *The Australian*, 11 March 1972.

Gleeson 1972
Gleeson, James, 'Whiteley Exhibit Disappoints', *The Sun*, Sydney, 1 March 1972.

Thomas 1972 (1)
Thomas, Laurie, 'Thoroughbreds that End Up On Canvas', *The Australian*, 21 March 1972.

'Artist Charged After Recital Scuffle', *The Australian*, 21 March 1972.

Boles 1972
Boles, Bernard, 'Paintings by Brett Whiteley', *The Review*, 15 April 1972.

Milgate 1972
Milgate, Rodney, 'Dangerous Rib-Tickling', *The Australian*, 15 April 1972.

Thomas 1972 (2)
Thomas, Laurie, 'Alchemy with a Poetic Impact', *The Australian*, 27 December 1972.

Thomas 1973
Thomas, Daniel, 'A Literal Autobiography in Eighteen Panels', *The Sydney Morning Herald*, 11 January 1973.

McGrath 1973
McGrath, Sandra, 'Whiteley: Potent Magician', *The Australian*, 13 January 1973.

Borlase 1973
Borlase, Nancy, 'Whiteley's Promised Land', *The Bulletin*, 13 January 1973.

Adams 1973
Adams, Bruce, 'Whiteley Rampant', *Sunday Telegraph*, Sydney, 14 January 1973.

Art and Australia [Sydney], vol.10, no.4, April 1973, pp.330–31

Thomas 1974
Thomas, Daniel, 'Whiteley's Love and Passion',

The Sydney Morning Herald, 10 January 1974.

Borlase 1974 (1)
Borlase, Nancy, 'Touching Depths of Agony', *The Bulletin*, 19 January 1974.

Borlase 1974 (2)
Borlase, Nancy, 'An Unexpected Whiteley', *The Bulletin*, 23 November, 1974.

'Criticism Welcomed', *The Australian*, 9 June 1975.

McGrath 1975
McGrath, Sandra, 'Whiteley's Homage to Matisse', *The Australian*, 25 October 1975, p.26.

Krausmann 1975
Krausmann, Rudi, 'Painting the Infliction of Life', *Aspect* [Sydney], vol.1, no.4, Summer 1975–76.

Art and Australia [Sydney], vol.13, Summer 1976, p.223.

Lynn 1976
Lynn, Elwyn, 'Brett Whiteley: the Grand Works', *Quadrant* [Sydney], October 1976.

McGrath 1977 (1)
McGrath, Sandra, 'The Making of an Authentic Genius', *The Australian*, 24 January 1977.

McGrath 1977 (2)
McGrath, Sandra, 'Cool, Cool Water', *The Australian*, 4 March 1977.

Eagle 1978 (1)
Eagle, Mary, 'Connor's Course More Even Than Whiteley's', *The Sun* [Sydney], 19 July 1978.

Eagle 1978 (2)
Eagle, Mary, 'Now it's the Archibald Event', *The Age* [Melbourne], December 1978.

McGrath 1978
McGrath, Sandra, 'Brett Whiteley's Alchemy', *Quadrant* [Sydney], September 1978.

Hoff 1978
Hoff, Ursula, 'Australian Paintings in British Collection', *Art and Australia* [Sydney], vol.16, no.2, December 1978, p.176.

McGrath 1979 (1)
McGrath, Sandra, 'Whiteley: The Artist as Hero', *The Weekend Australian*, 17 March 1979.

McGrath 1979 (2)
McGrath, Sandra, 'The Age of Reason', *The Weekend Australian*, 7 April 1979.

Lynn 1979
Lynn, Elwyn, 'Golden Haired Guru: Brett Whiteley', *Quadrant*, June 1979

McQueen 1979
McQueen, Humphrey, 'Brett Whiteley, *Art and Australia* [Sydney], vol.17, no.1, September 1979.

McGrath 1980
McGrath, Sandra, 'Brett Whiteley – Painting About his Friends', *The Weekend Australian*, 3 May 1980.

Williamson 1980
Williamson, Kristin, 'Whiteley', *The National Times*, 25 May 1980.

Art and Australia, vol.18, no.1, Spring 1980, p.14.

Rolfe 1980
Rolfe, Patricia, 'The Marketing of Brett Whiteley', *The Bulletin*, 29 July 1980.

Waldmann 1982
Waldmann, Anna, 'The Archibald Prize', *Art and Australia* [Sydney], vol.20, no.2, Summer 1982, pp.231–36.

Hughes 1983
Hughes, Karen Elizabeth, 'A Brett Whiteley Interview: The Van Gogh Period', *The Age Monthly Review* [Melbourne], 10 February 1983.

Holloway 1983
Holloway, Memory, 'Still Looking Good Despite the Clutter', *The Age*, Melbourne, 1 June 1983.

Clarke 1983
Clarke, Anthony, 'Whiteley Pays Tribute', *The Age* [Melbourne], 16 July 1983.

Maloon 1983
Maloon, Terence, 'Maloon on Whiteley on Van Gogh', *The Sydney Morning Herald*, 23 July 1983.

Nicklin 1985
Nicklin, Lenore, 'Wicked Whiteley's Surprised – He's Alive and Healthy', *The Bulletin*, 15 October 1985.

Lynn 1985
Lynn, Elwyn, 'Drawing Lines of Genius', *The Weekend Australian*, 26 October 1985.

Leonard 1985
Leonard, Christopher, 'How Whiteley Works', *The Sydney Morning Herald*, 28 September 1985.

Gray 1986
Gray, Robert, 'A Few Takes on Brett Whiteley', *Art and Australia* [Sydney], vol.24, no. 2, Summer 1986.

Adams 1987
Adams, Phillip, 'My Art, My Disease', *Tension*, [Melbourne], no.11, January–February 1987, pp.5–35.

Lynn 1988
Lynn, Elwyn, 'Whiteley Mystery Burns Bright', *The Weekend Magazine,* 9 July 1988.

McGrath 1988
McGrath, Sandra, 'True Colours', *Vogue Living* [Australia], vol.XXII, no.9, November 1988

Hawley 1990
Hawley, Janet, 'Brett Whiteley: The Art of the Warrior', *Good Weekend*, 17 February 1990, pp.16–26.

Allen 1990
Allen, Christopher, 'Would the Eye Match the Brush', *The Sydney Morning Herald*, 9 March 1990.

McGillick 1990
McGillick, Paul, 'The Whiteley Contradiction', *Financial Review*, 16 March 1990.

Mendelssohn 1990
Mendelssohn, Joanna, 'A case of too much', *The Bulletin*, 3 April 1990.

Lynn and Allen 1991
Lynn, Elwyn and Allen, Christopher, 'Luscious Ornaments', *The Independent Monthly* [Sydney], September 1991.

Robertson, Mendelssohn and Daws 1992
Robertson, Bryan; Mendelssohn, Joanna; Daws, Lawrence; 'Tributes to Brett Whiteley', *Art and Australia* [Sydney], vol.30, no.2,Summer 1992.

Hawley 1992
Hawley, Janet, 'Whiteley: The Lonely Exit of a Troubled Genius', *The Sydney Morning Herald*, 17 June 1992.

Date 1992
Date, Margot, 'Art of Generosity Smattered with Ego, Say Critics', *The Sydney Morning Herald*, 17 June 1992.

'The Crucial Art of Living Dangerously', *The Sydney Morning Herald*, 17 June 1992.

'Brett Whiteley' obituary, *Daily Telegraph*, London, 1992.

McKenzie 1992
McKenzie, Janet, 'Divided Self Sweeping Line' obituary, *The Guardian*, London, 18 June 1992.

'Brett Whiteley' obituary, *The Times*, London, 18 June 1992.

Delaruelle 1992
Delaruelle, Jacques, 'Whiteley and la Boheme', *The Sydney Review*, July 1992.

Heathcote 1992
Heathcote, Christopher, 'Whiteley's Fanciful Views of Some Paris Myths', *The Age* [Melbourne], 29 July 1992.

van Nunen 1992
van Nunen, Linda, 'The Other Side of Whiteley', *The Australian Magazine*, 31 October 1992.

Hawley 1993
Hawley, Janet, 'Two for the Road', *Good Weekend*, 3 July 1993.

James 1993
James, Bruce, 'Wendy's World', *Mode* [Sydney], August–September 1993.

Hawley 1994
Hawley, Janet, 'Still Life', *Good Weekend*, 2 July 1994, pp.18–24.

BOOKS

Aland and Darby 1991
Aland, J. and Darby, M., *Art Connections*, Melbourne: Heinemann, 1991.

Alley 1981
Alley, Ronald, *Catalogue of the Tate Gallery's Collection of Modern Art Other Than Works by British Artists*, London: Tate Gallery in association with Sotheby Parke Bennett, 1981.

Bonython and Lynn 1976
Bonython, Kim and Lynn, Elwyn, *Modern Australian Painting 1970–75*, Adelaide: Rigby Press, 1976.

Bonython 1980
Bonython, Kim, *Modern Australian Painting 1975–80*, Adelaide: Rigby Press, 1980.

Broinowski 1992
Broinowski, Alison, *The Yellow Lady: Australian Impressions of Asia*, Melbourne: Oxford University Press, 1992.

Davenport and Rees 1991
Davenport, R. and Rees, V., *Artifacts*, Sydney: McGrath-Hill, 1991.

Driscol and Whiteley 1986
Driscol, Michael and Whiteley, Brett, *Native Rose*, Cammeray NSW: Richard Griffin, 1986.

Fry 1984
Fry, E., *Gallery Images from the Collection of the Art Gallery of Western Australia*, Perth: St. George Books, 1984.

Hayes 1992
Hayes, S. and Gervasoni, C., *Artistic Insights*, Sydney: Harcourt, Brace, Jovanovich, Holt, Rinehart and Winston, 1992.

Hawley 1993
Hawley, Janet, *Encounters with Australian Artists*, St Lucia, QLD: University of Queensland Press, 1993.

Horton 1969
Horton, M. (ed.), *Present Day Art in Australia*, Sydney: Ure Smith Pty, Ltd., 1969.

Hunt 1994
Hunt, S., *The Archibald Prize*, Sydney: The Art Gallery of New South Wales, 1994.

Hunter 1991
Hunter, Lois, *The Australian Art Companion*, Sydney: Reed Books, 1991.

Hughes 1970
Hughes, Robert, *The Art of Australia*, Ringwood, VIC: Penguin, 1970 (1966).

Luck 1969
Luck, R.K., *A Guide to Modern Australian Painting*, Melbourne: Sun Books, 1969.

McGrath 1979 (3)
McGrath, Sandra, *Sydney Harbour*, Sydney: Jacaranda Press, 1979.

McGrath 1979
McGrath, Sandra, *Brett Whiteley*, Sydney: Bay Books, 1979.

Millar 1974
Millar, Ronald, *Civilized Magic: An Interpretive Guide to Australian Paintings*, Melbourne: Sorrett, 1974.

Murray 1989
Murray, Laura, *Great Australian Paintings*, Frenches Forrest: Child and Associates, 1989.

Pearce 1989
Pearce, Barry, *Australian Artists: Australian Birds*, Sydney: Angus and Robertson, 1989.

Pringle 1963
Pringle, John Douglas, *Australian Painting Today*, London: Thames and Hudson, 1963.

Rothenstein 1962
Rothenstein, J., *The Tate Gallery*, London: Thames and Hudson, 1962.

Smith 1991
Smith, Bernard with Smith, Terry, *Australian Painting 1788–90*, Melbourne: Oxford University Press, 1991 (1963).

Sturgeon 1987
Sturgeon, Graeme, *Australia: The Painters Vision*, Sydney: Bay Books, 1987.

Terry 1984
Terry, Martin, *Masterpieces of Modern Australian Painting*, Sydney: Bay Books, 1984.

Tesoriero and Nilson
Tesoriero, L. and Nilson, H., *Aspects of Art*, Marrickville: Science Press, 1993.

Thomas 1989
Thomas, Daniel, *Outlines of Australian Art: The Joseph Brown Collection*, 3rd Edition, South Melbourne: Macmillan Australian, 1989 (1973).

Whiteley 1979
Whiteley, Brett, *Zoo*, Melbourne: Pegasus, 1979.

Whiteley 1983
Whiteley, Brett, *Another Way of Looking at Vincent Van Gogh*, Melbourne: Richard Griffin, 1983.

EXHIBITION CATALOGUES

Robertson, Bryan, *The New Generation*, Whitechapel Gallery, London, 1964.

Thomas, Laurie, *Australian Painting and Tapestries of the Past Twenty Years: An Exhibition to Commemorate the Opening of the New South Wales House by Her Majesty 24 May 1972*: Worthing, Sussex Solitho Ltd, 1972.

Klepac, Lou, *Contemporary Australian Painting*, Perth: Art Gallery of Western Australia, 1978.

Slutzkin, Linda, *Art in the Making*, Sydney: The Art Gallery of New South Wales, 1979.

Three Years On: A Selection of Acquisitions 1978–1981, Sydney: The Board of Trustees, The Art Gallery of New South Wales, 1981.

Queensland Art Gallery: Selected Works, Brisbane: Queensland Art Gallery, 1983.

Smith, T. and Dixon, C., *Aspects of Australian Figurative Painting 1942–1962: Dreams, Fears and Desires*, Sydney: Power Institute of Fine Arts, 1984.

Thomas, Daniel (ed.), *Creating Australia: 200 Years 1788-1988*, Sydney: International Cultural Corporation of Australia, 1988.

Brett Whiteley: 162 Drawings 1960-85, Robin Gibson Gallery, Sydney, 1985.

Whiteley, Brett, *Regard de Côté*, Collingwood: Australian Galleries, 1990.

Biographical Notes

1939
Born 7 April, Sydney, Australia. Grew up at 18 Lucretia Avenue, Longueville.

1946
Won first art competition Annual RSPCA. Exhibition at Farmer's Blaxland Gallery for *The Driver Sits in the Shade But What About the Horse?*

1948
Sent to boarding school at Scots College, Bathurst.

1954
Saw Lloyd Rees's European paintings exhibition at Macquarie Galleries, Sydney.

Briefly attended Scots College, Sydney, 1954–55.

1956
Awarded first prize, Young Painters' Section, Bathurst Show, New South Wales. Left school mid-year, and worked in Sydney for Lintas Advertising Agency in the layout and commercial art department. Beryl Whiteley left Australia for London.

1956–59
Met Wendy Julius, who was attending the National Art School East, Sydney, where Whiteley and Michael Johnson occasionally drew at the Life Drawing Class. Sometimes attended sketch clubs such as John Santry's Sketch Club (also frequented by Lloyd Rees) on Thursday nights. Used the glasshouse at Longueville as a studio. Sporadically attended life drawing at Julian Ashton Art School. Painted on weekends around Bathurst, Sofala, Hillend and the south coast of New South Wales. Painted at Sydney Soup Kitchen and Night Refuge.

1959
Encouraged by Australian artist William Pidgeon, left Lintas in August to paint works for the Italian scholarship. In November awarded Italian Government Travelling Art Scholarship for 1960. The competition was judged by Sir Russell Drysdale at The Art Gallery of New South Wales. Whiteley submitted four paintings: *Sofala, Dixon Street, July* and *Around Bathurst.*

1960
Arrived on 25 February in Naples on board the *Fairstar*. March to May in Rome and Florence. Had an appartment in Rome near the Spanish Steps with Beryl. Visited Australian sculptor Stephen Walker, recipient of the same Italian scholarship, in Florence, and found a studio in the same building as Walker.

Brief visits to Paris and London. While in London took portfolio around galleries and was selected for a group show by McRoberts and Tunnard. On 14 June met Wendy in Paris and after two weeks they returned to the Florence studio.

20 July to 1 September exhibited in group show at McRoberts and Tunnard Gallery, London, with Tadashi Sato, Douglas Swan and Philip Weichberger. Three gouaches were sold for £18 and one was reserved at £9.

Travelled throughtout Italy, including Siena and Arezzo. Haunted the Uffizi Gallery immersed in work by artists of the fourteenth and fifteenth centuries, particularly Cimabue, Duccio and Piero della Francesca. In August spent three days in Venice to see the Biennale with Michael Johnson, visiting Morandi in Grizzana.

In November moved to London, 129 Ladbroke Grove W11, where Michael Johnson was already living. In December met British painters William Scott and Roger Hilton and other Australian artists then in London, including Arthur Boyd and John Passmore. Met Bryan Robertson, director of Whitechapel Gallery.

1961
Awarded a grant under the Dyason Bequest from The Art Gallery of New South Wales, which allowed Whiteley to stay in London. Awarded special Commonwealth Arts Advisory Board Scholarship enabling him to work in Paris from September to October. Awarded International Prix at the 2nd Biennale, Paris, des Jeunes Peintres et Sculpteurs.

In June represented The Australian National Committee at the International Association of Plastic Arts, organized by UNESCO at the Meeting of Young Painters.

Three paintings, *Untitled Red Painting* (1960), *Untitled White Painting* (1960) and *Untitled Dark Painting* (1961) selected for 'Survey of Recent Australian Painting' at Whitechapel Art Gallery, London. Introduced to Francis Bacon by Bryan Robertson

Work exhibited in The Wolfram von Eschenback International, Germany, and at the Burr Gallery, California.

Wendy left London, spending two months in New York over the summer with Beryl, also visiting Montreal and Toronto.

1962
Exhibited at the Stedelijk Museum, Amsterdam, and travelled in Holland with Australian artist Lawrence Daws.

Exhibited at the Berlin World Fair in the Stuyvesant Collection, then travelled to Baden-Baden, Stuttgart and to Venice for the Biennale.

Married Wendy Julius on 27 March at Chelsea Registry Office, London.

April to September travelled through Europe with his father, Clem, visiting Rome, Paris, Barcelona and the Haute Pyrénées, where they stayed with American painter George Sheridan. Clem returned to Australia (the last time Whiteley saw his father). With friend Wendy Paramour, the Whiteleys spent five months in the south of France in old farm houses at Sigean, from where they travelled to Spain and Germany.

In October travelled to the United States visiting New York, Connecticut and Washington. Met de Kooning. Returned to London in November and moved into 13 Pembridge Crescent, W11.

1963
Spent six and a half months completing *Summer at Sigean.* Afterwards commenced the bathroom series. Work selected for 'Australian Painting' exhibition at Tate Gallery, London, and 'British Painting In The '60s', which opened at the Whitechapel Gallery in London before touring Great Britain and Switzerland.

April in France.

On 3 May Clem Whiteley died aged 55.

Australian Group Show, Marlborough Gallery, London. Exhibited with Lawrence Daws, Jack Carrington Smith and Vaughan at The National Gallery of Rhodesia, Africa. 15 November to 22

December exhibited in the Dunn International, Fredericton, Canada, and Tate Gallery, London.

In December moved to Holman Hunt's old studio at 18A Melbury Road, London.

1964
Awarded International Drawings Prize for *Bather and Heater* (1964) International der Zeichnung, Darmstadt, Germany. Awarded travel grant from The Stuyvesant Foundation. Awarded Perth Festival Art Prize, Australia. From March to May exhibited in 'The New Generation 1964', Whitechapel Art Gallery, London, with *Woman in a Bath 5* (1963–64), *Bather and Mirror* (1964), *Figure at the Basin* (1963) and *Sketch for Large Mirror Painting* (1964).

From May to June travelled to Deya, Majorca.

Three works exhibited in Documenta III, Kassel, Germany: *Bather and Mirror* (1964), *Woman Washing Her Face* (1964) and *Woman Sitting on side of Bath* (1963).

6 November daughter Arkie born at St George's Hospital, London.

1965
Exhibited in De Hendendaagse Schilderkunst in Australia, France, Belgium, Germany and Italy.

'Treasures from The Commonwealth' Commonwealth Festival Exhibition, Burlington House, London.

From June to July travelled to Deya, Majorca

November to December exhibited *Untitled Dark Painting* (1963), and *Christie and Hectorina McLennan* (1964) in 'The English Eye', Marlborough-Gerson Gallery, New York. Exhibited in group show 'Marlborough Prints', at Marlborough New London Gallery, London.

Awarded T.E. Wardle Invitation Art Prize, Perth, Australia.

In December returned to Australia for the summer, staying at Whale Beach, north of Sydney.

1966
In February included in a group show with David Hockney and Arthur Boyd. Exhibited at Clune Galleries, Sydney, with The Zoo Graphics.

From 10 March to 16 April exhibition of the Mertz Collection 'The Australian Painters 1964–1966 at the Corcoran Gallery of Art in Washington DC, USA. *Woman in Bath* (1964), *Christie and Kathleen Maloney* (1964), *The Boxing Match* (1965), *Cheetah in Rillington Place* (1964) and *Head of Christie* (1964).

From 6 April to 22 May exhibited in 'British Graphics' at Museum Boymans-van Beuningen, Rotterdam. Exhibited in group show at Marlborough Graphics, Marlborough New London Gallery, London.

Returned to London via Calcutta mid-year.

Work selected for exhibition at Palais des Beaux-Arts, Brussels.

1967
Exhibited at Pittsburgh International Carnegie Institute, Pittsburgh, USA, and awarded Harkness Foundation Scholarship.

May to June travelled in Majorca, Tangier and Madrid, before sailing on the *Queen Mary* to New York in September. Moved into a penthouse apartment at the Chelsea Hotel.

Australian Group Exhibition, Whitechapel Gallery, London.

1969
In July fled New York for Fiji and lived in a *bure* at Navutuleva, about 45 miles along the coast from Suva. Spent five months in Fiji.

Group show at Cunard-Marlborough Gallery (on board *The Queen Elizabeth II* for the maiden voyage).

Fined £F50 in Suva for possession of a drug.

Returned in November to Australia, moving to Lavender Bay, Sydney.

1970–72
Involved with The Yellow House artist's community in Potts Point, Sydney.

1971
9–18 November showed in group exhibition 'The Bonsai Show', Australian Galleries, Melbourne.

Rented Gasworks studio in Waverton

1972
In February began work on *Alchemy*.

Exhibited in 'Australian Painters and Tapestries of the Past 20 Years' New South Wales House, London.

1973
In January completed work on *Alchemy*. Exhibited *Alchemy* at Bonython Gallery, Sydney.

In June travelled to Mauritius and Kenya.

1974
Quote from interview with Phillip Adams '(in 1974) moved from alcohol to more serious mind altering chemicals'.

Exhibited at The World Expo, Spokane, Washington, USA.

1975
Awarded Sir William Anglis Memorial Art Prize, Melbourne.

Included in 'Australian Painting' exhibition, People's Republic of China.

Moved from gasworks studio in Waverton to downstairs studio in Lavender Bay house.

1976
Archibald Prize for *Self-Portrait in the Studio*.

Sir John Sulman Prize for *Interior with Time Past* (genre painting).

1977
Wynne Prize for *The Jacaranda Tree (On Sydney Harbour)* (1977).

March to April in London.

In August stayed with Joel Elenberg at Arthur Boyd's Italian house, Casa Paletaio, in Pisa. Travelled to Venice, Florence and Rome.

1978
Wynne Prize for *Summer at Carcoar* (1977).

Sir John Sulman Prize for *Yellow Nude* (1978)

Archibald Prize for *Art, Life and the Other Thing* (1978).

June travelled to Bali. August in New Caledonia and back to Bali in September.

Exhibited four works at Cologne International Art Fair.

1979
Joel Elenberg shared studio with Whiteley in Lavender Bay.

1980
June to September in Bali with Joel Elenberg and his family, Anna and Zahava, until Elenberg's death.

1981
Moved to studio in Reiby Place, Circular Quay.

November in Vanuatu.

1982
Travelled to Spain, Germany, France. Returning to Australia, stopped in Rome to work with Walter Rassi on three etchings at Vigna Antoniniana, Rome.

1983
Travelled to Central Australia in the summer with Michael Driscoll and worked on publication *Native Rose*.

1984
Awarded Wynne Prize, The Art Gallery of New South Wales, for *South Coast After the Rain* (1984).

July in London.

1985
Purchased an old t-shirt factory in Surry Hills, Sydney, and converted it to a studio. Travelled to London in May; Wendy remained in England.

1986
Travelled to India to meet Wendy in Bombay and returned to Australia together.

1987
Travelled to London.

1989
Divorced from Wendy. May to August in London and Morocco, spending two months in Paris in an apartment on Rue de Tournon. Travelled for five weeks in Bali, Tokyo and Kyoto with Janice Spencer.

October in Byron Bay, New South Wales.

1991
Awarded Order of Australia (General Division) on June 10.

1992
Died at Thirroul, New South Wales, 15 June.

Solo Exhibitions

1962
9 March–31 March
Paintings and Gouaches
Matthiesen Gallery, London

1963
10 April–10 May
Brett Whiteley
Rudy Komon Gallery, Sydney

1964
23 April–23 May
Brett Whiteley
Marlborough New London Gallery, London

1965
October
Zoo Series and Christie Series
Marlborough New London Gallery, London

1966
31 January–17 February
Recent Works from London
Bonython Art Gallery, Adelaide

7 March–24 March
Recent Works from London
Kym Bonython's Hungry Horse Art Gallery, Sydney

27 September–14 October
23 Items by Brett Whiteley
Australian Galleries, Melbourne

1967
2 October–31 October
Deya – Majorca
Marlborough New London Gallery, London

1968
Brett Whiteley
5 February–21 February
Bonython Art Gallery, Sydney

May–June
Brett Whiteley: Recent Work
Marlborough-Gerson Gallery, New York

1970
June–July
Brett Whiteley
Bonython Art Gallery, Sydney

28 March–19 April
Brett Whiteley
Australian Galleries, Melbourne

1972
29 February–21 March
Portraits and Other Emergencies
Bonython Art Gallery, Sydney

28 March–21 April
Portraits and Other Emergencies
Australian Galleries, Melbourne

1973
Alchemy
Bonython Art Gallery, Sydney

1 June–19 June

Waves
Australian Galleries, Melbourne

1974
6 January–30 January
Drawings 1960–1973
Bonython Art Gallery, Sydney

19 November–3 December
Lavender Bay Series
Australian Galleries, Melbourne

1975
24 October–15 November
Thirty-six Looks at Four Sights on Three Themes: Recent Paintings, Drawings and Carvings
Bonython Art Gallery, Sydney

10 May–14 June
Brett Whiteley: Drawings
Marlborough Gallery, New York

1976
21 September–5 October
Recent Interiors, Still Lifes, Windowscapes, Sculpture and Ceramics
Australian Galleries, Melbourne

1977
February–March
Brett Whiteley Prints and Drawings
Susan Gillespie Galleries, Canberra

1 March–19 March
Rivers
Robin Gibson Gallery, Sydney

September
Recent Paintings and Drawings
Fischer Fine Art Gallery, London

November
Brett Whiteley: Prints
Robin Gibson Gallery

1978
12 July–25 July
Paintings, Drawings, and Three Scrolls
Australian Galleries, Melbourne

1979
10 April–5 May
Birds and Animals
Robin Gibson Gallery, Sydney

1980
Survey of Prints and Drawings 1964–1980
Impressions Gallery, Melbourne

26 April–17 May
Portraits, Crucifixions, (A Paddock at) Oberon
David Reid's Gallery (by Robin Gibson), Sydney

1981
14 July–7 August
Brett Whiteley: Prints
Greenhill Galleries, Perth

20 July–1 August
Graphics 1961–1981
Australian Galleries, Melbourne

20 September–4 October
Graphics 1961–1981
Kalamunda Gallery of Man, Kalamunda WA

3 October–31 October
Recent Nudes
Artist's Studio, Circular Quay, Sydney

1983
28 May–18 June
Life and Death
Australian Galleries, Melbourne

4 July–21 August
Another Way of Looking at Vincent van Gogh
The Art Gallery of New South Wales, Sydney

30 July–17 August
Some Recent Works: Birds (11) The Drought of 83 (7)
Robin Gibson Gallery, Sydney

July–August
Brett Whiteley – Recent Graphics
Philip Bacon Galleries, Brisbane

13 November–7 December
Brett Whiteley: Review of Prints 1976–1983
Chapman Gallery, Canberra

1984
12 July–28 July
Brett Whiteley
Australian Galleries, Melbourne

1985
19 October–6 November
150 Drawings From 1960–1985
Robin Gibson Gallery, Sydney

1986
October
Brett Whiteley: Graphics
The Newcastle Region Art Gallery, Newcastle

1987
27 January–22 February
Brett Whiteley: van Gogh Self Portraits
Greenhill Galleries, Perth

1988
14 April–2 May
Brett Whiteley: The Complete Graphics
(Christensen Fund)
Broken Hill City Art Gallery, Broken Hill

20 May–26 June
Brett Whiteley: The Complete Graphics
(Christensen Fund)
Nolan Gallery, Canberra

5 July–19 July
Birds
Artist's Studio, Surry Hills, Sydney

9–31 July
Brett Whiteley: Graphics
The Centre Gallery, Surfers Paradise

1990
1 March–26 March
Recent Paintings, Drawings, Photographs, Ceramics and Wood Carvings from Byron Bay, Marrakesh, Japan, San Gimignano–Tuscany
Australian Galleries, Sydney

1 March–6 May
Regard de Côté
The Art Gallery of New South Wales, Sydney

14 April–13 May
Brett Whiteley 1958–1989: The Central West
Orange Regional Gallery, Orange

1992
20 July–8 August
Paris–The Complete Regard de Cote Series Plus Works from Other Visits
Australian Galleries, Melbourne

1994
16 September–15 October
Brett Whiteley Drawings
Australian Galleries, Sydney